Issues in

Series Editor: *Anne Boran*

University of
Chester

In the Same Series

Implications
of
Globalisation

*Papers from a Conference held at
University College Chester,
November 2003*

Edited by Anne Boran and Peter Cox

Chester Academic Press

First published 2007
by Chester Academic Press
University of Chester
Parkgate Road
Chester CH1 4BJ

Printed and bound in the UK by the
Learning Resources Print Unit
University of Chester
Cover designed by the
Learning Resources Graphics Team
University of Chester

A catalogue record for this book is available
from the British Library

ISBN 978-1-905929-30-6

CONTENTS

Implications of Globalisation

CONTRIBUTORS

Dr Mark Bendall, following a First and PhD from Cambridge University, has published with US and UK publishers, including Fitzroy Dearborn (2001), Bowling Green University Press (2001), Greenleaf (2004) and Chester Academic Press (2006). His piece on Stakeholders and Corporate Social Responsibility appears in *Communication and Corporate Social Responsibility,* edited by Stephen May, Oxford University Press (2007).

Eclectic, integrated research spans representation and responsibility, spanning the fields of communications and criminology.

Mark is collaborating on a project on luxury and ethics with members of the United Nations Research Institute of Social Development, commencing a "Reading Bond" project, and contributing to studies of pedagogy.

Anne Boran is Head of the Department of Social and Communication Studies and senior lecturer in the areas of Political Economy and of Development Studies at the University of Chester. Her current research interests are labour/social movements and globalisation. She is series editor of the *Issues in the Social Sciences Series,* published by Chester Academic Press, and her publications include: *Crime: Fear or Fascination?, Gender in Flux* (co-editor: Bernadette Murphy), and this current volume, *Implications of Globalisation* (co-editor: Peter Cox). Anne teaches World Development, Latin America Area Studies, Global Political Economy and Globalisation.

Dr Peter Cox is a senior lecturer in Social Science at the University of Chester. His doctoral thesis, completed in 2002, explored Gandhian themes in the light of post-development theory and practice. His work is interdisciplinary in nature, ranging across the social sciences, and has a particular focus on community development in a range of contexts. His current research concerns the interaction of technologies of mobility, development and grassroots activism, with special reference to the importance of non-motorised transport. Peter is co-editor of *Cycling and Society* (Ashgate 2007) and is currently working on a book on Transport and Development.

Dr Robert Frith is a lecturer in International Relations at the University of Southampton. His main areas of academic interest are Globalisation and the Politics of the EU. His current research focuses on the legitimacy of transnational governance and the EU's democratic deficit.

Dr David Hall-Matthews is a lecturer in International Development in the School of Politics and International Studies at Leeds University. He has conducted research on famine and food security in both nineteenth-century India and contemporary Malawi. He has published a number of articles on the subject as well as a book, *Peasants, Famine and the State in Colonial Western India* (Palgrave Macmillan, 2005). He has also written about governance, democracy and corruption in Malawi and is now starting new research on a contemporary history of South Asia, commissioned by Blackwell.

Dr Hall-Matthews also teaches economic aspects of international relations, focusing on aid, trade and debt between the industrialised north and developing south. He has advised Liberal Democrat spokespeople in the British and European Parliaments on development issues, and served on policy working groups on International Development and International Trade and Investment for the Party.

Contributors

Dr Peadar Kirby is a senior lecturer in the School of Law and Government and co-director of the Centre for International Studies, both at Dublin City University. A former journalist with *The Irish Times*, he has published extensively on development and globalisation, with particular attention to the cases of Ireland and Latin America. He is the author of *The Celtic Tiger in Distress: Growth with Inequality in Ireland* (Palgrave, 2002) and of *Introduction to Latin America: Twenty-First Century Challenges* (Sage, 2003). His latest book, *Vulnerability and Violence: The Impact of Globalisation*, was published by Pluto Press in early 2006. He has published in many academic journals, including *New Political Economy*, *Globalizations*, *The European Journal of Development Research*, and *Administration*. He holds a PhD from the London School of Economics.

Dr Giles Mohan is a senior lecturer in Development Studies at the Open University. He is a human geographer who gained his PhD from Liverpool University in 1993. Since then he has taught geography and/or development studies at Liverpool University, the University of Central Lancashire, Portsmouth University and The Open University. He is a handling editor of the *Review of African Political Economy* and a member of the editorial boards of *Political Geography*, *Geography Compass*, and *The International Development Planning Review*. He has published numerous journal articles and chapters in books and is co-editor of *The politics of transition in Africa* (ROAPE Publications, 2002) and *Participation: From tyranny to transformation?* (Zed Books, 2004).

Dr Yacob Mulugetta teaches environment and development issues at the Centre for Environmental

Strategy, University of Surrey. He has over 10 years' experience in research and teaching in energy technology, environment and policy issues. He is currently involved in projects concerning energy consumption and climate change and its implications on local communities, with a particular focus on the inequalities of benefits and impacts associated with globalisation.

Dr Sally Theobald is a lecturer in Social Science and International Health at the Liverpool School of Tropical Medicine. Sally has a research, consultancy and capacity building/training portfolio on equity and TB, HIV & AIDS Treatment and Care. Much of this portfolio involves applying social science research methodologies and gender and poverty analyses. Sally works in collaboration with partners in Malawi, Kenya, Burkina Faso, South Africa and Thailand and has just returned from an 18 months' secondment as Technical Adviser at the REACH Trust, Malawi. She is also interested in gender and HIV mainstreaming in health and other development sectors.

Dr Rachel Tolhurst is a lecturer in Social Science and International Health at the Liverpool School of Tropical Medicine. Rachel has a background in gender and development. She completed her MA in Gender Analysis in Development at the University of East Anglia and her PhD at the University of Liverpool. Her research interests include gender equity and communicable disease (especially a focus on malaria, tuberculosis and HIV), maternal health and health systems development, including gender mainstreaming in the health sector and rural health financing and quality. She is currently working on research in China, Vietnam and Ghana.

FOREWORD

The fourth volume of Chester Academic Press's series on *Issues in the Social Sciences* is very welcome, performing an important function of disseminating new and original discussions of key research issues.

This collection of essays explores the processes, impacts and responses to the much debated and disputed phenomenon of globalisation in the contemporary world. In doing so, it very effectively draws back the curtain which obscures much of the discussion in contemporary research literature on the subject, which tends either to remain at the level of macro theory and processes or at the level of micro case studies which are not informed by any wider analytical framework, leading to a range of parallel discourses which rarely interconnect.

This book therefore fills an important space. Even the structure, which splits up the analysis of globalisation into three themes, performs a valuable task in illuminating the different sites for analysis and the importance of separating as well as connecting them. Written in a style which is intelligible, not only for students, but for academic and other readers from different disciplines, the introduction provides a clear exposition of the key debates which populate current conversations about global matters. By setting out the elements involved – economic, political and financial - and the key points of contention, including the uniqueness – or not – of the current phase of internationalisation of different aspects of the world economy, of economic and political pressures on the nation state and of the advantages – or not – of globalisation for the different groups within the world, the book offers readings that provide the basic vocabulary necessary for further research and analysis.   Key issues are explored, such as the demise – or not - of the nation state and the (changing) role of international companies and their transformation from multinational to transnational companies. A really intriguing dimension which emerges from these essays is the array of paradoxes displayed by the complex processes of globalisation and the way in which these impact at different sites of political and economic nodes of power. These include the fact that the new neo-liberal world order, regulated by supranational institutions, relies on the structures of the nation state to enforce these rules; the fact that entitlement failure, which contributes both to the causes and the consequences of famines in sub-Saharan Africa, can be both exacerbated and counteracted by globalisation; the ways in which the drivers of globalisation increase vulnerability to communicable diseases, but also offer new opportunities for the involvement of local communities and excluded groups to contribute to the construction of a pro-poor response to health crises; and indeed the complexities of migration flows and disasporic communities, which exhibit characteristics of both fluidity and sedimentation in different contexts.

At the level of responses, the book intelligently avoids the usual heroic local struggles approach; instead it includes the responses of the post-9/11 superpowers, seeking to assert their national hegemony within an out of (their) control world, as well as successful examples of local resistance against prevailing political and ecological threats. This is indeed a valuable collection, which will be welcomed by students and researchers alike.

Professor Ruth Pearson
Director, Centre for Development Studies
School of Politics and International Studies
University of Leeds
March 2007

ACKNOWLEDGEMENTS

Many thanks to the co-authors of this volume for their excellent contributions; most particularly to those who contributed early and have waited patiently while the rest of us dragged our heels! We hope it has been worth the wait. A warm thank you also to Professor Ruth Pearson from the University of Leeds for her well-crafted foreword to the volume.

Our students have, yet again, chosen a topic worthy of intense argument and debate. Thanks to them for their enthusiastic involvement in, and enjoyment of, the subject. Thanks to colleagues in the Department of Social and Communication Studies who have, as ever, creatively engaged with the theme, providing practical and academic support, and who make the annual conference an enjoyable and stimulating event.

Lastly, our very sincere thanks and appreciation go to Peter Williams, Managing Editor of Chester Academic Press, whose patience and exacting standards make this series possible. His contributions are always apt and pertinent.

Anne Boran and Peter Cox

INTRODUCTION

This volume raises searching questions about the nature and implications of globalisation. It targets not only some key features identified with the processes of globalisation but, most importantly, explores its impacts on real nations and people. In order that we may begin to investigate the impacts that globalisation has across a range of areas, we first need to clarify the range of meanings attributed to the term, and to outline the different attitudes that it provokes among those who observe it, who analyses it and who feel its impact in contrasting contexts.

The term itself is deeply contested, presenting a multiplicity of definitional challenges. A number of different classificatory schemata have been advanced to help us navigate these contested positions. We argue for a fourfold grouping, arising from the understandings attached to the various phenomena of globalisation. The first approach (traditionalist) denies that globalisation is a significant phenomenon. Nayar (2005) describes this group as "agnostic", highlighting their ambiguity towards the idea that contemporary globalisation is significantly different from previous waves of internationalisation. The second approach (by positive globalisers) enthusiastically endorses the changes that globalisation brings, and is sometimes referred to as the "enthusiast" or "advocate" approach. Notably, advocacy of globalisation is not the exclusive property of either the political left or right, neo-liberal enthusiasm being paralleled by those on the more traditional left who see the possibility for increased internationalism and the forging of global solidarities. A third approach (by sceptics) recognises globalisation as worthy of serious study and criticism because of its negative impacts. Again, this position crosses traditional political divides. Our final group of commentators (transformationalist) argue that globalisation must be examined because of its perceived creative potential for change, whether negative or positive. The degree of ambivalence in this final group is important, as it understands globalisation as a series of phenomena with widely variant results, whose significance lies in the transformation of constraints and opportunities that it brings to the contemporary socio-political world, requiring a re-examination of traditional suppositions concerning social inequality, justice, structures and agency.

Whatever the theoretical position adopted, there is recognition that profound changes are making an impact on societies around the world. The patterns of both continuity and disjunction witnessed in contemporary social, political and economic change lead to contrasting theoretical responses: the same transformations being regarded by some as radically different in nature to what has gone before; by others, simply as variation within historical continuity.

In what Harvey (1989) terms time/space compression, the world appears to be shrinking in terms of perception and reach. Whilst capital may be the driver of these changes, technological innovations have provided the means whereby rapid globalisation has been facilitated. The technological revolutions of the last decades of the 20th century have made all corners of the earth accessible through sophisticated transport and communication networks. The speed of transmission and the digitisation of information, resulting in the capacity for instantaneous data transfer, provide the "push" factors for economic, political and cultural changes around the world (Lyon, 1988).

As a result of these changes in mobility, spatial perceptions and relations have changed, so that, according to Scholte (2000), supra-territorial relations between people

Introduction

have assumed more significance. Global reach enables distant events to shape local ones and vice versa, national boundaries become increasingly permeable and global players increase in significance and operate across them, with less and less hindrance. Low (economic) cost travel and transport facilitate the movement of both people and goods. Integrated communications technologies make connections across the globe immediate, so that physical distance is, theoretically, no longer a problem. Ideas, information, goods, finance and services can move freely, in growing size and intensity of global flows (Held & McGrew, 2000), helping to integrate the world and shrink it.

These processes are not, however, neutral. They carry implications. These implications are the focus of analysis of this volume. The chapters encompass three broad themes integral to the study of globalisation: *Key players and processes; Consequences and impacts; and Responses and resistance.*

Economic processes are frequently seen as core to the discussion about the significance of globalisation. Scholte (2000) identifies three types of globalisation. Firstly, *internationalisation*, or the crossing of boundaries; this occurs, for example, through trade and has been significant since pre-colonial times. Secondly, the opening of borders through *market liberalisation*, which has become increasingly significant since 1945 and which has been accompanied by the expansion of Multinational Companies [MNCs]. Scholte's third type, *globalisation* proper, is identified by the transcendence of borders when production and consumption become increasingly delinked from the geography of distances, a process dating from the 1980s onwards. Hirst & Thompson (1996) argue that contemporary globalisation is merely an extension of earlier phases of internationalisation. A variation on this

3

continuity can be seen in the writings of Shiva (e.g., 1998), who describes these three waves as cumulative forms of colonialism. By way of contrast, Giddens (1990) and Held and his collaborators (2000), whilst accepting this continuity, argue that the intensity of contemporary patterns requires us to interpret them as qualitatively as well as quantitatively different. The latter two types (or stages) of globalisation, particularly the last, are distinguished from the first because of the sheer scale and intensity of global flows, and the global impact of communications.

The key global agents of these profound changes are MNCs, helped by technological developments, liberalised financial markets (from the 1970s onwards), and neo-liberal ideology (institutionalised in what became known in ideological terms as the "Washington consensus") adopted by global financial institutions and then imposed on dependent governments. Combined with a negation of the role of the state in economic development, these processes, John Gray (1998) has argued, created perfect conditions for the global spread of economic liberalism. As a result of these changes, the multinationals transmuted into Transnational Corporations [TNCs], not only crossing borders, but transcending them, unfettered from their local and national origins: a process highlighted by Firth in his chapter in this volume. Positive advocates of globalisation insist that this model produces rapid economic growth, but sceptics contend, conversely, that the balance of power has shifted too radically in favour of the big economic players, even to the extent of undermining the nation state (Beck, 2000). This latter position is perhaps most succinctly summed up in the phraseology of one of its most vociferous proponents, David Korten (2001): *When Corporations Rule the World*. Consequently, we see that issues of power relations emerge as one of the most important implications of globalisation, whether one takes a positive or sceptical view of its significance.

Many of the TNCs, acting as primary global players and advocates of deeper and more intense globalisation, command more wealth than most nation states in the world (Dicken, 2003), so the implications of economic globalisation in terms of costs and benefits to subjects, as well as agents, need close scrutiny. The first three chapters of the volume focus on globalisation processes, each directing analysis predominantly, though not exclusively, at different actors within these processes: *the neo-liberal market, the state and citizens.*

Key players and processes

The first chapter examines neo-liberal market claims. Peadar Kirby, in an ambitious and insightful chapter, "Implications of Globalisation: Present Imperfect, Future Tense?", takes as a starting point Robert Cox's analysis of approaches to strategic decision-making. One of these starts with acceptance of current thinking, adapting it to new circumstances in such a way that it improves on a given social order, while the second tries to identify and understand the nature of historical processes, so that change can be directed to produce desirable outcomes for society. Given the rival claims made about the impacts of globalisation, with one side extolling its capacity to deliver immense benefits, particularly in its purer "free market" form, while the other criticises its capacity to deliver a skewed uneven form of development, Kirby seeks to discover which framework provides the best basis for future decision-making by agents of development.

For evidence to interrogate the claims made of globalisation, Kirby draws on the examples of two economies that have wholeheartedly embraced globalisation of a more orthodox neo-liberal kind: Ireland and Latin America. He asks whether, in light of the evidence, the best model of decision-making should involve the adaptation of the existing systems in those countries to deal with imbalances and challenges or whether a more radical solution aimed at a different, more balanced, social order is required. Evidence on Ireland, a very late economic developer, confirms that, from the 1990s, strong inward investment and an open economy was accompanied by strong economic growth, based primarily in the information technology, pharmaceutical and financial services sectors, fostered and encouraged by an active state sector, offering low taxation levels, investment funding and an educated and skilled workforce. This model of globalisation was seen to deliver not only rapid growth, but also falling unemployment rates, growth in average earnings and a rise in living standards: a "Celtic Tiger", the envy of struggling economies around the world. However, this liberal economic model is, the evidence suggests, accompanied by a growth of inequality, a polarisation in the share of income, an increase in relative poverty and growing educational and health inequalities. In a rolling back of state, commitment to a relational share of wealth has declined and, Kirby argues, a model of globalisation that polarises, providing economic success together with high social cost, has been adopted.

Latin America, in contrast to Ireland, had, in the course of the 20th century, developed a reasonably integrated industrial base in its stronger economies. Economic restructuring as a consequence of the debt crises entailed a shift away from state-guided, inward-oriented development to liberalisation and inflows of Direct Foreign Investment. Evidence of a return to growth in the mid-1990s, control of inflation and a shift away from dependence on the export of primary products, together with democratic political stability throughout the region, all point to a success story for globalisation. However, a slowdown towards the end of the 1990s and the early years of the new millennium, together with increased polarisation of wealth distribution and increasing concentration of employment in the informal sector, signalled pause for caution. Closer analysis points to a model of development that relies heavily on two types of production: the processing of primary natural resources, using capital intensive production methods, and labour intensive, mainly female, assembly industries, located along the Mexican Border. These industries provide few internal linkages or high wage employment, weakening capacity to generate demand and trade. Although Latin American states have continued to commit more funds to social spending, even as growth contracts, the pattern has structural economic weaknesses that generates high levels of poverty and weak social development.

Both case studies support the claims of positive globalisers that globalisation generates rapid economic growth, but does not deliver increased benefits for all sectors of society. The evidence, Kirby asserts, supports anti-globaliser claims that global capital has become more powerful. Consequently, nation states are more sensitive to the demands of capital and less prepared to protect the social needs of citizens. Continuance on the current path is likely to generate an increasingly tense future, with yet greater structural weaknesses and greater social polarisation. In order to create a more equitable form of development, the solution would seem to require a more radical response, a rethinking of global relations as outlined in Cox's second model.

There is a tendency within political economy debates about globalisation to assume that the nation state is an increasingly helpless pawn in the hands of global capital and perhaps to underestimate the capacity of the state to mediate the impacts of globalisation, or to resist totally buying into the Washington consensus. Kirby's evidence demonstrates nuanced differences in state responses, at least in mediating the benefits of globalisation to citizens via commitment to social expenditure, although less so, perhaps, in relation to state/global capital relations. How the nation state interacts with powerful global actors on the one hand, and with its own citizens on the other, is central to debates about models of development. It is to this crucial point about the nature of state/capital relations to which Robert Frith turns his attention in his chapter "Multinational Corporations and the Democratic State: Friend or Foe?"

As distinct from the "type" or "phases" categorisations of globalisation, this chapter locates distinctions around the centrality or otherwise of the state in cross-border economic exchanges. "Internationalisation" (a term supported by Hirst & Thompson to reflect the true nature of the phenomenon) locates the territorial state as key to economic exchanges between discrete territorial units, whereas "globalisation" refers to the notion of supra-state, deterritorialised flows. Similarly, the term "MNC" reflects the location of business within a system of national territorial links, whereas "TNC" reflects companies that operate with no such ties. Firth qualifies the globalisation thesis and reaffirms the continued importance of the nation state in economic activity, depending on the size of state generated Gross Domestic Product [GDP] and the re-embedding of capital flows within nation state regulatory frameworks. Multinational companies still depend on state-endorsed corporate contracts and private property rights, and are facilitated or encumbered by state policy-making, particularly in relation to technological infrastructure. There is clearly an interpenetration of space of flows (markets) and space of place (state).

However, Firth recognises a number of qualitative differences in relation to the current global political economy and the growth in the globalisation of the production of goods, services, finance and Research and Development [R&D], all of which, whether nationally located or not, are aimed at global markets. Global political authority has been ceded to major global institutions like the International Monetary Fund [IMF], the World Bank and the World Trade Organization [WTO]. Networks of firms, innovative research centres and rapid knowledge transfer facilitates global supply chains.

A significant difference in the structure of global flows lies in a shift from trade in durable goods and national resources (hard economy) to the service and entertainment economy. Firms like Nike focus on branding and image, but outsource actual production. The main trade is in information, images, entertainment, films, advertising, brand names and merchandising. So there is, in effect, something new going on.

Firth looks at two arguments suggesting a threat to the nation state. The first is the increasing disjuncture between the structure of the globalising economy and the territorial state, undermining state policy control. Cross-border mergers and acquisitions and intra-firm trading that can undermine state attempts to tax profits are examples of this process. The second relates to the increasing mobility of capital in the global economy, which allows companies to switch production locations in pursuit of greater profits. The notion of a *competitive state* suggests a state reaction that works to create competitive conditions in order to keep companies territorially located. Such responses by nation states, it could be argued, lead to the convergence of national economic structures to the lowest common denominator, in terms of compliance to TNC demands and consequently a shrinking of welfare commitments to citizens. On the other hand, perceptions of state and market have shifted so radically (as implied by cognitive perspectives) that the notion of *the regulatory state* might capture current consumer and state perceptions of the state as one that creates an enabling environment for the provision of public goods by the market, rather than direct state provision of those goods, thus blurring the old boundaries of what traditionally was regarded as the role of the state and that of markets.

What are the implications for democracy, usually conceived as territorially bound, of this type of shift? Orthodox notions of democratic legitimacy are constituted by effective *output-oriented* legitimacy, judged by the effectiveness of state control of policy within its borders, and *input-oriented* legitimacy gained through citizen representation in policymaking. From the orthodox perspective, the problem in relation to globalisation rests in the threat to both if the state allows itself to be a vehicle that represents the interests of global economic actors within the state, at a cost to its own citizens; a notion captured in Sasson's term *economic citizenship*. On the other hand, powerful nation states actively shape globalisation and the actions of multinational corporations through the overarching regulatory regional (European Union [EU]) and global institutions (IMF, World Bank, WTO), to which state power is ceded. In an interesting case study of the biotechnology industry, Firth explores these competing claims and perceptions, highlighting how the primacy accorded to economic organisations facilitates the ranking of consumers and shareholders above citizens as the relevant community in relation to government decision-making. However, as the issue of genetically modified organisms demonstrates, citizens are not passive, either as consumers or citizens. Political protest and action contest the knowledge claims of both state and market in this case and have forced some notable back-tracking.

Firth concludes that, while there is some blurring of roles between states and markets, in that states employ the tools of the market and the market takes on some state roles, both states and multinational companies remain powerful actors in the contemporary world, making decisions about ownership, distribution and regulation of key resources.

In his chapter, "Globalisation of What? Power Knowledge and Neo-Colonialism", Peter Cox engages with the origins and inadequacies of the current model of globalisation, particularly in relation to citizenship. Situating himself within the continuity framework of globalisation, Cox's analysis unmasks the myth that globalisation is simply about economic and political processes. Locating the epistemological basis for the current model of globalisation in Western narratives of modernity, Cox argues that this world view emerged explicitly within a historically defined, territorially located, European context of the Enlightenment, when scientific laws, secularism and economic development came to be defined as the only valid knowledge framework worth having. Diffused as universal norms, initially through colonialism and empire, currently through neocolonial economic and political globalisation processes, this hegemonic narrative elevates a linear view of economic development and progress to the status of an immutable logic, failing totally to recognise the ethnocentric location of its knowledge base. Effectively, through processes of internalisation of this knowledge and value system by those outside the core successful market economies, it becomes self-perpetuating and legitimatised through the process of neocolonialism, driven by the dominant economic powers. This negates cultural values and processes that do not fit the model and can, as a consequence, justify peripheralisation, exclusion and exploitation. Cox traces a line from colonialism to current globalisation that locates nations in a hierarchy of power justified by the nearness or distance from the Western liberal economic model.

Are the dominated trapped, devoid of agency, within this global order? Just as Marx argued that every social order held within it the seeds of its own destruction, so Cox argues that global spaces and channels of domination create conditions for resistance and counteraction, which can subvert them to endorse a different set of values based on the celebration of plurality, intercultural exchange and hybridity. This makes stepping outside the dominant framework at least possible, though not inevitable, because of the forces of co-option and neutralisation constantly employed against critics of the dominant neo-liberal model.

Together, these three chapters examine contrasting aspects of the state, markets and citizens that make up the key players within globalisation. They are involved in networks of complex interaction that are often contradictory and sometimes profoundly obfuscatory. These need to be studied at micro level, as well as through macro analyses, in order to understand them more clearly. The processes brought into play by globalisation, as well as its own internal dynamics, can be better understood by reference to specific cases. It is to these consequences and impacts that the next group of chapters turns.

Consequences and impacts

David Hall-Matthews introduces the particular phenomenon of famine in order to examine the evidence for globalisation's impact on this enduring phenomenon. Such a specific focus can enable the reader to interrogate globalisation in order to understand the relative validity of the various positions taken towards it, as outlined at the start of this chapter. After providing a clear survey of current understandings of the causes of famine, he proceeds to unravel the patterns in which these causal factors are entwined with the market, the state, and citizen actors involved in globalisation.

Globalisation not only changes the patterns of production and distribution of primary goods but, as noted previously, also lessens the role of the state in key domestic intervention. These twin actions give credence to the claim that globalisation may make the occurrence of famine more likely, through its secondary effect on entitlements. However, this is not entirely a one-sided process and Hall-Matthews draws our attention to the potentially positive impacts of globalisation, in terms of the improved capacity for pre-empting and responding to famine. That such pre-emption does not occur more frequently is a result of the failure of political will rather than directly because of globalisation processes. Indeed, he concludes that the failure is ultimately one of insufficient globalisation: it should not be limited merely to the liberalisation of markets and the benefit of elite players, but must become a process involving all levels of society for it to become more equitable.

Bringing both continuity and contrast to the previous chapter, Sally Theobald and Rachel Thompson examine how globalisation impacts upon people's vulnerability to tuberculosis and HIV. Again, both negative and positive aspects are clearly visible. Whilst vulnerabilities are certainly increased, there are also increased opportunities for citizens to develop relevant expertise, and for increased campaigning possibilities that may have even more profound long-term effects. The authors importantly delineate the gendered impact of globalisation. The clear linkage between poverty and infectious disease rates mirrors the parallel linkage between gender and impoverishment. Thus, we witness a complex interweaving of factors in which, although it may be impossible to predict rates of infection, clear patterns of vulnerability emerge.

Dealing with these vulnerabilities requires attention, not only to the issues of poverty, but also to questions of gender roles, expectations and inequalities. It is apparent that existing patterns of response, shaped by agreements such as the Agreement on Trade-Related Aspects of Intellectual Property Rights [TRIPS] and the manufacturing interests of transnational pharmaceutical businesses, reflect the dominance of economic globalisation's processes. However, the concurrent globalisation of knowledge and information has resulted in a loosening of the exclusive grip that such large economic players hold. The opportunity arises for previously silent voices to become engaged in health advocacy and even delivery. New alliances and forms of action are created in the very spaces opened up by globalisation. So, despite the gloomy picture of increased infection rates, we must also acknowledge that there are many positive factors emerging from current health care and disease prevention practices and initiatives. The challenge of globalisation is to engage with the opportunities.

The complexity of the health impacts of globalisation is examined in further detail by Anne Boran in her examination of the consequences of cross-border movements of peoples. Again, the pattern is one of increasing vulnerabilities. However, it is important to look beyond the headlines and to consider the reality of the patterns of cross-border movement. Starting with Koser's classification of historically changing patterns of migration, she then continues to bring together the many and varied influences that create hazards and risks for both migrants and destinations. The increased flow of goods and services, so characteristic of contemporary globalisation, must be understood as inevitably bringing with it increased cross-border flows of peoples, either as citizens or as permanent or temporary migrants. She argues for a change of policy regarding the movement of peoples. Whilst in former times migration has often appeared to be an aberration, its location within a globalised economic and productive structure requires considered long-term responses that deal with it as a concomitant part of the movement of goods and services.

Once more, the picture is one of an unequal pattern of impacts. Under current policy arrangements, the vulnerabilities of the weakest in society tend to be the least well protected. The not inconsiderable numbers of migrants from More Economically Developed Countries [MEDCs] become invisible, whilst migrants from Less Economically Developed Countries [LEDCs] are stigmatised. It should be possible to see migrants of all sorts as potential assets, rather than painting them as potential risks. This theme of cross-border movement is continued in the following chapter by Giles Mohan.

Mohan focuses in particular on the African diaspora and explains the complex patterns of change and development that accompany settlement of diasporic communities in new locations. Whilst historically this may have occurred for many involuntary reasons, Mohan also emphasises the voluntary element involved in these movements.

Through examining the community structures, values and relations of Ghanaians in Milton Keynes, this micro level analysis is able to shed considerable light on the transmission of values and ideas, as well as on the more familiarly discussed issue of remittances and their role in economic development. Thus he sheds light on the manner in which developmental processes in a globalised context can be multifaceted and more enriching than might have formerly been expected. However, the reality of the "sedimentation" of diasporic communities and relations in contemporary society requires us, he argues, to re-evaluate the importance of place and of fixity within globalisation. The emphasis for analyses of globalisation may be on flows and movements, but it is as well to remind ourselves that not everything is in flux. Even within cross-border movements that initially speak to us of fluidity and the dissolution of boundaries, the underlying process may be rooted in traditional notions of territoriality.

Responses and resistance

In considering the impact of globalisation, it is very easy to become engaged entirely within a world of academic discussion. In this final section, we are reminded that globalisation is a process that directly affects people's lives and livelihoods, and provokes visceral and emotional responses.

This final theme, responses and resistance to globalisation, thus addresses two very different outcomes of globalisation. The first explores the way in which the governments of dominant states (particularly the United States, and to a lesser extent Britain,) respond to globalisation's impact on their hegemony in a way that can be seen as akin to fascism. The other focuses on civilian anti-globalisation responses.

Despite endorsing, indeed promulgating, the Washington consensus, it is possible even for a superpower like the United States to lose out to competitors in a global market place. Other competing powers, such as China, are "leaner" and "meaner" in economic terms than the USA and can potentially build up power bases that might inevitably challenge the superpower's economic and political position. Such potential challenges for hegemony might, it could be argued, generate reactions by the threatened state that will attempt to confirm and secure its continued dominance. Mark Bendall, in his chapter, "The Slowly Simmering Frog: Notes on Pre-fascism and Globalisation", argues that empire, in the sense of political and military expansionism in the interest of economic domination, lies at the heart of the "War on Terror". Bendall examines the extent to which this thirst for domination, supported by its military industrial complex, is justified and driven by fascist, or at least, authoritarian ideology. Drawing on Harvey's (2003) analysis of the relative American economic decline in the context of globalisation, involving declining oil stocks, polarisation of wealth and increased unemployment, Bendall argues that such decline is countered by state repression and hegemonic control, both domestically and in defined "enemy" territory.

The War on Terror provides a smokescreen to distract attention from economic decline, as well as providing the opportunity to asset-strip in order to bolster economic strength. Continuity of key personnel with a neoconservative ideology across succeeding administrations in the USA, Bendall argues, endorsed fascist ideas to justify attacking those defined as "the enemy". Rhetoric constructed difference in terms of a clash of civilization (Huntington, 1996) or in terms of progressive or regressive worlds, integrated or not into the global economy. Parallels can be drawn with traditional fascist ideas that push a strong nationalist line, defining enemies in moralistic terms such as "evil" and "threats" and justifying their elimination,through collective state-led action. This message appealed strongly to both neoconservatives and to evangelical Christians, both of them groups used to good effect to support the Bush Administration. The internal contradictions of the message, use of uncivilised methods to contain and extract information while preaching democracy, differential accountability before international law, and indeed the arrogance that justified going to war without the support of the United Nations, all point to fascistic tendencies in this state and in its ally, Britain, according to Bendall.

Growing surveillance and authoritarian legislation, both in the USA and the UK, form part of the dark side of globalisation, asserts the author, leading to a serious erosion of civil liberties. A worrying aspect of this trend seems to be a lack of reaction by civil society, lulled into inaction by fear; a fear generated by the state, in collusion with the media. Can we categorically say that the present US government and its British ally are fascist in intent and direction? Bendall stops short of arguing this, claiming instead that there are necessary, but insufficient, elements of fascism present; a condition he defines as pre-fascist.

Bendall's chapter paints a picture of a civil society that is manipulated and democratically undermined by the state. However, there is a risk of underestimating the ability and power of civil society to sift out the "truth", if not immediately, then eventually. This brings an inevitable backlash that hits where it hurts, by voting out the government. Indeed, the indications are that a backlash might have already begun in the United States, and even earlier in Britain, and that civil society does come to see these contradictions and resents being misled, with predictable consequences.

Yacob Mulugetta, in his chapter, "Globalisation: The Battle for Solidarity and Effective Resistance", discusses new social movements as contextual responses to the negative consequences of neo-liberal globalisation: growing inequalities and indebtedness, subsequent environmental and labour problems, and the degradation of public welfare services, particularly in the South. Mulugetta maps the consolidation of neo-liberal dominance and its consequences for the nation state, for multinational capital and for civil society, arguing that old ways of resistance, based largely on class as a badge of identity, for example, are no longer sufficient. A reconceptualisation is needed that recognises multiple, interacting, subject positions that may be difficult to separate out; for example, that of woman, worker, environmentalist, immigrant and protestor. Collective action, therefore, does not necessarily depend on homogeneity. However, the problem of such a decentred view of the subject is that opposition constantly risks fragmentation.

Mulugetta recognises the diversity of civil society groups and admits to a diversity of responses to the challenges of neo-liberal driven globalisation. These can range from identification with the process, attempted reform in order to limit its negative impacts, or complete rejection of it. Multinational capital and, indeed, governments react in a time-honoured manner of co-option or attempted neutralisation of the new (in historical terms) social actors. Mainstreaming of "concerns", like those of environmentalists, is one such typical response. Adoption of softer policy approaches by international institutions, such as the IMF and the World Bank, and developing policies that involve civil society organisations in the disbursement of aid and policy formulation, successfully deradicalises and co-opts such organisations into the agenda of governments and multinational companies. Mulugetta demonstrates how easy this is for big companies, by drawing on some interesting case studies of such co-option: Shell in Peru and the McDonald's/Environmental Development Fund co-operation. The McLibel case demonstrates how difficult it is to confront companies like McDonalds.

Acknowledging the maxim that power concedes nothing without demand, Mulugetta points to some successful action by, for example the Ilisu Dam opposition groups in Turkey and the Zapatista movement in Mexico. He concludes that social movements today must fight to strengthen links between like-minded groups in order to oppose effectively the processes of neutralisation and co-option by governments and by supranational organisations, keen to buy off opposition. This means opposing organisations willing to comply with the neo-liberal agenda at the local level in return for easy access to funding and influence, and strengthening alliances with like-minded organisations at the international level: in short, a recognition of the power of linking the local with the global, and visa versa, as a means of achieving successful social action.

We finally come full circle, therefore, from the key players and processes, through the impacts and consequences of globalisation, to the responses it generates. Perhaps what is most striking is the insistence throughout on the importance of citizen action, as a key player in globalisation. However one understands or defines it, and whatever one's particular analytical response to globalisation, the repeated theme emerges that current patterns of globalisation, with their emphasis on the market and the state, are incomplete without significant citizen input. It is at the micro level of human activity that the macro processes of globalisation are ultimately felt and from where reaction and response should naturally be anticipated. These responses may clearly draw on a wealth of different understandings and approaches, corresponding to the myriad of situations and interlinked pressures that create any given particularity. The implications of globalisation therefore are many and this volume simply begins the process of analysing them.

References

Beck, U. (2000). *What is globalization* (P. Camiller, Trans.). Cambridge: Polity Press. (Original work published 1997).

Cox, R. W. (2002). *The political economy of a plural world: Critical reflections on power, morals and civilization.* London: Routledge.

Dicken, P. (2003). *Global shift: Reshaping the global economic map in the 21st century.* (4th ed.). London: Sage Publications. (Original work published 1986).

Giddens, A. (1990). *The consequences of modernity.* Stanford, CA: Stanford University Press.

Gray, J. (1998). *False dawn: The delusions of global capitalism.* London: Granta.

Harvey, D. (1989). *The condition of postmodernity: An enquiry into the origins of cultural change.* Oxford: Basil Blackwell.

Harvey, D. (2003). The new imperialism. Oxford: Oxford University Press.

Held, D. (Ed.). (2000). *A globalizing world?: Culture, economics, politics.* London: Routledge, in association with the Open University.

Held, D., & McGrew, A. (Eds.). (2000) *The global transformations reader: An introduction to the globalization debate.* Cambridge: Polity Press.

Hirst, P., & Thompson, G. (1996). *Globalization in question: The international economy and the possibilities of governance.* Cambridge: Polity Press.

Huntington, S. P. (1996). *The clash of civilizations and the remaking of world order.* New York: Simon & Schuster.

Korten, D. C. (2001). *When corporations rule the world.* (2nd ed.). Bloomfield, CT: Kumarian Press.

Koser, K. (2000). Asylum policies, trafficking and vulnerability. *International Migration,* Special Issue 2000/1, 91-111.

Lyon, D. (1988). *The information society: Issues and illusions.* Cambridge: Polity Press.

Nayar, B. R. (2005). *The geopolitics of globalization: The consequences for development.* Delhi: Oxford University Press.

Scholte, J. A. (2000). *Globalization: A critical introduction.* Basingstoke: Palgrave.

Introduction

Shiva, V. (1998) *Biopiracy: The plunder of nature and knowledge.* Totnes: Green Books. (Original work published 1997).

IMPLICATIONS OF GLOBALISATION: PRESENT IMPERFECT, FUTURE TENSE?

Peadar Kirby

New thinking comes about in two ways. One way is by adapting established knowledge to new events and circumstances through incremental adjustments. The other way is by projecting thinking forward so as to attempt to understand the nature of the historical process and how to control it towards achieving desirable outcomes. This way includes normative choice along with realist assessment of possibilities. These two approaches coexist during periods of fundamental change in world order. They express different power positions struggling for control over the future. The first gives precedence to the established order and seeks to adjust it to new needs. The second opens the way for more radical change (Cox, 2002, p. 76).

Globalisation is a term full of paradoxes. It has, over a short period of time, come to occupy a central place in academic and public discourses, yet there is no consensus as to what exactly it means or, indeed, whether it actually exists. Among academics, we have those, usually economists with a strong neo-classical leaning, who see it as ushering in a period of unprecedented prosperity around the globe, if only anti-globalist movements can be prevented from promoting a retreat to forms of protectionism. These are known as the positive globalists. On the other hand, there are those, usually termed the sceptics, who see in the discourse of globalisation an ideological tool to prise open national economies so that multi-national companies (usually Western) can get more opportunities for profit-making. Such people tend to take a very pessimistic view of the future, particularly for the poor and for the developing world (Held & McGrew, 2002).

These issues, therefore, alert us to the complexity of the term globalisation and of the social processes it seeks to express. Yet, instead of advancing our understanding, the globalist and the sceptical approaches often obscure it even further, since they are largely based on theoretical presuppositions, rather than on any thorough interrogation of the evidence. The great benefit of the title of this collection, and of the conference at which its assembled papers were given, is that it makes no assumptions about globalisation. In a way that avoids the determinism of both the globalist and the sceptical approaches, it invites us to examine the implications of globalisation and, based on this examination, to ask what kind of present we have and what kind of future we might expect. Since there is general agreement among all analysts that we have a present that is far from perfect (though analysts of different theoretical persuasions might identify differently what they regard as the imperfections of the present), the real question raised by the title relates to the future, and specifically to what kind of future globalisation holds in store for us. It therefore suggests an interrogation of what currently is perhaps the single most important question facing anyone who considers globalisation – from anti-globalisation activists, through policy-makers and government ministers, to academics.

Responding to the invitation of the title, this paper will therefore offer a partial answer to this most important question. It will do this in three sections. The first will outline what this central question is. Section 2 will draw on evidence from the author's own research as a basis for suggesting an answer to the question. The research examines the impact of globalisation in two places, Ireland

and Latin America. By looking at two very different parts of the world, both of them places where processes we label globalisation (such as economic liberalisation, a development model that gives priority to attracting foreign investment and to extensive insertion into global trade flows, and a state that facilitates these market-led processes) have been actively and consistently promoted by public authorities for at least two decades, key economic and social impacts of globalisation can be identified and the contours of the present situation in these areas mapped out and characterised. Section 3 will then discuss what this evidence tells us as a way of answering the key question posed in Section 1. The final section will draw conclusions.

1 - Globalisation's key question

The chapters of this book describe many of the features of today's world order that highlight just how imperfect it is: features such as poverty and inequality, environmental pressures, exploitation of workers, HIV/AIDS, refugee and migrant flows, food insecurity and famine, and the violence of the powerful against the poor. The present is, without doubt, frighteningly imperfect. While we could have very sharp disagreements about the extent of these problems, about how one interprets them and about their causes, all would agree that they exist. Where the more substantial basis for disagreement arises is in relation to the future. Do present trends offer grounds for hope that the future will be better? It is in answer to this question that the most fundamental disagreements arise, disagreements that embody what Robert W. Cox, in the quotation that opens this chapter, calls "... different power positions struggling for control over the future".

Implications of Globalisation:
Present Imperfect, Future Tense?

Cox is widely regarded as one of the most innovative and influential theorists of today's world order, a towering figure of radical social thought at a time when a narrow, bland and complacent orthodoxy dominates social discourse in the media and in academia. In identifying the debates taking place on globalisation as struggles for power over the future, he alerts us to the significance of what is at stake; namely, the ability to define the ways in which that future is going to be built. For Cox, globalisation is "... the salient emerging reality around which the knowledge struggle now clusters" (2002, p. 76); this means that the fundamental questions being discussed in relation to globalisation are of primary importance in the whole field of social thought today. In elucidating the fundamental positions that constitute this knowledge struggle, Cox presents two. The first projects present trends incrementally into the future, so that the range of possibilities open to us is limited to a further modification and development of what we have at present. This is a "more of the same" scenario. Cox's second position, however, is far less constrained. This dares to ask what kind of world we would like to see in the future; in other words, it is more a normative position. It then seeks to identify as rigorously and realistically as possible how this kind of world can be brought about, largely through human agency and struggle. As he says, the first of these two positions "... gives precedence to the established order and seeks to project it to new needs" (p. 76), whereas the second "... opens the way for more radical change" (p. 76). Much of his own work, especially his latest book, *The Political Economy of a Plural World* (2002), is concerned with identifying the basis and possibilities for such radical change.

In the light of Cox's treatment, we can now identify what was called "... the single most important question facing anyone who considers globalisation" in the introductory section of this chapter. This relates to what can be done to shape a better future, and the fundamental disagreement is as follows: one side argues that what is needed is *more* globalisation, namely a deepening and intensification of the trends that are shaping today's world, whereas the other side argues that this will only make matters worse and that instead we need a *different* form of globalisation, one that will foster a more humane and sustainable world, in which values of solidarity and the public good prevail. It is difficult to overemphasise what is at stake here, since the outcome of this fundamental disagreement will largely determine the ways we approach social change. As Cox puts it, "History goes on and has the potential to shape new structures of thought and of political authority. The opportunity now opens to develop the forms of knowledge conducive to such innovation and to bring them into the power struggle over the future" (2002, p. 77).

This chapter offers a modest contribution to establishing the grounds on which a decision could be made between the two positions on this fundamental disagreement. In other words, which position is right and how do we decide this? The chapter will do this by presenting evidence in the next section on the impact of globalisation in Ireland and in Latin America, establishing the causal connections between this evidence and the processes we label "globalisation". By establishing that globalisation is the cause of the imperfect present described in Ireland and in Latin America, it will highlight what future is likely to be in store if these trends are deepened and intensified.

2 - Globalised societies

According to the widely referenced globalisation index published by the US academic magazine *Foreign Policy*, Ireland is the most globalised country in the world (A. T. Kearney, Inc. & *Foreign Policy*, 2002, 2003). Latin America, too, is a region that has embraced globalisation with zeal, opening its economies, reforming its states, and faithfully implementing the advice of the World Bank and the International Monetary Fund [IMF]: "It is therefore the closest we have to a laboratory test case of the globalizing orthodoxy at the dawn of the new millennium" (Kirby, 2003a, p. 202). For these reasons, examining the impact of globalisation in these two areas reveals what can be expected of it. This section examines the ways in which both areas have globalised, the structural impact of this on their productive economies, and the sort of societies that have resulted.

a) Ireland:

Ever since the liberalisation of its economy in the late 1950s and early 1960s, Ireland has developed an industrial base which depends overwhelmingly on very high levels of foreign industry established for the export market; particularly, but not exclusively, to the European Union [EU]. While this provided moderate levels of economic growth and development up to the 1990s, the years 1994 to 2000 witnessed an unprecedented economic boom in Ireland. Its average Gross Domestic Product [GDP] growth of 7.6% per annum between 1990 and 2001 was the third highest in the world over this period - behind China and Singapore, but far ahead of all of its nearest neighbours in the EU. The significance of this boom can only be fully appreciated in the light of Ireland's record up to then. In the late 1980s, a leading Irish historian wrote that the country's performance was "... the least impressive in Western Europe, perhaps in all Europe, in the twentieth century" (Lee, 1989, p. 521). All that changed in the 1990s, as high economic growth translated into increases in employment that averaged 4.7% per year between 1993 and 2001, with the level of employment growing from 1.15 million at the beginning of this period to 1.65 million in the first quarter of 2000, an increase of over half a million people. As Ireland's National Economic and Social Council [NESC] put it: "This was completely unprecedented in Irish economic history and was the fastest growth of employment in the OECD in this period" (2003, p. 11). Unemployment fell from 15.9% of the workforce in 1993 to 4.3% in 2000, with the numbers of those unemployed falling from 222,500 to 74,900. The long-term unemployed - those out of work for longer than a year - fell from 8.9% of the workforce to 1.6%. As a result, average earnings grew by 25% in real terms over the period 1987-2000 but, with reductions in personal taxation, real take-home pay for those on average manufacturing earnings increased by 60% for a single person and by 54% for a married person. This led to a convergence in living standards towards the EU average: in 1987, private consumption expenditure per capita in Ireland was only 72% of the EU average, whereas by 2002 it was estimated to be 95% (NESC, 2003, p. 57). In reference to the successes of the East Asian "tiger" economies in the 1980s, Ireland came to be known as the Celtic tiger.

Globalisation quickly came to be seen as the reason for this remarkable economic turnaround, with success owing "... much to the enthusiasm with which Ireland has ... approached the globalisation of its economy and the opening up of its society to outside influences" (Fitz

Gerald, 2000, p. 55). Sweeney examines the connection further, arguing that "... the impact of globalisation on Ireland has been profound and in many ways has brought great benefits to the majority of people in most, though not all, areas" (2003, p. 210). Describing Ireland as "... one of the most open economies in the world", he points to the fact that the value of Ireland's exports and imports in 2002 was 176% of the country's GDP, while Ireland is also the largest recipient of Foreign Direct Investment [FDI] in the world on a per capita basis. Ireland is, therefore, perhaps "... the case study for understanding how globalisation can bring success to a late-developing economy" (Sweeney, pp. 215-16). But this has not happened without very active state involvement, which attracted foreign investment through the incentive of low taxes on corporate profits, described by the managing director of the state's Industrial Development Agency [IDA] from 1981 to 1990, Padraic White, as "... the unique and essential foundation of Ireland's foreign investment boom" (Mac Sharry & White, 2000, p. 250). Over the decades, the IDA honed its strategies, so that it became very successful at identifying high-growth sectors of the international economy appropriate to Ireland and then attracting to the country some of the key global companies in those sectors. Information technology, pharmaceuticals and financial services were among the key sectors that drove the Irish boom. Furthermore, the state has consistently invested in education, thereby providing a skilled workforce for the many multinational companies setting up in Ireland and, through successful diplomacy, it managed to win far higher levels of structural funds per capita from the European Union than any other member state received, which contributed some €12 billion in grants to the Irish economy between 1989 and 2001 (Kirby, 2003b, p. 28).

In these ways, therefore, Ireland seems to offer a shining example of a form of globalisation that has the potential to turn around the economic prospects of late-developing countries. This is how it is being widely seen around the world, especially in Latin America and in the countries of Central and Eastern Europe, which hope to emulate its success. Yet the present is far from perfect in Ireland, as there is another, darker side to its economic success, which led Kirby to characterise the Celtic tiger as a case of "... economic success and social failure" (Kirby, 2002, p. 5). Examining the distributional impact of the economic boom on Irish society serves to illustrate this darker side. Poverty is perhaps the most common way in which distributional issues are treated. In the Irish case, data on poverty have become a battleground, since the picture presented depends entirely on one's definition of poverty. The Irish government likes to emphasise what it calls "consistent poverty", a definition based on the percentage of households that fall below relative income poverty lines, *and also* experience deprivation, in that they lack one or more items on a list of eight basic indicators of deprivation, which include new rather than second-hand clothes, a meal with meat, fish or chicken every second day, a warm waterproof overcoat, and adequate heating. The percentage of Irish households in "consistent poverty", whose income was half the average income, fell from 9% in 1994 to 5.1% in 2000. However, even those who compile such data urge that deprivation indicators be amended to take account of "... the way poverty itself can be reconstituted in terms of new and emerging social needs in a context of higher societal living standards and expectations" (Nolan et al., 2002, p. 63). This acknowledges that poverty is always a relative concept. Looking at trends in relative poverty under the Celtic tiger reveals a far less benign situation, as the percentage of households whose income was below half the average income increased from 18.6% to 25.8% over this period. Data also reveal a consistent growth in the depth of poverty below each income line, meaning that "... those falling below relative income thresholds are falling further and further behind the middle of the income distribution" (Nolan et al., 2002, p. 22).

Consistent with the growth in relative poverty, surveys also show a growth in inequality during the 1990s, after 20 years of remarkable stability in Irish income distribution data. For example, data from the Central Statistics Office [CSO] show that the share of national income going to all households except the top 10% declined between 1994 and 2000, with the biggest decline being experienced by the poorest households (Nolan, 2003, p. 135). As with all survey data, this almost certainly severely underestimates the share of the top 10%, as the rich consistently understate their income in such surveys. A comparison between Ireland and other countries is provided by the Human Poverty Index for 17 industrialised countries, contained for the first time in the *Human development report 1998* of the United Nations Development Programme [UNDP]. It constitutes a more multifaceted measure of poverty, including not just income, but also education, health and unemployment. From 1998 to 2003, Ireland occupied the second lowest place (the United States was in the lowest place) on the index, although other countries changed their positions, up or down (United Nations Development Programme, 2003, p. 248). This range of evidence shows that Ireland has become a much more polarised and unequal society as a result of the economic boom.

These data, however, fail to capture the range of inequalities that characterise post-Celtic tiger Ireland. Inequality at regional level, between the West of the country, which for over 100 years has seen steady outmigration and falling population, and the East, where the fast growing capital city is located, has been exacerbated. The Eastern region absorbed 90% of public investment over the period, while employment in foreign multi-national companies located in the East increased from under 35% of permanent employment in all such companies in Ireland in 1993 to over 48% by 2000, a dramatic rise (NESC, 2003, pp. 16-17). Gender inequalities showed a more mixed trend. While women's participation in the labour force increased from 39% in 1994 to over 50% in 2002 (with almost half of the increase being in part-time employment), Ireland has the lowest activity rate in the EU for women with children under five years of age, owing to the lack of provision for childcare.

A final structural inequality relates to housing. As Drudy and Punch point out, until 1994 new house prices increased broadly in line with the consumer price index, house building costs (labour and materials) and average industrial earnings. Since 1994, however, house prices have diverged significantly from these other indices and have increased at a significantly faster rate than house building costs (Drudy & Punch, 2001, p. 248). Nationally, the ratio of the average price of new houses to average industrial earnings (a ratio of housing affordability) increased from 4.33 in 1990 to 5.29 in 1997 and to 7.40 in 2000, while in Dublin the ratio went from 5.34, to 6.32, and to 9.70. Prices for second-hand houses increased even more (NESC, 2003, p. 83). The average price of a house increased from €100,000 in 1996 to €290,000 in 2003 (*permanent tsb/ESRI House Price Index*, available at the website: www.permanenttsb.ie/house-price-index/). As a result, "... access to home ownership based on principal incomes has been eliminated for low-to-average-income households and an increasing number of middle-to-higher income households.... access to owner occupation is now limited to joint mortgage holders with combined incomes considerably higher than national average wages" (Downey, 1998, p. 34). Meanwhile, the number of public authority houses being built declined from 2,960 in 1995 to 2,204 in 2000, despite the fact that the number of families on waiting lists more than doubled. As a direct consequence, the number of those who are homeless in Ireland has increased from 2,172 in 1993 to 5,581 in 2002; a figure regarded by the Simon Community as an extremely conservative estimate ("New Homeless Figures", 2003).

Perversely, as social need has increased, state social provision has declined. While Irish social expenditure increased in real terms throughout the 1990s, as a proportion of Gross National Product [GNP] it has fallen steadily from 12.3% in 1992 to 7.8% in 2000, and as a proportion of GDP from 10.9% to 6.6% over the same period. The Irish welfare state "... continues to exhibit the defining characteristics of the residual, or liberal, welfare state model" (Timonen, 2003, p. 21). Structural inequalities have also become more deeply entrenched. While educational participation has steadily increased over recent decades, Smyth and Hannan (2000, p. 117) find "... a notable persistence in educational inequalities by social background". They find a widening gap between the professional and unskilled manual groups in terms of access to full-time third-level education over the past two decades. Thus, the available evidence points to the fact that education tends to further marginalise those who come from more disadvantaged backgrounds. Inequalities are more pervasive in the health care system, where the state actively supports a two-tier system. Wren describes it as "... an extraordinary system":

Consuming 10 per cent of national income yet denying care to many families. Consuming nearly one-quarter of government spending yet fostering two-tier access to hospitals. Channelling state funds into private for-profit hospitals. Channelling them into preferential care for private patients through tax relief for insurance, subsidised charges for private accommodation in public hospitals and the payment of public salaries to hospital consultants while they earn private fees. The ill-considered use of state funds to subsidise and promote private care contrasts with the resistance of government to improving access to primary care for those who cannot afford it (Wren, 2003, p. 363).

Perversely, she finds that "... access to free primary care has become more restricted as national wealth has grown", as the state raised medical charges, but failed to increase income eligibility for medical cards (Wren, 2003, November 17).

These outcomes are not accidental, but are a direct consequence of Ireland's economic success. For, as already stated, this success has been based on a strategy of using low taxes on manufacturing profits to gain a competitive edge in attracting foreign investment. Furthermore, wage competitiveness has been maintained by a policy of trading moderate wage rises for cuts in income taxes. As a result of this policy mix, Ireland has fallen further and further behind all other EU states in social spending and in tax receipts. Between 1993 and 2000, Irish government expenditure on social protection has fallen from 20.2% of GDP to 14.1%, while the average EU expenditure has fallen from 28.8% to 27.3% over the same period. Meanwhile, Irish government current tax and non-tax receipts have decreased from 38.6% of GDP to 33.8% over this period, while the EU average has increased from 43.2% to 43.9% (Kirby, 2003b, p. 41). The Irish state has become a low-tax, low-spend state, ever more dependent on market forces to achieve social outcomes and with a greatly weakened ability to provide quality infrastructures or services, or to counteract with any effectiveness the polarising impact of market forces. It finds itself caught amid contradictory pressures: economists tell policy-makers that they must further reduce spending and taxation to maintain competitiveness (Sachs, 1997, p. 62), while those concerned with social problems call for increased social spending (Nolan, O'Connell, & Whelan, 2000, p. 352). The evidence points to the fact that the former have more influence over policy than the latter. Ireland's economic success is based on a model of development that creates an ever more polarised and unjust society. Far from being a model of success in the era of globalisation, Ireland is a model of the social cost of economic success under the conditions of globalisation.

b) Latin America:

Latin America's opening to globalisation happened under conditions very different from those of Ireland. Plunged into its worst recession since the 1930s by the international debt crisis that broke suddenly upon the region in 1982, and under pressure by the World Bank and the IMF to adopt the tenets of the "Washington Consensus", Latin American governments moved swiftly to liberalise trade, to open up their financial systems as a way of attracting foreign investment and to reduce government intervention in the economy by privatising state enterprises. In this way, they put an end to a 50-year period of inward-oriented development, led by the state, in a bid to lay the foundations of a national industrial base manufacturing for the local market that they had previously imported (a strategy known as Import Substitution Industrialisation or ISI). By the early 1990s, the region was returning to economic growth, attracting increasing levels of foreign investment and becoming deeply integrated into global trade flows. Governments sought to ensure a climate of macroeconomic and fiscal stability, so as to keep the investment they had and to attract more, establishing themselves as responsible players in the global marketplace and putting behind them the region's image of political instability and of government interference in the economy. As Weaver put it: "... the market, rather than the government, [had become] the principal mechanism for regulating society, resolving conflicts, and determining directions of change" (2000, p. 181).

During the first half of the 1990s, the results seemed very promising. Economic growth reached an annual average of 4.2% between 1990 and 1994 and, after net capital outflows in the 1980s (associated with payments on the region's huge foreign debts and the lack of foreign investment in the region), Latin America became again a net recipient of capital inflows, reaching some 3% of GDP between 1990 and 1999. Furthermore, as the decade progressed, more and more of these inflows were constituted by FDI: namely, investment in industries and services, instead of portfolio investment in the region's bonds and stock markets, a form of investment that is notoriously volatile, since it withdraws at the first sign of financial trouble. FDI grew more than five-fold, from an annual average of $18 billion in 1990-94 to a high of $103 billion in 1999, before falling back under the impact of the US economic downturn. By the late 1990s, over three-quarters of total investment flows to Latin America were in the form of FDI. The region registered one of the world's highest rates of growth in merchandise trade, both in volume and in value. Between 1990 and 2001, the export of goods from Latin America and the Caribbean grew by an annual average rate of 8.4% in volume and by 8.9% in value. These rates were exceeded only by China and the most dynamic Asian countries. Furthermore, the nature of the goods being exported by the region showed a marked change. The share of primary products (such as coffee, sugar, copper, tin and oil) in the region's total exports fell from 73.5% in 1985 to 44.3% in 2000, while that of high-, intermediate- and low-technology manufactured goods grew from 24.3% in 1985 to 52.3% in 2000. Workers were moving out of the agricultural sector and into manufacturing and, particularly, services. Inflation, which had reached over 1,000% annually in some Latin American countries in the 1980s and early 1990s, was reduced from an average of 877% for the region as a whole in 1993 to 8.5% in 2003. Apart from strictly economic matters, the region's reintegration into the international political system helped strengthen its links with North America (through the Summits of the Americas) and with Europe (through the annual Latin America–EU Summit), reinforcing democratisation throughout the region. In these ways, Latin America appeared to be approximating more and more to the industrialised countries of the North. Globalisation seemed to be spurring development in a way that had eluded the region throughout its history.

Mexico's financial crash at the end of 1994, however, served as a wake-up call to Latin America. Not only did it plunge Mexico into a severe recession (though it recovered from this more quickly than was expected), but the whole region's growth declined to a lacklustre 2.5% for the second half of the 1990s, collapsing to virtually nothing in 2001 and to -0.4% in 2002, as the downturn in the United States took its toll. By 2003, FDI had fallen back to $29 billion, close to its level in the mid-1990s, while investment as a percentage of GDP had fallen to 18%, its lowest level since the early 1970s. These trends highlighted the weaknesses and vulnerabilities of the region's new model of development. Surveying the 1990s, the UN Economic Commission for Latin America and the Caribbean [ECLAC] finds it paradoxical that the most successful sectors in Latin America have been ones that do not trade, such as transport, communications, energy and financial services, while manufacturing has suffered the most, especially in more traditional, labour-intensive sectors such as clothing, footwear, leather manufactures and furniture, because of the impact of imports. Instead, the emerging industrial strengths of what the ECLAC researchers Katz and Stumpo (2001, pp. 138, 141) call the "... new Latin American economic model" are centred on two "... great dominant models of productive and trade specialization":

- The first, centred on Brazil, the Southern Cone (Chile and Argentina) and some Andean countries (Colombia and Peru) is based on the processing of natural resources, producing industrial commodities such as vegetable oils, paper and cellulose, iron and steel, wine, and fishmeal. These productive activities involve the intensive use of natural resources and are processed in capital-intensive automated plants, using little labour. They are products for which international demand grows slowly and they involve mature technology, with few opportunities for technological innovation.

- The second, centred on Mexico and Central America, is based on assembling electrical goods, computers and clothes, principally for the US market. Some of this work is done in *maquiladoras*, the products of which constitute almost a half of Mexico's exports. These assembly plants employ mostly low-cost labour, are largely non-unionised, and have been condemned for their coercive labour practices. They therefore have a record of high labour turnover. While providing jobs and badly needed foreign exchange, they have been criticised for their low level of linkages to the rest of the economy (and for thus not stimulating the development of other productive sectors) and for having little interest in developing the skills of their workforce.

Owing to lack of active government support, many industrial sectors producing capital goods and machinery and developing indigenous technological innovations have declined. The United Nations Conference on Trade and Development [UNCTAD] (2003, p. 141) sums up the impact of the two models that are now dominant: "Both types of activity have relatively low domestic-value-added content, and neither provides the kind of transformation of the domestic production and export pattern that would allow trade to become an engine of growth". As a result, ECLAC (2002, p. 178) points out that "... despite the region's economic turnaround in the 1990s, its rhythms of economic growth continue being significantly inferior to those before the debt crisis".

As with Ireland, therefore, it is difficult to argue that globalisation has been beneficial for most Latin Americans. Poverty has remained very high, affecting 43.9% of the population in 2003, higher than at any time since the mid-1990s, while the number of people living in poverty has grown from 200 million in 1990 to 204 million in 1997, and to 225 million in 2003 (ECLAC, 2004, p. 3). Similarly, inequality in income distribution, a characteristic of the region since colonial times, "... has stubbornly resisted efforts to reduce it" (ECLAC, 2004, p. 8). It is interesting that, unlike Ireland, Latin American governments have consistently increased their social spending since the early 1990s, rising from 10.1% of GDP in 1990 to 12.1% in 1996-7, during a period of economic growth, but continuing to rise from 12.1% to 13.8% of GDP between 1997 and 2000-01, despite a slowdown in economic growth. Alongside this, however, the economy is itself generating poverty, owing to the fact that more than 6 out of every 10 new jobs created is in the informal economy, characterised by low incomes, flexible or non-existent contracts, lack of social security cover and poor conditions of employment. The informal economy's share of all new jobs created rose from 67.3% in 1990-94 to 70.7% in 1997-99, while ECLAC (2004, p. 9) concluded that "... precarious employment conditions, in terms of contractual status and social security coverage, probably became even more widespread in 2003". In this way, the changing nature of employment is reshaping the region's social structure. As ECLAC (2000, p. 68) puts it, "... there is every indication that the occupational structure has become the foundation for an unyielding and stable polarisation of income". The effects on society are expressed graphically by the well-known Argentine political scientist, Guillermo O'Donnell:

> The sharp, and deepening, dualism of our countries severely hinders the emergence of broad and effective solidarity. Social distances have increased, and the rich tend to isolate themselves from the strange and disquieting world of the dispossessed. The fortified ghettos of the rich and the secluded schools of their children bear witness to their incorporation into the transnationalized networks of modernity, as well as to the gulf that separates them from large segments of the national population. (cited in Kirby, 2003a, p. 116)

Finally, this growing social polarisation is undermining the region's economic growth since, as unemployment has grown in the early years of the new millennium and wages have fallen, domestic demand is unable to act as a stimulus to economic recovery. As UNCTAD (2003, p. 146) concluded, "... policies introduced in response to the debt crisis have left many countries in the region in conditions as fragile as those prevailing in the 1980s".

3. - *Interrogating globalisation's claims*

Ireland and Latin America present different examples of how opening up economies to the global flows of capital, trade and production that characterise globalisation end up reconfiguring and restructuring societies. More than analysing economic performance at any particular moment in time, therefore, it is important to examine the ways in which globalisation has structured two sets of relationships. The first is the relationship between national societies and global flows of capital, trade and production: the issues to focus on are the sorts of productive capacities fostered and how embedded and enduring they are. The second set of relationships relates to the ways in which the productive economy serves the needs of society, particularly of the most vulnerable: the issues to focus on are poverty, inequality and social provision. An examination of how globalisation is configuring these two sets of relationships provides the basis for answering the important question posed in Section 1: "Does a deepening of globalisation offer the prospect of a better future or do we need to reshape globalisation?".

In answering this question, the globalists make two claims. The first is that globalisation results in higher economic growth, and the second is that higher growth helps the poor at least as much as it helps everyone else.

Does the evidence presented on Ireland and Latin America bear out these claims? The answer to the first claim is a partial "Yes", with the case of Ireland in particular seeming to vindicate strongly the claims of the globalists. However, if we examine more than simply rates of GDP/GNP growth per annum, both cases examined here point to the greater vulnerability that reliance on global flows entails. With regard to Ireland, there is now evidence that the Central and Eastern European countries joining the European Union in 2004 are more attractive than Ireland for FDI, highlighting just how dependent the Irish success has been on winning very high levels of foreign investment. By contrast, indigenous industry remains relatively weak. For all its differences, Latin America shows similar structural vulnerabilities. No country in the region has been as successful in attracting FDI as has Ireland, but the growing role of foreign investment in all the region's countries has created a two-tier economic structure, with the dynamic sectors being heavily dependent on outside investment and weakly linked to the domestic economy. The steady decline in such investment since 2000 highlights the vulnerabilities that result. The second claim made by the globalists, namely that economic growth benefits the poor as much as it does other sectors of the population, is clearly refuted by the cases presented here, most dramatically by the case of Ireland, where the structural features that have helped the economy to boom have also severely eroded the state's welfare capacity. The evidence, therefore, strongly supports the conclusion that more globalisation will indeed make the future for Ireland and for Latin America more tense.

The position of the so-called anti-globalists also rests on two claims. The first is that the present dominant form of globalisation results in increasing the power of global capital at the expense of the power of the national state.

The second claim follows on from the first: namely, that globalisation increases social polarisation, producing few winners, but many losers, and thereby undermines social cohesion and sustainability. Both claims are borne out by the evidence presented here. In consciously trying to foster deeper linkages with global flows, both the Irish state and the states of Latin America have become much more subservient to the demands of global capital and much less able to protect their own citizens or to provide them with quality and accessible social services - not that any of them were very successful in the latter task, but they aspired to be so. The overwhelming weight of evidence points to the fact that globalisation has increased the polarisation of societies in Ireland and in Latin America, undermining social cohesion and sustainability with sometimes dramatic results, as in the growing "crisis of governability" that is evident in many Latin American countries. This therefore supports the argument that what is required, if we are to aspire to a better future for all, is a form of globalisation in which strong public authorities, whether national or transnational, can regulate and govern market flows, ensuring that they serve, in a sustainable and equitable way, the public good. Needless to say, how this can be done raises another complex set of questions, to our understanding of which the work of Robert Cox makes a major contribution.

Conclusions

If the present is imperfect, what does the evidence tell us about the future? Examining the implications of globalisation through presenting evidence from Ireland and Latin America, it can be concluded that globalisation as we have it today sunders the bonds through which public authorities restrained the market for the good of society. The results of this liberation of market forces have been unpredictable: it has generated an economic dynamism side by side with economic and social marginalisation and it has done so both in the context of booming economies (as in Ireland for much of the 1990s) and when growth was more sluggish (as in Latin America). Furthermore, these polarising processes are now structural features of these societies, so that they will worsen until such time as these structures are changed in fundamental ways. These conclusions therefore illustrate Cox's two positions on globalisation. The first projects present trends into the future, with change being at most incremental; this is what will give us an ever more tense future. The second position will require more radical change if we seek a future that is more humane and stable.

Responses to this are varied. Many individuals submit themselves to the ever more intense competitive pressures it engenders, often at great personal cost. Others react against it, involving themselves in protest activities, in proposing alternatives and in mobilising support for these. There is an increasingly visible reaction in the return to local forms of living, especially through organic farming, local production and distribution co-operatives, handcrafts, and what is often labelled "alternative living". Though easily dismissed, this is a trend that is involving ever larger sections of the population (Korten, 1999). The growing power and pervasiveness of the criminal economy indicates another response to globalisation, as people find alternative sources of livelihoods (sometimes extremely lucrative ones) in crime, gangs, and informal networks trafficking drugs, women and children, diamonds and arms. Finally, some strike back through forms of counter-systemic violence, expressing a logic of revenge. The impact of this on all our societies and individual lives has grown astonishingly fast in the wake of 9/11 (Kaldor,

2001). The future for all, winners, losers, and those desperately caught in between, is more and more tense.

References

A. T. Kearney, Inc., & *Foreign Policy* (2002, January/February). Globalization's last hurrah?. *Foreign Policy*, 38-51.

A. T. Kearney, Inc., & *Foreign Policy* (2003, January/February). Measuring globalization: Who's up, who's down?. *Foreign Policy*, 60-72.

Cox, R. W. (2002). *The political economy of a plural world: Critical reflections on power, morals and civilization.* London: Routledge.

Downey, D. (1998). *New realities in Irish housing: A study on housing affordability and the economy.* Dublin: Dublin Institute of Technology, Consultancy and Research Unit for the Built Environment.

Drudy, P. J., & Punch, M. (2001). Housing and inequality in Ireland. In S. Cantillon, C. Corrigan, P. Kirby, & J. O'Flynn (Eds.), *Rich and poor: Perspectives on tackling inequality in Ireland* (pp. 235-261). Dublin: Oak Tree Press, in association with the Combat Poverty Agency.

Fitz Gerald, J. (2000). The story of Ireland's failure – and belated success. In B. Nolan, P. J. O'Connell, & C. T.

Whelan (Eds.), *Bust to boom?: The Irish experience of growth and inequality* (pp. 27-57). Dublin: Institute of Public Administration.

Held, D., & McGrew, A. (2002). *Globalization/anti-globalization*. Malden, MA: Blackwell Publishers.

Kaldor, M. (2001). *New and old wars: Organized violence in a global era*. (Rev. ed.). Cambridge: Polity Press.

Katz, J., & Stumpo, G. (2001). Regímenes sectoriales, productividad y competitividad internacional. *Revista de la Cepal, 75*, 131-152.

Kirby, P. (2002). *The Celtic tiger in distress: Growth with inequality in Ireland*. Basingstoke: Palgrave.

Kirby, P. (2003a). *Introduction to Latin America: Twenty-first century challenges*. London: Sage Publications.

Kirby, P. (2003b). *Macroeconomic success and social vulnerability: Lessons for Latin America from the Celtic tiger*. Santiago: United Nations Economic Commission for Latin America and the Caribbean.

Korten, D. C. (1999). *The post-corporate world: Life after capitalism*. San Francisco: Berrett-Koehler.

Lee, J. J. (1989). *Ireland 1912-1985: Politics and society*. Cambridge: Cambridge University Press.

Mac Sharry, R., & White, P. A. (2000). *The making of the Celtic tiger: The inside story of Ireland's boom economy.* Cork: Mercier Press.

National Economic and Social Council (Ireland). (2003). *An investment in quality: Services, inclusion and enterprise.* Dublin: Author.

New homeless figures do not tell the whole story. (2003, June). *Simon News, 6,* p. 2.

Nolan, B. (2003). Income inequality during Ireland's boom. *Studies: an Irish Quarterly Review, 92* (366), 132-150.

Nolan, B., Gannon, B., Layte, R., Watson, D., Whelan, C. T., & Williams, J. (2002). *Monitoring poverty trends in Ireland: Results from the 2000 Living in Ireland survey.* Dublin: Economic and Social Research Institute.

Nolan, B., O'Connell P. J., & Whelan, C. T. (Eds.). (2000). *Bust to boom: The Irish experience of growth and inequality.* Dublin: Institute of Public Administration.

Sachs, J. D. (1997). Ireland's growth strategy: Lessons for economic development. In A. W. Gray (Ed.), *International perspectives on the Irish economy* (pp. 54-63). Dublin: Indecon Economic Consultants.

Smyth, E., & Hannan, D. F. (2000). Education and inequality. In B. Nolan, P. J. O'Connell & C. T. Whelan

(Eds.), *Bust to boom?: The Irish experience of growth and inequality* (pp. 109-126). Dublin: Institute of Public Administration.

Sweeney, P. (2003). Globalisation: Ireland in a global context. In M. Adshead & M. Millar, (Eds.), *Public administration and public policy in Ireland: Theory and methods* (pp. 201-18). London: Routledge.

Timonen, V. (2003). *Irish social expenditure in a comparative international context.* Dublin: Institute of Public Administration.

United Nations Conference on Trade and Development (2003). *Trade and development report, 2003: Capital accumulation, growth and structural change.* New York: United Nations.

United Nations Development Programme (1998). *Human development report, 1998.* New York: Oxford University Press.

United Nations Development Programme (2003). *Human development report, 2003: Millenium development goals: A compact among nations to end human poverty.* New York: Oxford University Press.

Implications of Globalisation:
Present Imperfect, Future Tense?

United Nations Economic Commission for Latin America and the Caribbean (2000). *Social panorama of Latin America, 1999-2000*. Santiago: Author.

United Nations Economic Commission for Latin America and the Caribbean (2002). *Globalización y desarrollo*. Santiago: Author.

United Nations Economic Commission for Latin America and the Caribbean (2004). *Social panorama of Latin America, 2002-2003*. Santiago: Author.

United Nations Economic Commission for Latin America and the Caribbean (2004, January 9). Unemployment rate stays at record levels. *ECLAC Notes, 32,* 9.

Weaver, F. S. (2000). *Latin America in the world economy: Mercantile colonialism to global capitalism*. Boulder, CO: Westview Press.

Wren, M.-A. (2003). *Unhealthy state: Anatomy of a sick society*. Dublin: New Island.

Wren, M.-A. (2003, November 17). Chronic consequences as medical card safety net slowly disappears. *The Irish Times*.

MULTINATIONAL CORPORATIONS AND THE DEMOCRATIC STATE: FRIEND OR FOE?

Robert Frith

Introduction

"With the exception of the nation-state, the Trans-National Corporation [TNC] generates more controversy and attention in international political economy than any other single actor" (Goddard, 2003, p. 435). This controversy is, perhaps, most pronounced in respect of the contested relationship of the Multinational Corporation [MNC] with the national democratic state. Disagreement abounds with respect to the novelty of contemporary levels of internationalised trade, globalised production and market integration: of the consequences – if any - for the sovereignty and autonomy of the modern state and its continued effectiveness in providing a range of public goods, and ultimately the implications of these issues for us as citizens and consumers. This chapter reviews the range of arguments and evidence concerning the features of contemporary economic globalisation, and its relationship to the state. It does so in order to evaluate whether economic globalisation constitutes a new set of challenges to the sovereign authority and power of the modern territorial state, or whether it continues to remain, in Aristotle's phrasing, "... the most sovereign and inclusive association" (as cited by Cerny, 1995, p. 596).

This chapter makes the case that transformations in the contemporary global economy are qualitatively different, rather than simply denoting a quantitative expansion of international trade between states. It is argued that these transformations - in particular the growth of diffused and globalised networks of production, services, finance, and Research and Development [R&D] - raise serious challenges in relation to the governance control and democratic legitimacy of the state. Thus, whilst claims regarding a borderless world are viewed to be premature and misleading, at the same time those sceptical arguments which maintain that the modern state at the beginning of the 21st century is a similar beast to that of 100 years ago are also rejected as inaccurate.

Specifically, it is argued that the globalisation of economic activity marks the "denationalization" (Zürn, 2000, p. 187) and "deterritorialisation" (Scholte, 2000, p. 46) of economic spaces. Thus, even if we accept arguments that the scope of the transactions is not yet fully global, they "... still cause a problem for national governance simply because the social space to be governed is no longer national" (Zürn, p. 187). This is significant in two distinct but related respects. Firstly, it raises important questions concerning the governance control of the territorially bounded state – whether it can continue to provide effectively the range of public goods which the national citizenry of advanced industrial states have come to expect in the post-war period (Cerny, 1995). The second issue concerns misgivings in relation to the efficacy of territorially constituted democracy, when citizens are increasingly exposed to forces originating outside of their national states (Held, 1995).

In the context of the incongruity between the territorially bounded state and increasingly globalised and diffuse modes of economic activity, Goddard posits that " ... perhaps the best hope for restoring equilibrium is an enlargement of political society to a new level of organization capable of bringing TNCs under jurisdictional control" (Goddard, 2003, p. 437). Such prescriptions raise profound normative questions concerning the relevant political authority and community: "Who rules, by what means, in whose interests and to what purpose?" (McGrew, 2002, p. 343). Whilst sceptical interpretations contend that the global political system remains underpinned principally by territorially limited and discrete national states, which govern for, and in the name of, a national citizenry, the argument presented here adopts the position that the processes of globalisation "... are leading to the crystallization of multilayered and asymmetric institutions and patterns of authority, and within this structural context, the fragmentation and refocusing of actors' identities and objectives" (Cerny, 2000, p. 22). The dimensions of economic activity – productive, service, financial, and R&D - are organised within networks, in which the space of place (the territorial state) interpenetrate the space of flows (the globalising economy), which at best only partly fit our standard political maps (Castells, 1996, p. 378; Toulmin, 1999, p. 907): hence Goddard's observation that the multinationals' constituents are not a territorially delimited national citizenry, but globally dispersed shareholders (2003, p. 437). Thus, the "... direct correspondence between authority, territory, community and economy" established by the Westphalian order - characterised by the dominance of the modern territorial state and interstate system - is being profoundly destabilised in the context of globalisation (Devetak & Higgott, 1999, p. 487).

Despite the challenges placed upon the state in the contemporary globalised context, it is not absolved of its social, political and economic responsibilities. These global transformations in the spheres of production, service, finance and R&D have not occurred, as it were, from somewhere "out there". Instead, the state is co-author of these processes and is hence constitutive of globalisation as much as globalisation is constitutive of the state: "... globalization shapes the state and is, at the same time, what states make of it' (Clark, 1999, p. 55). Accordingly, globalization is not simply a material structure that constrains state behaviour, "... but is itself reflective of movement in ideas about what states are, and what roles they can best perform" (Clark, p. 173). Simply put, globalisation is partially the outcome of the ideas that states hold about themselves and their material environment. The emphasis upon ideas alongside material factors "... as the building blocks of international reality" reflects a broadly constructivist perspective (Ruggie, 1998, p. 33).

This constructivist view of globalisation - as constitutive of a set of ideas about what states are and what roles they can best perform - is used to reflect upon contemporary discourses about the relative efficacy of the state and market for the provision of collective goods. In particular, it is argued that our perception of the efficacy of the alternative institutions of state and market[1] will partially construct our relations to the contemporary political-economy as citizens and consumers. This in turn raises profound questions regarding the viability of democratic politics and its perceived utility to contribute towards self-determination in the context of globalisation.

It is a reflection of the importance ascribed to ideas that this chapter gives particular attention to the transformations in the global knowledge structure - the realm of ideas and beliefs, which, according to Susan Strange (1994, p. 136), "... is undergoing the most rapid change" in the context of globalisation. It is suggested that

---

[1] For an argument that suggests states and markets should not be construed as distinct institutions, and which is largely contrary to the position I advance here, see Kay, 2004.

it is in the context of the knowledge structure that we can witness the latest set of (re)negotiations between the public and private spheres concerning the provision of collective goods, and our respective constitution as citizens-cum-consumers.

Organisation of the chapter

With these aims and objectives in mind, the following argument is split into three parts. The first reviews the conceptual landscape. It begins by considering the evidence concerning the contemporary changes in the patterns of global trade, production, services and R&D to evaluate whether they are best expressed by the term internationalisation, retaining an orientation to state-centric political maps; or globalisation, suggesting the increasing importance of diffused space of de-territorialised flows. While accepting many of the material and ideational insights of the globalisation perspective, a number of arguments which partially qualify the globalisation thesis are acknowledged. In particular, processes of re-territorialisation and location-branding, which reaffirm the continued importance of the territorial state and yet are integral aspects of contemporary globalisation, are highlighted. Acknowledging the interpenetration of the space of flows (market) and the space of place (state) (Ruggie, 1993, p. 144; Anderson, 1996, p. 173) provides the opportunity to conceptualise the variety of competing, yet converging, loyalty claims that are generated by both states and corporations and partially constitute people as citizens-cum-consumers.

Building on the conceptual analysis of the first part of the chapter, the second evaluates the challenges globalisation poses to the continued legitimacy of the territorial state. It focuses on the challenges to the continued effectiveness – i.e. the control and autonomy - of the state and the limits of territorially bounded democracy. The third, and final, part of the chapter applies these concepts and arguments to the global biotechnology industry – an exemplar of the knowledge economy.

Internationalisation or globalisation?

Goddard (2003, p. 437) claims that multinational corporations may be regarded as "... the major vehicle for the globalization of international production". Compelling data can be marshalled to support this claim. In 2002, there were 64,000 multinational corporations, which owned 870,000 foreign affiliates. The value added by foreign affiliates ($3.4 trillion) was estimated to account for about a tenth of world Gross Domestic Product [GDP]. MNCs' global sales reached £18 trillion and they employed more than 53 million people abroad (United Nations Conference on Trade and Development [UNCTAD], 2003, p. 14). Despite these staggering figures, sceptical commentators contend that the world remains far less globalised than the data suggest. The relevant question, pose De Grauwe & Camerman (2002, p. 313), is "... how the size of the multinationals has evolved relative to that of countries". Comparing the value added by MNCs with the GDP of states provides a useful indicator of their relative sizes.[2] Using this yardstick, De Grauwe & Camerman find that, of the 100 largest economies, 63 are countries and 37 are

---

[2] Grahame Thompson (2003, p. 407) notes that "... one of the often-quoted illustrations of the nature of modern corporate power is to compare the size of companies to that of nation-states", using corporate sales income and the GDP of states, and rightly points out that this methodology is flawed because "... GDP is a value-added measure, while sales income is not" and corporate value-added "... is typically between 20 per cent and 30 per cent of turnover".

corporations. Moreover, their historical comparison suggest that, in the year 2000, the 50 largest industrial corporations were slightly smaller in relation to world GDP than in 1980 (2002, pp. 314-318). Slightly different data over a different time-series, published by UNCTAD (2002), gives a slightly different picture, indicating the increased relative importance of multinationals compared with countries. In this regard, their data indicates that the value-added activities of the 100 largest multinationals have grown faster than those of countries in recent years, accounting for 4.3% of world GDP in 2000, compared with 3.5% in 1990. Nevertheless, the data suggests only a very small increase in the relative size of MNCs compared to states (0.8%). Furthermore, the value-added created by the 37 largest corporations represents less than 4% of the value-added created by the top 37 countries; confirming resolutely, in absolute terms, the overwhelming contribution of states to world GDP (De Grauwe & Camerman, 2002, p. 320).

Regardless of contemporary wrangling, by adopting a more extended historical perspective, additional evidence is available that casts further doubt on claims relating to the supposedly unprecedented levels of contemporary globalisation. Compared with the belle époque of 1890-1914, global economic integration in the contemporary period shows very little difference in terms of trade, capital transfers and movements in people (Hirst & Thompson, 1999, chap. 2). In this respect, Ngaire Woods (2000, p. 2) notes that: "Transnationalism and interdependence were buzzwords not only twenty years ago, but even eighty years ago, not to mention in the nineteenth century". The period of the belle époque was "… precisely the era during which nation-states and national economies were being forged", and thus there is very little reason to suppose that contemporary conditions pose a real threat to national sovereignty or autonomy (Held & McGrew, 2002, p. 46).

Despite clear continuities, to conclude that the contemporary global political economy is ostensibly similar to that of 100 years ago is unsatisfactory. Whilst interdependence may not be unique to the late 20th and early 21st centuries, we can identify a number of significant qualitative differences in the structure of the contemporary political economy, in terms of the growth of globalised production in goods, services, finance and R&D. Even where corporations remain primarily national, their products are increasingly aimed at global markets. These changes have been partly authored by the core industrialised states themselves and have been reinforced by the extension of political authority into the international sphere through the creation and empowerment of global regulatory institutions, such as the World Trade Organisation [WTO], International Monetary Fund [IMF] and World Bank, alongside a series of regional institutions such as the European Union [EU] and state-sanctioned private and public-private networks of governance (Woods, 2002).

Those who are sceptical of claims regarding the transformative impact of globalisation largely portray it as the increasing movements – in goods, capital and people - across borders. Jens Bartelson (2000, p. 184) terms this view of globalisation as intensified *transference* "... between pre-constituted units", which can be adequately captured by the term *internationalisation* (Hirst & Thompson, 1999, pp. 7-10). If global integration is simply interpreted along these lines, the term *globalisation* becomes redundant (Scholte, 1997, p. 430). However, *internationalisation* is only one dimension of global economic integration. Far more significant in relation to the globalisation thesis is the development of global networks by multinational corporations, which have replaced the Fordist production-line that incorporated all aspects of the process (Woods, 2000, p. 3), and whose production "... is considerably greater than the level of world exports, and encompasses all the world's major economic regions" (Held & McGrew, 2002, p. 48). For Robert Cox (1993, p. 260), this justifies speaking of a globalised economy, that is "... an economic space transcending all country borders", alongside an already existing internationalised economy "... based on transactions across country borders". These networks are composed of the "... segmentation of functions" (Goddard, 2003, p. 441), which introduce "... differentiation – both of distinct stages of the production process and of increasingly complex and variable production-line tasks themselves" (Cerny, 1995, p. 613). Exemplary in this regard is Nike, whose core activities involve the marketing and branding of their sports wear, whilst the fabrication of the goods is outsourced to contractors (Goddard, 2003, p. 441). The advent of increasingly advanced information-communication technology enabling real-time communications, in conjunction with national liberalisation policies, allows the same global restructuring in the service and financial sector also (Cable, 1999, pp. 15-18; 1995, pp. 32-34). An ostensibly national service, such as rail transport, is enmeshed in the global network, with National Rail Enquiries announcing, in November 2003, their plans to move their call centre to Bangalore, confirming likely labour-cost savings of up to £25 million over the next five years (Clark, 2003, p. 9). As regards the financial services sector, Vincent Cable (1999, p. 12) remarks that it is perhaps the "... one field in which globalization may begin to approximate to the truly global ... where financial firms increasingly function as globally integrated businesses, not just as multinational companies". Increasingly, research and development is conducted outside of the "home" country and focuses on truly innovative activities, rather than product and process modification. Investment in R&D is directed towards regions which have locational advantages in terms of a highly skilled workforce, rather than in natural resources or low-cost labour. Locational advantages in R&D and other knowledge intensive activities often arise as an outcome of "clustering", which brings about competitive advantages by bringing firms and innovative research institutions such as universities and science centres into close geographical proximity (Goddard 2003, pp. 449-450). These "districts" or "agglomeration economies" are integrated into wider global networks, forming complex global supply chains (Phillips, 2000, p. 50). These institutional innovations are closely connected with the technological imperatives expressed in an advanced knowledge economy. In particular, networks provide the arrangements for the development of mutually beneficial alliances, mechanisms for the rapid knowledge transfers required by alliance capitalism and enhanced protection of temporary monopolies on the appropriation of specialised knowledge (Phillips, pp. 40-42).

However, as Cerny (2000, p. 29) remarks, these transformations in the global economy "... only represent the supply side of the equation". Even when multinational corporations could reasonably be described as internationalised rather than globalised, it remains the case that their goods and services are increasingly aimed at globalised markets (Cerny, p. 29). In this regard, Susan Strange (1995, p. 59) comments: "It is the markets, not the enterprises that are multinational". For Benjamin Barber (2000, p. 280), the globalisation of the markets is associated with a shift from trade in durable goods and natural resources – what he refers to as the "... hard economy of the industrial/manufacturing world" - towards the "...

service and information economy". In this respect, he suggests that "... trade as we cross the millennial threshold is in information, in images, in entertainment and in ideas; it is in films and advertising and brand-names and merchandising". Such arguments regarding the development of global consumer brands seem persuasive when we are informed that 69% of three-year-olds recognise the golden arches of McDonald's, whilst half of four-year-olds do not know their own name (Hill, 2003).

The continued relevance of the state

Despite these qualitative shifts towards a globalised economy, images of a borderless world are misleading. The territorial state remains a core institution in the constitution, regulation and extension of globalised economic activity. Even in the context of an increasingly "weightless" economy, characterised by information flows circulating through digitised space, place remains important. Virtualised and disembedded economic flows are again re-embedded within the national regulatory borders of the territorial state (Sassen, 1996, p. xii). In no meaningful sense can we talk of a single global economy. Indeed, the state's continuing role as the principal guarantor of corporate contracts and private property rights (Sassen, p. 27), in conjunction with governments' position as "... central agents affecting the organisation of industry through selective or strategic policy decisions surrounding the national technology infrastructure" (Phillips, 2000, p. 42), suggests the continued importance of place, in relation to the successful functioning of the contemporary global knowledge economy.

In their disavowal of the globalisation thesis, Hirst & Thompson carefully distinguish between TNCs and MNCs. The distinction is premised on the continued importance of the "home base" for multinationals, whereas truly transnational corporations are genuinely footloose and without a specific national identification (Hirst & Thompson, 1999, p. 11). Whilst Vivien Schmidt (1995, p. 79) contends that "... multinationals have been coming closer to the 'stateless' ideal", Peter Van Ham (2002, p. 254) is surely right to point out that the "so-called 'country-of-origin effect' plays an important role in consumers' purchase decisions (viz., 'German cars' and 'Japanese cameras')." Thus, location branding is an increasingly necessary activity in order to provide positive territory images on customers' mental maps. In this regard, Van Ham (p. 252) predicts that "... the time is rapidly approaching when territorial entities can no longer afford not to jump on the 'brand-wagon' – it's branding or bust".

Whilst territorial location may retain its resonance in relation to the provision of regulatory authority and corporate branding strategies, this re-territorialisation of economic activity does not necessarily reinforce any sense of symmetry between territory, authority and political community: i.e. the assumed set of relationships which have constituted the political maps which have traditionally made sense of the respective fields of international relations, international political economy and political theory.

Branding, claims Van Ham (2002, p. 255), is not only about "... selling products, services and ideas, it is not only about gaining market share and attention, it is also about managing identity, loyalty and image". In short, one of the central purposes of branding is to generate loyalty claims upon actors amidst an environment of alternative and competing claims. Consumers are encouraged to develop emotions of identity and loyalty with certain corporate product brands and citizens are encouraged to develop and deepen civic ties to their state, whilst the contemporary state is required to generate loyalty claims on multinational corporations and in relation to its citizenry. Whilst state-centric models of international relations, international political economy and political theory assumed equivalence within these claims, the loyalties generated by them under conditions of globalisation are increasingly divergent. It is around these competitive loyalty claims that the arguments concerning the future *meanings* of governance, control and autonomy in relation to the national state, and the continued veracity of territorial modes of democracy, emerge.

Governance, control and autonomy

The arguments concerning the impact of economic globalisation on the future governance, control and autonomy of the contemporary state are broadly twofold. Firstly, it is argued that there is an increasing disjuncture between the structure of the globalising economy and the territorial state, which undermines the state's policy control (Clark, 1999, p. 91). In these terms, Philip Cerny (1995, p. 598) speaks of a growing incongruence in the "... political economies of scale" between the political-institutional and the economic-organisational structures. An increasingly important trend in corporate restructuring has been the growth of cross-border Mergers and Acquisitions [M&As] (Scholte, 2005, p. 180), which reached an all-time high of 7,894 cases in 2000, of which 175 were worth more than $1 billion (UNCTAD, 2003, p. xiii). Whilst the number and value of M&As fell in the years immediately following, in 2006 they returned to levels that were "... close to those achieved in the first year of the cross-border M&A boom of 1999-2001" (UNCTAD, 2006, p. xvii). This has raised the significance of intra-firm trading and estimates suggest that it now accounts for one third of aggregate global trade flows (Goddard, 2003, p. 438). This creates considerable problems for tax raising purposes, which require national regulatory authorities to attribute global profits to a specific locale. This is an incredibly complex task, which requires that revenue authorities not only calculate the transfer-value of goods and services, but the appropriation of research gains, patents, trademarks and copyrights among the firm's affiliates. This task is further exacerbated by the opportunity for transfer-pricing, in which firms can manipulate the assignment of the price and value of trades within the corporation in order to reduce their overall tax burden (Goddard, pp. 438-439).

The second sense in which the policy control and the autonomy of the state are deemed to be undermined concerns the increasing mobility of capital in the contemporary globalised economy. Briefly put, the argument suggests that technological advances allow multinationals to relocate their production in response to market changes in the pursuit of profit maximisation (Woods, 2000, p. 7). In this regard, Scholte (1997, p. 435) points to the "country hopping" exploits of Nike which, during a five year period, closed 20 factories and opened 35 others – "... many of them thousands of miles away" (Scholte, p. 435). Indeed, since the early 1970s, Nike has relocated its production from Japan to South Korea, Taiwan, Indonesia, China, Thailand, Vietnam and Malaysia, in response to rising costs and organising labour (el-Ojeili & Hayden, 2006, p. 66). In order to remain competitive and continue to attract globally mobile multinationals, states are required to adopt similar sorts of policies. Such policies are principally associated with the adoption of low corporate tax regimes, shifts from redistributive to infrastructural investment, flexible labour markets and so forth. Philip Cerny (2000, p. 30) encapsulates this set of transformations regarding the function of the state by introducing the notion of the *competition state*, "... aimed at making economic activities located within the national territory, or which otherwise contribute towards national wealth, more competitive in international and trans-national terms".

Predictions that these transformations will simply lead to convergence in the structure of national economies, or a "race to the bottom" in terms of national welfare provision, are an oversimplification. Fritz Scharpf (1997) highlights the continuing significant structural and institutional differences within European welfare regimes. Thomas Bernauer and Christoph Achini (2000, pp. 253-4) find no evidence to support the claim that globalisation has a negative impact in areas of expenditure that are not considered vital for international competitiveness: i.e. expressly redistributional expenditure. Nevertheless, evidence remains equivocal and UNCTAD (2003, p. xv) suggests that regulatory changes adopted by national authorities are increasingly favourable to Foreign Direct Investment [FDI]. In order to make sense of this apparent tension, we can distinguish between structural and cognitive perspectives of the competition state.

The structural perspective avers that states are constrained by the structural context of contemporary economic globalisation. Thus, whilst acknowledging the continued prevalence of different state forms in the medium term, Cerny (1997, p. 251) contends that "... pressures for homogenization are likely to continue to erode these different models where they prove to be economically inefficient in world markets and therefore unattractive to state and market actors". The implication in Cerny's work (p. 266) is that, whilst presently existing in "myriad forms", pressures for convergence will ultimately render the neo-liberal state *the* competition state form. As noted by Clark (1999, p. 104), this argument for the competition state is underpinned by a structural logic similar to that of Waltzian neo-realism – ostensibly substituting the determining structure of the global capitalist economy for that of anarchy.

In contrast, the cognitive perspective claims that competition states "see" themselves differently in the late 21st century - what Thomas Biersteker (2000, p. 150) refers to as "... changes in orientation". Whilst perhaps sitting uneasily with his, ultimately structural, argument, Cerny (1997, p. 256) emphasises globalisation's "crucial feature" as a discourse, altering "... the ideas and perceptions which people have of the empirical phenomena which they encounter ... which may restructure the game itself". From this perspective, the "... rise of the regulatory state" – concerned with providing an enabling-environment rather than direct provision of public goods - denotes a shift in perception of what statehood entails, and a re-evaluation of the border between the state and the market (Majone, 1994, p. 77). Van Ham (2002, p. 255) notes a branding consultant's remarks that "... governments don't want to run things any more ... the role of Government today is to inspire rather than control". Such a comment does not merely reflect the respective possibilities and limitations of states and markets under a particular set of structural constraints. More fundamentally, it expresses a change in their inter-subjective relations and a renegotiation of their constitutive precepts. As a consequence, it is suggested that "... commercial and political/territorial brands become harder to distinguish" (Van Ham), together with their respective "behavioural modes" (Cerny, 2000, p. 34).

The town of Celebration, Florida, established in 1994 by the Disney Corporation as a simulacrum of the post-war American suburban town, provides an exemplar of the blurring between corporate and political brands. Its leitmotif: "... commitment to community, education, health, technology, and a sense of place" (Celebration Company, c1999), sounds more reminiscent of a public authority than a commercial corporation. This corporate experiment constitutes a radical challenge to the self-understanding of both state and community and unsettles the distinctions between public and private modes of provision. Likewise, Richard Rosecrance (2002) points to a change in the organisation of states, which parallels the transformations in corporate organisation. Alongside the growth of "virtual" corporations, such as Nike, which provide R&D, product design, financing and marketing functions, but do not actually manufacture the product themselves, so too, he suggests, we are witnessing the rise of the virtual state, as advanced industrial states contract-out their productive functions to market actors in developing states, whilst retaining their "head" functions. As a consequence of such developments, "… the market rises as a direct provider of services, and the state contracts its role in the market" and, as a result, "… the citizen emerges with a greater independence of the state and greater contracting ability' (Rosecrance pp. 449-450). The notion of a weakening of the bonds between the citizen and the state can elicit normatively positive responses. A highly developed model which responds to these challenges is David Held's notion (1995; 2002) of cosmopolitan governance, which commends citizens' full incorporation of a variety of sub-national and supranational political communities alongside their membership of the national state. However, such orientations are not inevitable. The following questions continue to be posed: whether one wants a corporation rather than a city council or national state making these types of collective decisions and whether claims of consumer loyalty are to trump the traditional claims of citizenship (demos). This requires that we revisit those longstanding questions of who rules, by what means, on whose behalf and for whose benefit; the fundamental arguments that constitute the very ground of democracy.

Democracy

Orthodox formulations of democracy are usually conceived in territorially delimited terms, which "... assume a 'symmetrical' and 'congruent' relationship between political decisions-makers and the recipients of political decisions" (Held, 1995, p. 16). In fact, we can discern two specific, but interrelated, dimensions of democratic legitimacy. The first of which, following Fritz Scharpf, (1997, 1999), we may refer to as "output-oriented" – that is, in terms of the effectiveness of the state's policy control, the contours of which have been outlined above. The other aspect – input-oriented legitimacy - refers to opportunities of voice and representation through which citizens can shape and influence policy (Scharpf). The threat to input-oriented legitimacy or, more simply, democracy, in terms of the globalisation thesis is constituted by a reversal in the flow of democratic accountability that is imagined in the orthodox formulation (Clark, 1999, p. 94). Thus, instead of the state providing democratic institutions through which domestic constituencies impose demands upon the international domain, "... states are becoming transmission belts from the global into the national economic spheres" (Cox, 1993, p. 260). In a useful phrase, which again highlights the blurring of commercial and political/territorial brands, Sassen (1996, p. 41) speaks in terms of "economic citizenship", to denote the aggregation of economic rights belonging to corporate global actors rather than individuals.

In response to these claims that globalisation disrupts territorially-bounded democracy, Clark (1999, p. 156) enquires whether or not these outside-in formulations of globalisation eroding democracy are misconceived, asking instead whether "... the (un)democratic state generates globalization?" The serious implication arising from Clark's question concerns the political origins of globalisation, and hence perhaps the need for political solutions to the challenges it presents. At the outset, this requires that we ask ourselves: "Who am I?" (Brown, 1995, p. 9), or perhaps, "Who do I want to be?" The tentative answers we offer to such questions will delineate the normative political-economic boundaries concerning the appropriate role of the state and market and ultimately our constitution as citizen-cum-consumer.

In order to flesh-out some of these abstract arguments, the final section of this chapter will briefly apply the conceptual analysis to the contemporary contests concerning the respective roles of the state and market in the production, trade, regulation and ownership of biotechnology, our constitution as citizens-cum consumers, and the implications for democracy.

The State Incorporated vs. the Political Corporation: Citizen-cum-consumer in an age of globalisation.

Estimates suggest the globalised biotechnology industry to be worth around £70 billion ($113 billion) at the turn of the millennium (Russell & Vogler, 2000, p. 1), although projections are circulating which suggest that the European biotechnology market could be worth over €100 billion ($101 billion) by 2005 and that by the end of the decade global biotechnology markets could exceed €2,000 billion ($2,016 billion) - (European Commission, 2002, p. 12). The world market for genetically modified [GM] crops and food, alone, was estimated to be worth about $17 billion in 2002, and it is estimated that the wider application of GM crops – for the production of vaccines, renewable sources of energy, and so forth – could be worth about $100-$500 billion by 2020 (Bernauer, 2003, p. 6).[3]

Scholte links the emergent biotechnology sector with the "… ever widening range of commodification under globalizing capitalism" (2005, p. 172). The industry exhibits characteristics which strongly resonate with the notion of a *globalised*, rather than simply *internationalised*, industry – one constituted by complex networks, segmented production chains, and innovations closely connected with the technological imperatives expressed in an advanced knowledge economy. The sector is characterised by a demarcation between smaller Dedicated Biotechnology Firms (DBFs) and larger multinational corporations within the context of a division of innovative labour, in which multinational corporations utilise the expertise and intermediate products and services of DBFs in globalised supply chains, providing access to financial and managerial resources to the DBFs in return (Russell & Vogler, 2000, p. 2; European Commission, 2001, p. 8). These collaborations between the market actors are partly structured on the basis of geographical proximity, leading to the development of regional clustering in biotechnology activities (Allansdottir et al., 2002, chap. 5; European Commission, 2001, p. 9). The benefits of clustering are

---

[3] The figures given in brackets have been converted into $US, rounded to the nearest dollar, using current prices as of January 1, 2000. The $US prices are provided simply in order to allow the reader to compare roughly the various estimates cited. The price conversions were calculated using the full currency converter provided on *The Economist* website:
http://www.economist.com/markets/currency/fullconverter.cfm.

associated with effective and efficient knowledge transmission between actors, access to relevant laboratory and research expertise in centres of excellence - such as major universities - and the development of other supporting institutions, like venture capital and patent lawyers (Allansdottir et al., pp. 45-46, 59; European Commission, 2001, p. 9). These clusters are not only based on "... dense internal or local relations, but also by the ability to establish strong and varied external ties with other clusters" (Allansdottir et al., p. 56). The development of outward-oriented ties appears to be an increasing trend and is associated with "... the need to get access to state-of-the art knowledge, wherever it might be located" (Allansdottir et al., p. 59). It is this latter aspect which is perhaps most significant for our purposes. As Russell & Vogler (2000, p. 4) remark: "Modern biotechnology is fundamentally about knowledge. It is effectively an information-based *enabling* [original italics] technology, with DNA and its manipulation ... at its heart".

Employing Strange's notion (1994, p. 121) of the knowledge structure, "What knowledge is discovered, how it is stored, and who communicates it by what means to whom and on what terms", reveals the continued dominance of the large multinationals who, whilst outsourcing research to the small firms and universities, continue to control commercially the knowledge generated (Williams, 2000, p. 78). New varieties of Genetically Modified [GM] crops are designated by brand names – such as Novartis's *Bt 176 Modified Maize* - and protected though the assertion of intellectual property rights. The award of a patent is highly significant, because it constitutes "... a legal boundary between the overlapping private and public domains of knowledge" (Williams, p. 69). In effect, it constitutes the border between the state and the market, and in so doing denotes the legitimate realm of each. This is highly contentious, especially in view of the fact that intellectual knowledge is often the outcome of both public and private research. The primacy accorded to economic organisations above the political-administrative institutions ranks consumers and shareholders above citizens as the relevant community in relation to governance decisions. The control of genetic material, such as in Genetically Modified agricultural crops, becomes a matter of market forces, the expression of consumer preferences and consumer rights, instead of reflecting the voices and representations of political citizenship. Moreover, the state is partially constitutive of this process. Margaret Beckett's 2004 speech to the House of Commons on the commercial planting of GM crops in the UK is instructive in this regard. Notions of citizenship were tangentially alluded to via references to "stakeholders" and public dialogue. However, the speech concluded that ultimately "... *customers* [italics added] want a clear regime for traceability and labelling so that they can make their own choices".

However, to invoke an image of an absolute shift from the public realm of politics to the private sphere of economics is misleading. Barber's image (2000, p. 275) of capitalist markets having been "... ripped from the juridical and legislative box of regulatory institutions and civil infrastructure" is inaccurate. Rather, as noted earlier, the global extension of multinational corporations has been intimately associated with a deeply invasive complex of public-private global rules, which are institutionalised and enforced by the extension of state power through overarching regional and global regulatory organisations such as the EU and the WTO. The Intellectual Property Rights [IPRs] of private corporations over genetically manipulated life forms are adjudicated and enforced by the World Trade Organisation's Agreement on Trade-Related

Aspects of Intellectual Property Rights (WTO/TRIPS) regime, giving rise to situations where states protect the interests of foreign firms above that of their citizens (Williams, 2000, p. 72). In so doing, Sassen's notion of *economic citizenship* is given form at the expense of citizenship rights located in the individual.

Again, though, we may be in danger of pushing the argument too far. Economic citizenship has not simply replaced individual citizenship, even if the notion does provide key insights with respect to the contours of corporate power and authority in the contemporary world. Since the mid-1990s, the issue of Genetically Modified Organisms [GMOs] has provided a locus for sustained and energetic political activity, in which people have protested as citizens (as well as consumers) in relation to their development and commercial production (Levidow, 2007, p. 122). Their actions as citizens have required governments throughout the EU to engage in debates with civil society, thus signifying the resilience of the public sphere. Illustrative in this regard is the UK government's initiative *GM Nation?: The Public Debate*.

Similarly, in response to the rising controversy surrounding GM products, EU governments have been increasingly hostile to the commercial application of agricultural biotechnology, illustrating the continued importance of territorially based governance even for globalised industries. Beginning in February 1997, a number of governments prohibited approved GM products from their territories, on the basis of environmental and human health concerns, and sustained their objections for over a decade until the biotechnology companies indicated that these varieties were no longer for sale and their market withdrawal was confirmed by the European Commission (European Commission, 2007). Alongside these restrictions on approved products, the member states decided to impose an EU-wide moratorium on any new approvals in 1999, which remained in place until May 2004 (Pollack & Shaffer, 2005, pp. 341, 346); while in March 2003, Austria - one of the states already prohibiting approved GM products - proposed to make the region of Upper Austria a GM-free zone (Pollack & Shaffer, p. 345).

In sum, the emergent biotechnology sector inhabits increasingly globalised economic spaces and contributes towards the generation and control of socially relevant knowledge (e.g. the risks and benefits of genetic manipulation). However, it remains the case that the processes of de-territorialisation and denationalisation are incomplete and globalised economic activity is, ultimately, re-embedded in the territorially based authority of the state. Accordingly, while citizens continue to contest the knowledge claims made by multinational corporations and states subject their commercial activities to public forms of governance, they will continue to unsettle the boundary between the public and private domains of the knowledge structure.

Conclusion

The principal concern of this chapter has been to elucidate the arguments regarding the relationship between the state and the multinational corporation - otherwise described as "... the state and the market" (Palan, 2000, p. 3) - in the contemporary period of economic globalisation. In order to do so, it has considered a number of issues. Firstly, arguments pertaining to contemporary economic globalisation as a unique phenomenon were outlined. The differences between quantitative and qualitative aspects were highlighted and, whilst it is largely accepted that in many ways 19th century economies were as integrated as contemporary economies, it has been contended that contemporary economic globalisation is *qualitatively* different. The contemporary features of globalised production networks and the segmented production of goods, services and R&D should be emphasised in this regard. However, the most radical transformations in the contemporary economy concern the salience of the knowledge structure in (re)negotiating long-standing debates about what constitutes power, where it is located, for what purpose it is used and for whose benefit. Of particular concern should be the movement towards the privatisation of knowledge, which radically reconstitutes the relationships and identities of state, community and market.

Within the orthodox perspectives of both International Relations [IR] theory and democratic theory, state, community and economy have been held as congruent. The state rules on behalf of its citizens, effectively managing a range of public goods, especially from a macroeconomic perspective. Democratic institutions provide the citizenry with channels of voice and representation to express their political opinions. In turn, the effective provision of public goods and democracy provide the territorially delimited state with legitimacy. However, under conditions of economic globalisation, this democratic settlement seems increasingly strained, as the state (re)negotiates the multiple claims pressed upon it. New meanings are being ascribed to citizenship, statehood and market, in which private and public solutions are seemingly increasingly substitutable (Cerny, 2000, pp. 33-34).

These new relations are neither inevitable nor determined by the logic or efficiency of global markets. Economic globalisation is in a very real sense the result of a reorientation of the state – what we may call, following Ian

Clark (1999), the "globalising state". Globalisation is not simply an outside-in process, but one that is actively shaped by the most powerful states, through global institutions such as the WTO. This global economy has not anarchically spun into "hyper space", as Barber (2000, p. 275) would have us believe. Instead, the activities of private corporate actors have benefited considerably from the extension of the states' juridical boundaries into the international sphere, perhaps extending its sovereign authority beyond its territorial borders (Cable, 1995, p. 37), and thereby providing a common regulatory framework. Nevertheless, the impact of these new structures in relation to the principles and practices of democratic citizenship is not benign. Moves toward private provision of collective goods - including services and knowledge - destabilise traditional conceptions of citizenship and the bundle of rights which it normally entails. Political spaces do still exist; however, their future vibrancy depends upon citizens thinking as citizens and not merely as consumers. It requires that we value the public as well as the private. When increasingly large numbers of young people can claim to have voted for contestants on the *Big Brother* television programme, but not in the local, national or European elections, we surely should give pause for thought.

In view of the apparent erosion of state autonomy and territorial democracy, Toulmin (1999, p. 911) suggests that "… it is no good merely complaining about the power of multinational corporations. Instead we should copy them". It seems that this is already happening, but not in the simple linear direction suggested by Toulmin. When states are employing Public Relations [PR] managers and corporations are increasingly involved in the provision of collective goods, including territorial brands, it becomes less and less clear who is copying whom. Moreover, it seems that more of the same will not resolve any of the ambiguities that are raised. The Disney Corporation (ca. 2003) wants to "... bring the magic of Disney to those in need" by lending a "Disney Hand". Corporations may want to be our friend, but we need to ask ourselves what the price of this friendship may be, in terms of the future vigour of politics and democracy. Both multinational corporations and states are vastly powerful actors in the contemporary world - institutions through which key decisions are taken in respect of the ownership, distribution and regulation of key resources. When the cutting edge of the global economy is the generation, ownership and allocation of knowledge, then increasingly it is in terms of the knowledge structure that these contests will occur.

References

Allansdottir, A., Bonaccorsi, A., Gambardella, A., Mariani, M., Orsenigo, L., Pammolli, F., et al. (2002). *Innovation and competitiveness in European biotechnology*. Luxembourg: Office for Official Publications of the European Communities.

Anderson, J. (1996). The shifting space of politics: New medieval and postmodern territorialities? *Environment and Planning D: Society and Space, 14*, 133-153.

Barber, B. R. (2000). Can democracy survive globalization? *Government and Opposition, 35*, 275-301.

Bartelson, J. (2000). Three concepts of globalization. *International Sociology, 15,* 180-196.

Beckett, M. (2004, March 9). Speech by the environment secretary, Margaret Beckett, to the House of Commons concerning the commercial planting of genetically modified crops. *The Guardian.* Retrieved March 9, 2004, from: www.guardian.co.uk/print/0,3858,4876154-103528,00.html

Bernauer, T. (2003). *Genes, trade, and regulation: The seeds of conflict in food biotechnology.* Princeton, NJ: Princeton University Press.

Bernauer, T., & Achini, C. (2000). From 'real' to 'virtual' states?: Integration of the world economy and its effects on government activity. *European Journal of International Relations, 6,* 223-276.

Biersteker, T. (2000). Globalization as a mode of thinking in major institutional actors. In N. Woods (Ed.), *The political economy of globalization* (pp. 147-171). Basingstoke: Macmillan Press.

Brown, C. (1995). International political theory and the idea of world community. In K. Booth & S. Smith (Eds.), *International relations theory today* (pp. 90-109). Cambridge: Polity Press.

Cable, V. (1995). The diminished nation-state: A study in the loss of economic power. *Daedalus, 124* (2), 26-53.

Cable, V. (1999). *Globalization and global governance.* London: Pinter.

Castells, M. (1996). *The rise of the network society.* Cambridge, MA: Blackwell.

Celebration Company. (c1999). *Community.* In Celebration, Florida: The official website. Celebration, FL: Author. Retrieved November 16, 2003, from: http://www.celebrationfl.com/community/communit y.html.

Cerny, P. G. (1995). Globalization and the changing logic of collective action. *International Organization, 49,* 595-625.

Cerny, P. G. (1997). Paradoxes of the competition state: The dynamics of political globalization. *Government and Opposition, 32,* 251-274.

Cerny, P. G. (2000). Structuring the political arena: Public goods, states and governance in a globalizing world. In R. Palan (Ed.), *Global political economy: Contemporary theories* (pp. 21-35). London: Routledge.

Clark, A. (2003, November 13). Power cuts forcing phone jobs abroad. *The Guardian,* p. 9.

Clark I. (1999). *Globalization and international relations theory*. Oxford: Oxford University Press.

Cox, R. W. (1993). Structural issues of global governance: Implication for Europe. In S. Gill (Ed.), *Gramsci, historical materialism and international relations* (pp. 259-289). Cambridge: Cambridge University Press.

De Grauwe, P., & Camerman, F. (2002). How big are the big multinational companies? [Electronic version]. *Tijdschrift voor Economie en Management, 47*, 311-326.

Devetak, R., & Higgott, R. (1999). Justice unbound?: Globalization, states and the transformation of the social bond. *International Affairs, 75*, 483-498.

Disney Corporation ([ca. 2003]). *Disney Hand*. Burbank, CA: Author. Retrieved November 16, 2003, from: http://disney.go.com/disneyhand/.

el-Ojeili, C., & Hayden, P. (2006). *Critical theories of globalization*. Basingstoke: Palgrave Macmillan.

European Commission. (2001). *Towards a strategic vision of life sciences and biotechnology: Consultation document*. [Luxembourg: Office for Official Publications of the European Communities].

European Commission. (2002). *Life sciences and biotechnology: A strategy for Europe.* Luxembourg: Office for Official Publications of the European Communities.

European Commission (2007, March 26). *Questions and answers on the regulation of GMOs in the European Union: [MEMO/07/117].* Brussels: Author.

Gill, S. (1995). Globalisation, market civilisation, and disciplinary neoliberalism. *Millennium: Journal of International Studies, 24,* 399-423.

Goddard, C. R. (2003). Defining the transnational corporation in the era of globalization. In C. R. Goddard, P. Cronin, & K. C. Dash (Eds.), *International political economy: State-market relations in a changing global order* (pp. 435-456). (2nd ed.). Basingstoke: Palgrave Macmillan.

Held, D. (1995). *Democracy and the global order: From the modern state to cosmopolitan governance.* Cambridge: Polity Press.

Held, D. (2002). Law of states, law of peoples: Three models of sovereignty. *Legal Theory, 8,* 1-44.

Held, D., & McGrew, A. (2002). *Globalization/anti-globalization.* Malden, MA: Blackwell.

Hill, D. (2003, November 11). The kids aren't alright. *The*

Multinational Corporations and the Democratic State

Guardian. Retrieved November 14, 2003, from: http://www.guardian.co.uk/g2/story/0,3604,1082152, 00. html.

Hirst, P., & Thompson, G. F. (1999). *Globalization in question: The international economy and the possibilities of governance.* (2nd ed.). Cambridge: Polity Press.

Kay, J. (2004). The state and the market. *The Political Quarterly, 75* (S1), 74-86.

Levidow, L. (2007). The transatlantic agbiotech conflict: A policy problem and opportunity for EU regulatory strategies. In R. Falkner (Ed.), *The international politics of genetically modified food: Diplomacy, trade and law* (pp. 118-137). Basingstoke: Palgrave Macmillan.

Majone, G. (1994). The rise of the regulatory state in Europe. In W. C. Müller & V. Wright (Eds.), *The state in Western Europe: Retreat or redefinition?* (pp. 77-101). Ilford: Frank Cass.

McGrew, A. (2002). Between two worlds: Europe in a globalizing era. *Government and Opposition, 37,* 343-358.

Palan, R. (2000). New trends in global political economy. In R. Palan (Ed.), *Global political economy: Contemporary theories* (pp. 1-17). London: Routledge.

Phillips, R. (2000). Approaching the organisation of economic activity in the age of cross-border alliance capitalism. In R. Palan (Ed.), *Global political economy: Contemporary theories* (pp. 37-52). London: Routledge.

Pollack, M. A., & Shaffer, G. C. (2005). Biotechnology policy: Between national fears and global disciplines. In H. Wallace, M. Wallace, & M. A. Pollack (Eds.), *Policymaking in the European Union* (pp. 329-351). (5th ed.) Oxford: Oxford University Press.

Rosecrance, R. (2002). International security and the virtual state: States and firms in world politics. *Review of International Studies, 28,* 443-455.

Ruggie, J. G. (1993). Territoriality and beyond: Problematizing modernity in international relations. *International Organization, 47,* 139-174.

Ruggie, J. G. (1998). *Constructing the world polity: Essays on international institutionalization.* London: Routledge.

Russell, A., & Vogler, J. (2000). Introduction. In A. Russell & J. Vogler (Eds.), *The international politics of biotechnology: Investigating global futures* (pp. 1-10). Manchester: Manchester University Press.

Sassen, S. (1996). *Losing control?: Sovereignty in an age of globalization.* New York: Columbia University Press.

Scharpf, F. (1997). Economic integration, democracy and the welfare state. *Journal of European Public Policy, 4*, 18-36.

Scharpf, F. W. (1999). *Governing in Europe: Effective and democratic?* Oxford: Oxford University Press.

Schmidt, V. A. (1995). The new world order, incorporated: The rise of business and the decline of the nation-state. *Daedalus, 124* (2), 75-106.

Scholte, J. A. (1997). Global capitalism and the state. *International Affairs, 73*, 427-452.

Scholte, J. A. (2000). *Globalization: A critical introduction.* Basingstoke: Palgrave.

Scholte, J. A. (2005). *Globalization: A critical introduction.* (2nd ed.). Basingstoke: Palgrave Macmillan.

Strange, S. (1994). *States and markets.* (2nd ed.). London: Pinter.

Strange, S. (1995). The defective state. *Daedalus, 124* (2), 55-74.

Thompson, G. F. (2003). Globalisation as the total commercialisation of politics? *New Political Economy, 8*, 401-408.

Toulmin, S. (1999). The ambiguities of globalization. *Futures, 31*, 905-912.

Implications of Globalisation

United Nations Conference on Trade and Development (2002, 12 August). *Are transnationals bigger than countries?* [Press release]. Geneva: Author.

United Nations Conference on Trade and Development (2003). *World investment report, 2003: FDI policies for development: National and international perspectives.* New York: United Nations.

United Nations Conference on Trade and Development (2006). *World investment report, 2003: FDI from developing and transition economies: Implications for development.* New York: United Nations.

Van Ham, P. (2002). Branding territory: Inside the wonderful worlds of PR and IR theory. *Millennium: Journal of International Studies, 31,* 249-269.

Williams, O. (2000). Life patents, TRIPs and the international political economy of biotechnology. In A. Russell & J. Vogler (Eds.), *The international politics of biotechnology: Investigating global futures* (pp. 67-84). Manchester: Manchester University Press.

Woods, N. (2000). The political economy of globalization. In N. Woods (Ed.), *The political economy of globalization* (pp. 1-19). Basingstoke: Macmillan.

Multinational Corporations and the Democratic State

Woods, N. (2002). Global governance and the role of institutions. In D. Held & A. McGrew (Eds.), *Governing globalization: Power, authority and global governance* (pp. 25-45). Cambridge: Polity Press.

Zürn, M. (2000). Democratic governance beyond the nation-state: The EU and other international institutions. *European Journal of International Relations, 6,* 183-221.

GLOBALISATION OF WHAT?
POWER, KNOWLEDGE AND NEOCOLONIALISM

Peter Cox

Introduction: What precisely is being globalised?

The intense discussions in academia concerning globalisation that have taken place over the past decade have matured and extended their reach and implication. Globalisation is now a language and process that reaches into the discursive realm of media reporting and political rhetoric, shaping and creating realities as it does so. Amongst the competing and contested languages and debates, two broad camps, of sceptics and enthusiasts, can be discerned.

A further layer of complexity over the implications of globalisation has been opened up by Michael Hardt and Antonio Negri's *Empire* (2001), together with the profusion of works of commentary and dispute that have followed on its publication (e.g. Passavant & Dean, 2004). It is into this realm of debate that I want to make tentative steps in the course of this chapter, which does not attempt to grapple in depth with Hardt and Negri's thesis, but to work around some of the underlying themes that are raised in the juxtaposition of globalisation debates and those concerning both the contemporary nature of imperialism and its relationship to the processes of globalisation. As the central concern of Jan Nederveen Pieterse's important work *Globalization or Empire?* (2004), the intersection of these two areas is proving a fruitful direction for current discussion of some central themes in political sociology. This chapter is, therefore, a small contribution to the linking of two debates, rather than a full exposition of either, and a suggestion that knowledges, and the nature of knowledges and their validity claims, are areas that may benefit considerably from greater exposition and theoretical treatment. When knowledge is power, then what counts as knowledge is of vital importance in social relations. It is the argument concerning the legitimacy of power and knowledge raised by globalisation as it is experienced in social life that concerns this chapter.

To explore these issues, I shall focus attention on some of the broader implications of current globalisation practices and trends. The chapter is intended to consider what lies beneath the surface of the phenomena, and to reveal some of the assumptions that all too readily get passed over in the usual concentration on the events themselves. Hence my initial question in the chapter title: "The Globalisation of What?" Just exactly what is it that is being globalised, that we are seeing arise as a global phenomenon? To address this, it is worth reviewing a number of more widely used descriptions of globalisation and examining both what they reveal and, perhaps even more valuably, what they obscure and omit.

Globalisation is ...

Defining terms in such a fraught debate is always difficult, but we may usefully approach issues through the much referenced definitions provided by some of the most widely quoted sources. For Anthony Giddens, writing at the start of the debates on globalisation, the earliest points of recognition that require the use of a neologistic buzzword are those that draw attention to the transgeographical nature of socio-political life: "... the intensification of worldwide social relationships which link distant places in such a way that local happenings are shaped by events occurring many miles away and vice versa" (Giddens, 1990, p. 64).

In one sense, this might be thought of as no more than a re-imagining of the internationalist dreams of the nineteenth-century labour movement and the rise of an international proletariat to counter the internationalisation of capital. But Giddens insists that this phenomenon was one of a new era of capitalism, bound up, not in the pre-passport era of steam travel, but in the automated and technologically driven later twentieth century, an era in which the technological capacity of the age was equal to the imaginations of its power brokers.

This theme is further developed in Waters's suggestion that the distinction to be understood is that the physicality of geography is no longer the barrier it may have been in the past: "A social process in which the constraints of geography on social and cultural arrangements recede and in which people become increasingly aware that they are receding" (Waters, 1995, p. 3).

Further, it must be noted that this process is not merely one of technical changes, but of a concomitant change in the consciousness of those globally affected by these processes. This latter point, of people's increasing awareness of the changes, hints at an ambiguous, but overall somewhat positive, potential in globalisation. Its own internal contradictions create the possibility for the release of, or creation of, emancipatory dialogues from below – if the "people" can become sufficiently aware of the implications of these social processes.

Indeed, the tension between images of globalisation from above and globalisation from below have become essential themes of much of the dialogue surrounding globalisation over the past decade. The emergence of grassroots activist critiques of neo-liberal globalisation, such as the World Social Forum (see its web-site at http://www.forumsocialmundial.org.br/), with its annual global gatherings, accompanied by regional activist forums, point towards the salience of this analysis of globalisation. Notably these activist critiques, broadly sympathetic to the wider range of activism grouped sociologically under the banner of the New Social Movement [NSM] as extensively analysed by Arturo Escobar (see Escobar, 2000), have also generated a new wave of more classically left critiques, whether self-defined as Maoist, Marxist-Leninist or other (see, for example, the World People's Resistance Movement [WSF] at http://www.wprm.org). These latter groups revert explicitly to a more conventionally recognisable anti-capitalist stance, highlighting capitalism's historic globalising tendency and the need for a counter-movement with similarly expansionist aims of internationalist solidarity, even when particular actions and resistances (revolutionary activities) are locally situated. The re-emergence of classical Marxist debates, complete with complex factional claims and counter-claims, re-energises the nineteenth-century perspectives suggested above. We also see here the necessary echoes of a series of debates within political sociology of the possibility of, and future of, the very idea of emancipation in the context of a globalised realm: a debate mapped out in the collection entitled *Emancipations, Modern & Postmodern* (Nederveen Pieterse, 1992) and still a vital, ongoing and vibrant focus of discussion (e.g. Burbach, 2001; Venn, 2006).

The detail of the conflicts between the two paradigmatic forms of grassroots activity – over whether the WSF's activity, for example, is merely reformist counter-revolutionary, or whether it exhibits a novel or postmodern form of political activism and engagement – need not detain us here for too long. However, these arguments point towards a fundamentally important issue, which lies at the heart of this chapter. The challenge of globalisation is not just one of making adjustments to contemporary trade arrangements, capital flows, or political arrangements. Nor is it limited to confronting, or accommodating to, the political hegemony of nation states and their alliances, and the strategies and tactics necessary to gain greatest leverage or advantage in these political relations. Rather, there is an epistemological challenge being highlighted under the present conditions that we call globalisation. Knowledge and its grounds for legitimation, linking through to values and therefore to ideological justification, are as much a matter of contest as any physical arrangements or geographical delimitation.

Returning to our understandings of globalisation, Beck distinguishes a number of processes at work within the complexity of phenomena given the catch-all description of globalisation. He gives a definition of globalisation as: "… the *processes* through which sovereign national states are criss-crossed and undermined by transnational actors with varying prospects of power, orientations, identities and networks" (Beck, 2000, p. 11).

More importantly, Beck makes a conscious distinction between globalisation and two other associated but, as he outlines them, dissimilar ideas: "globalism" ("the view that the 'world market' is now powerful enough to supplant political action") and "globality" ("from now on nothing that happens is a local event").

Although Beck's definition has the ring of authenticity to it, and has the advantage of alerting us to the complex dynamics and ambivalence of globalisation and its variant phenomena and readings, it must be countered that, when considered in terms of power and knowledge, the division of globalisation into component parts risks becoming insufficiently clear about the interweaving of globalisation and exploitation. That is, it delinks the technical processes, which may be described as the mechanisms of globalisation, from their social and political components. Put another way, Beck succeeds in isolating the technologies of globalisation from the social forces that shape and form them. Sufficient work exists on the social construction of technologies to alert us to the fact that this delinking results in a dehistoricised and depoliticised narrative, justifying the outcomes without questioning their basis in political process and the exercise of social, political and economic power. Indeed, it is important to recognise that, as a process, globalisation is itself a technology and therefore must be analysed with the same scrutiny as any other technology, not treated as a determinist force with its own predetermined teleology.

Reverting to the immediate discussion of globalisation, this process of dehistoricisation fails particularly to express the history of colonialism that underpins transnational action in the economic field. Globalism and globality, as defined above, are inextricably part of Beck's globalisation, not distinguishable from it, because these phenomena are both interdependent and causally interrelated in complex entanglements. Moreover, in the context of current debates, these points of view are employed by various actors to justify one another. Separating them, even if only for scholarly or heuristic clarity, can serve dangerously to obscure the importance of the intertwining of these processes within an historical and political set of deliberate actions. The agency required to bring about globalisation is part of its identity, not separate from it.

It can therefore be argued that processes of globalisation and the perspectives of globalism and globality are also declarations of particular epistemological assumptions. In order to arrive at such perspectives and interpretations of the present era, certain knowledges must be assumed and shared. Globalisation and knowledge are therefore intimately linked: globalization makes presumptions about the world and the story of a particular historiography implicit within it. By knowledge, of course, I mean here an epistemology: not just the things we know, but the assumptions that lead us to that knowing; the ways in which we understand knowledge itself; the boundaries which govern what is acceptable and valid knowledge.

It is therefore germane to consider implications of globalisation in terms of ways of interpreting the world, of our understanding of histories and destinies - where we have been and where we might be going - that go along with it. In the political context, the ordering and valuation of knowledge may be of greater import than the socio-economic globalisation to which much of the political concern is directed. When interpreted in terms of knowledge, globalisation emerges, not simply as a problem of socio-geography and the ordering of economic and cultural processes, but as an excuse and a justification for the continuation of some very destructive forms of exploitation.

Globalising knowledge

In this vein, it is appropriate to draw attention to a couple of definitions which point us in a clearer direction as to what it is that is being globalised. Firstly, Barker (extending Robertson, 1992) notes that: "Globalization is constituted by a set of processes which are intrinsic to the dynamism of modernity and as a concept refers both to the compression of the world and the intensification of consciousness as a whole" (Barker, 1997; as reprinted in Benyon & Dunkerly, 2000, p. 42).

Globalisation of What?

Secondly,

> ... globalization is a direct consequence of modernization. The epochal transformation of social structures and ideas that began in Western Europe has had as one of its most important consequences the spread of key aspects of modernity to encompass the entire globe, particularly a world capitalist economy and the system of sovereign states. (Beyer, 1992, p. 3)

Both these explorations point towards the central observation that not everything is being globalised. In fact, it is a very particular set of practices and arrangements that is being globalised. But at the same time, the processes of globalisation are universal in their reach. It is in this vein that we can see Hardt and Negri's exploration of "empire" as particularly pertinent. Significantly, their emphasis is on the deterritorialising nature of imperial sovereignty because of its multilayered, one might almost say totalising, complexity. Whilst not everything is being globalised, the globalisation described by "empire" encompasses human experience to the exclusion of any notion of an "outside" or an exterioriority. "In this smooth space of Empire, there is no *place* of power – it is both everywhere and nowhere. Empire is an *ou-topia*, or really a *non-place*" (Hardt & Negri, 2000, p. 190). Again, the emphasis here is not on the territorialised spaces of globalisation, but on the non-geographicality of the underlying power structures enacted by the globalised hegemony of certain exclusive knowledges. The question then arises: what is being lost or delegitimised in the hegemony of "empire"?

To clarify: keeping within the context of power and knowledge indicated in the title of this chapter, the "increased flow" apparent under globalisation looks to be a very one-way channel. Globalisation of knowledge is fundamental to the creation of "empire" and is a pervasive process, expanding one set of epistemological assumptions to incorporate and subordinate all other ways of knowing. The two definitions of globalisation quoted above are illustrative of a wide body of writing exploring and exposing how the transnational increase in flows of goods and services that characterises globalisation is carried, at least in part, on a universalisation of a set of assumptions and narratives which are understood to be the cornerstones of European modernity. So what are these characteristics?

Modernity has been built on the legacy of the European Enlightenment, with its grand utopia of a meaningful history, universal civilization, and the possibility of progress. These ideals have been expressed in a range of ideas, such as the cumulative truth of scientific knowledge, of history as a developmental progression from the primitive to the civilised, of secular reason and rationality overcoming superstition and magic as the means of understanding what is real. Whilst Western academics debate whether or not these grand narratives are still valid currency in the conditions of gross material surplus in the post-industrial nations of the "global North", processes of globalisation act to universalise these narratives across the planet. Regardless of whether or not we are at the "end of history", it is hard for most critical thinkers to conceive of a future outside these narratives of modernity.

Thus, even the common narratives of emancipation and resistance emanating from within the centre are structured within the dominant frameworks that have justified globalisation's colonial past.

My argument is therefore that despite, or even because of (but that opens up another set of arguments beyond the immediate scope of this chapter), the scepticism towards grand narratives in the West, one of the more hidden processes of globalisation is the diffusion of these aspects of modernity as global norms. Globalisation, then, is more than just a descriptive term for a set of ambiguous processes; it is a powerfully normative term. It acts as a master frame, suppressing all other possibilities as simply not credible or viable. In this sense, then, globalisation is akin to the processes of empire

As a momentary diversion, one could suggest further that globalisation, based on the existence of transnational actors, indicates that there must also exist transnational communicative codes. The universalisation of key narrative aspects of modernity acts as the medium by which such transnational actors can be created, beyond the limitations of particular cultural frames: thus supporting the imperial code of globalisation.

So, to summarise the plot so far: focusing on the power of knowledge in globalisation leads us to suspect that globalisation is more than just an economic phenomenon, and more than an increase in the depth and intensity of economic and cultural flows. It represents the universalisation of influence of a particular understanding of the world; that understanding being given the shorthand of modernity.

It is for this reason that Ashis Nandy, one of India's foremost cultural commentators, has described globalisation from the perspective of the recipients (more frequently simply referred to as its "victims") as a "modernist cultural totalitarianism" (see Buell, 2000). The answer to the question in the title, "What is being globalised?", must be, "A framework of knowledge derived from a particular socio-geographic history: that of Western Europe". It is certainly not the knowledge of the world one encounters when speaking with those outside of the beneficiaries of dominant markets, whether in First or

Third Worlds. Global communications technology certainly provides the potential for anyone to have a web presence anywhere in the world, but we must also acknowledge that, language exclusivity aside, the data flow is hardly symmetrical between the global North and the global South. (This is even disregarding the intergovernmental treaties that exist to formalise the inequality of these exchanges.)

Globalisation and history

It is vital to stress at this point therefore that globalisation is not a "natural event". It is not an ahistorical happening that takes place within a cultural and political vacuum. It is part of an ongoing set of processes, mapped into the very idea of history that lies at the heart of Western narratives of self-identity. It is a corollary of the particular European chronicle of a meaningful history, with its narrative of progress from primitive to civilised, from tradition to modernity.

As such, the current wave of globalisation can be seen - as both Robertson (1992) and Held, McGrew, Goldblatt and Perraton (1999) point out - as an integral part of the ongoing historical relations of European expansionism, starting in the fifteenth century with the "voyages of discovery". However, the part of the jigsaw missing from both Robertson's and Held et al.'s depictions is that European global expansion has historically taken the form of imperialism (conquest and direct political control from the metropolis) or colonisation (establishment of immigrant colonies mimicking the metropolis, supported by slavery or indentured labour), resulting in colonialism (the condition of subjection of those experiencing imperial rule). Therefore, in a globalised world of increasing commodity and information flows, the flow of power and knowledge is almost entirely one-way, because such flows are governed by power relations stemming from the reality of historical precedents; to be more explicit, a history of global relations structured by the legacy of empire and colonialism.

Examining this historical legacy again from the point of view of the recipient, we can usefully turn to a description from the academic and activist Vandana Shiva:

> Globalization has occurred in three waves. The first wave was the colonization of America, Africa, Asia, and Australia by European powers over 1,500 years. The second imposed a Western idea of "development" during the postcolonial era of the past five decades. The third wave of globalization ... is known as the era of "free trade". For some commentators, this implies an end to history; for the Third World, it is a repeat of history through recolonization. The impact of each wave of globalization is cumulative, even as it creates discontinuity in the dominant metaphors and actors. And each time a global order has tried to wipe out diversity and impose homogeneity, disorder and disintegration have been induced, not removed. (Shiva, 1998a, p. 105)

We can call this recolonisation a neocolonialism, or a new form of colonialism. I use the term to indicate that what is being established today is not just a set of economic arrangements, but the cultural hegemony of modernity. Where colonialism was the condition of the subjection of those whose lives were shaped by the institutions of imperialism, neocolonialism can be used to describe the condition of those whose lives are shaped by the institutions of economic globalisation. Nor is it entirely synonymous with Hardt and Negri's "empire", for the reasons outlined above.

If we accept that the current situation merits the description of another form of colonisation, then we should also bear in mind the understandings that arise from studies of the impact of colonialism. This not only affects those colonised, but also has a dehumanising effect on the colonisers. Neocolonialism projects a myth of the ultimate superiority of the social and political institutions, the economic arrangements, the lifestyles and the values of the global North.

Viewed exclusively from the point of view of the former imperial nations, current events could appear to vindicate the entire history of domination if, on reaching independence, the former colonies sought nothing more than to replicate the value systems of the former masters. We, as those who dominate today's globalisation processes, bow down to the notion that the form of organisation found in today's global North is the best way of organising human society; that it is the one true path to salvation.

The power relations of globalisation

Through the second half of the twentieth century, the relationship between the industrial nations of the Euro-American North-West and the former colonial nations has been shaped by the ideology of developmentalism: the transfer of expertise, knowledge and production techniques from the developed to the "developing". The unspoken assumption is of the ignorance of the primitive and the traditional, cured by generous donation from the imperium. No matter that the immiseration of generations is inseparable from the history of exploitation. For our contemporary version of the technology transfer, the epistemological or knowledge transfer of globalisation, this means the globalisation of "... priorities, patterns and prejudices of the Occident" (Shiva, 1998b, p. 169). In a context of a history of not just uneven, but asymmetrical, power relations, globalisation can only mean the imposition of one set of norms and priorities on another.

Whilst not wanting to equate globalisation exclusively with capitalism, it nevertheless remains valid that the primary source of and almost exclusive basis for value in contemporary Western society is both economic and utilitarian. (One could add that this is necessarily so, given the narrative of secularisation in modernity.)

Thus it can also be argued that the discourses of globalisation and sustainable development operate together to narrow the range of possible futures; to shape processes and options for social change towards the "smooth functioning" of technocratic solutions to the management of social change at a global level (Williams & Ford, 1999). Hence, because of the reality of unequal power relations, Beck's distinction between globalisation and globalism collapses. Globalisation may be a minor irritant in the context of the North but, for the majority of the world's population in the nations of the global South, it is no more than a new wave of colonialism.

We see this explicitly when we examine commentaries on globalisation that originate outside the world of Western academia. For example, K. S. Krishnaswamy writes: "There is manifestly a sympathetic relationship between privatisation and globalisation, since both are predicate on the principle of 'efficient' resource use – 'efficient' that is to say, in the free market sense of private benefit" (Krishnaswamy, 1993, p. 94). He goes on to argue that: "The most disadvantageous aspect of globalisation is the clear loss of independence in policy-making" (p. 108). The language of economic globalisation does not simply describe an existing phenomenon, but goes further, and forecloses any options in the future. It chases any vision of other possible social and value arrangements into the realms of fantasy: e.g. the primary concern of social change becomes not what possibilities exist, but how to achieve a predetermined end. The problematic of the development process is no longer conceived of as a self-guided and self-determined search for better ways of living, but as a problem of finding the quickest and easiest transition to a liberal market economy.

One illustration of the way in which globalisation becomes this crude globalism (to refer back to Beck's distinction) can be seen through the work of Philip McMichael (1996). He argues that the decentralisation of state power (a key factor in globalisation processes) also leads inevitably to the centralisation of power in the economics of neo-liberal capitalism, as the conventional checks and balances that have provided other means of assigning cultural value to social goods, services and activities decline in reach.

So the core values originating within the historically powerful and dominant nations – i.e. the present and former colonial powers (in which we must include the USA – are spread by means of conquest and trade. More importantly, these values are diffused throughout the reach of these empires; that is, these values become internalised by those who start out on the receiving end, and become in turn the basis of the value system of the elites of those nations, who can reinforce their own power over their subjects. Unfortunately, this trickle-down is an ultimately unsustainable process that leads, not to an overall raising of standards and conditions, but to increasing divergence of wealth and opportunity.

Neocolonialism, knowledge and power

What does neocolonialism do? Firstly, it establishes a hierarchy of values, privileging the experiences and insights of the coloniser over those of the colonised. Globalisation can be seen as a process of hierarchical structuring of global power relations. The value of cultures, traditions, processes and social relations is measured by their distance from the notional centre.

This distance is measured not in physical terms, but in both socio-cultural terms and in temporal terms.

- Socio-cultural distance indicates the ease with which the social and cultural institutions, including governance, can be incorporated in the dominant economic and political forms of Western free market capitalism and liberal democracy.

- Temporal distance indicates how far in time a particular culture is from the "now" of Western capitalism. This presupposes that nations and cultures are interpreted within a developmental and primarily linear notion of history. Western "civilisation" is naturally the most "advanced" on the timeline. Note also that this process is most pernicious in its closure of the future. If there is a future, it is limited to the current reality of the dominant West.

But just when all looks entirely bleak, we can acknowledge that the obverse of dominant codes and spaces is that they always carry, within and of themselves, their own resistances. Resistance and intercultural exchange are increasingly vibrant. Because channels are created for neocolonial domination, these conduits can be subverted or used as counter-channels. There are always counter-currents and, even more important, ways which do not try and oppose the overwhelming force, but operate on different sets of values entirely.

The positive side of globalism has been the celebration of plurality and the rediscovery and celebration of hybridity. It is not to be underestimated – the upside of the recognition of socio-cultural distance as partly illusory in a world of modern communications, etc. However, the presence of hybrid forms and intercultural exchanges is no guarantee of justice. Music of protest can be sidetracked as a process of commodification of the "other", in which the exotic is celebrated, but only as filtered through and commodified by the economic and cultural filters of the dominant partner. Some examples illustrate the ambiguity of counter-currents.

"World music" ceases to be an exchange and becomes just another commodity for Sony in their worldwide empire. "Ethnobotany" identifies the traditional knowledge of healing plants, etc., but its downside is that it reduces this knowledge to an object of capitalist ownership. Even dissent is packaged and reinterpreted in recognisable forms, thus rendering it as familiar "opposition", which challenges only within recognisable narrative categories. For example, women's activism to prevent deforestation in the Himalayas (the Chipko movement) has long ceased to be evaluated in terms of their own understandings of struggle, but is (re)interpreted as an example of either a struggle over ownership of the means of production or as a form of deep ecology. (In my own research elsewhere, I have indicated that witnesses suggest that it is both and neither, and has many other dimensions not seen as relevant: e.g. about sacred space, meaning, magic, etc.)

Conclusions: Pathways to plural futures

For us, as citizens of the privileged global North, the damage inflicted by neocolonialism on our own integrity is less obvious. If we just look to those whom we are conventionally inclined to view as the victims of globalisation for solutions, we risk missing the damage that neocolonialism does to us, shaping us to foreclose our vision of a worthwhile life and to reduce it simply to a problem of how to make the most money with the least effort.

Ashis Nandy's vital insights and extensive analyses of the impact of colonialism show us that the victimiser is dehumanised by participation in the extension of these power games. The knowledge/epistemological assumptions of globalisation repeat and reinvent the same distorting patterns to be seen in colonialism, according to Nandy (1983). He argues that colonialism deforms masculinity into aggression, whilst subjugating the perspectives of women, children and age. It places "other" societies into categories of the feminine and the childish, reading these as either permanently inferior or acceptable only when they conform to the styles of the dominant narrative.

Neocolonialism urges us to believe our own myths of superiority: that we have discovered the "right way to live"; that we are the most successful civilisation, the best country in the world. As Buell points out, according to Gandhian practice, "... full liberation means not only healing the oppressed but also the oppressors of the consequences of their oppression" (Buell, 2000, p. 313).

The struggle for freedom in the power relations of global neocolonialism requires not simply supporting claims for all nations to have equal rights or representation in the global marketplace, though this is necessary. It requires finding ways and possibilities that step outside the limitations of the framework altogether.

What interests me, in terms of understanding oppositions and resistance to the power of globalisation, is that traditions do exist for which the narratives of secular salvation have little relevance. They work through weakness, not by taking hold of the power wielded by the centre or the dominant, but by ignoring it and making it non-pertinent. There are possibilities of shaping possible futures, but they do not lie within the conventional remit of narratives of modernity. These futures take many fluid forms, and often are not even seen as pertinent movements or paths of liberation, since they fall outside those channels defined by modernity as possible forms of dissent.

For example, the work of Nandy and others (see, for example, Lal, 2000; Nandy, 2004) points towards what was originally called a critical traditionalism. The term is oxymoronic within the terms of the critical hermeneutic of modernity, and deliberately so. Nandy's central argument, from an Indian perspective, is that India is neither Western nor Non-Western; it is Indian. The fatal flaw of colonial and neocolonial visions is that they are only able to conceive of alternatives within their own existing cognitive frameworks. Critical and dissenting traditions are legitimised within the hegemony of modernity. However, this results in the paradox that only those courses of action that do work within the narratives of modernity are recognised as legitimate possibilities of dissent. Other approaches, or narratives, can be labelled as anachronistic, romantic, idealistic, etc. Hence, we also see close parallels between a whole range of contemporary dissent and dissidence, whether social postmodernism, post-colonial criticism, or multicultural feminism (West, 1990).

To summarise: understood in terms of power, globalisation offers a narrative of secular salvation rooted in a uniquely Western European philosophic religious tradition, reinterpreted through a variety of political forms through the ages. Through its universalising extension of the founding motifs of modernity, globalisation appears to hold out a promise of salvation by means of the redemption narratives of science, reason, progress and nationalism. Technically speaking, it is a form of soteriology, a redemption myth. Unfortunately, it is one that has taken material form in exploitation and domination. The nature of the narratives by which salvation is secured demands a greater or lesser degree of submission. Since the hypermasculinity distorting the centre is based on the celebration of aggression, conflict is therefore a function of the process, not an unfortunate by-product. Closer interrogation may even serve to make us suspicious of the soteriological motif itself. But perhaps more modestly, by taking seriously voices from outside the West, we might understand how the myth of our own superiority has damaged us, as well as the "obvious" victims of neocolonialism; so that, as we seek to make a better world, we may start by addressing our own profligacy and question our own institutions and lifestyles, before deciding on the proper course of action for others.

References

Barker, C. (2000) *Global television.* In J. Benyon & D. Dunkerley (Eds.), *Globalization: The reader* (pp. 107-109). London: Athlone Press.

Beck, U. (2000). *What is globalization?* (P. Camiller, Trans.). Cambridge: Polity Press. (Original work published 1997).

Beyer, P. (1992) The global environment as a religious issue: A sociological analysis. *Religion, 22* (1), 1-19.

Buell, F. (2000). Ashis Nandy and globalist discourse. In V. Lal (Ed.), *Dissenting knowledges, open futures: The multiple selves and strange destinations of Ashis Nandy* (pp 309-334). New Delhi: Oxford University Press.

Burbach, R. (2001). *Globalization and postmodern politics: From Zapatistas to high tech robber barons.* London: Pluto Press.

Escobar, A. (2000). *Notes on networks and anti-globalization social movements.* [Paper] prepared for Session on Actors, Networks, Meanings: Environmental Social Movements and the Anthropology of Activism, 2000 AAA Annual Meeting, San Franscisco, November 15-19.

Giddens, A. (1990). *The consequences of modernity.* Stanford, CA: Stanford University Press.

Hardt, M., & Negri, A. (2000). *Empire.* Cambridge, MA: Harvard University Press.

Held, D., McGrew, A., Goldblatt, D., & Perraton, J. (1999). *Global transformations: Politics, economics and culture.* Cambridge: Polity Press.

Krishnaswamy, K. S. (1993). Privatisation, globalisation and Swadeshi: Which way lies the solution? In K. S. Narayana Swamy & T. Krishna Murthy (Eds.), *Sustainable development: The Gandhian perspectives* (pp. 91-118). Bangalore: J. C. Kumarappa Birth Centenary Committee.

Lal, V. (Ed.). (2000) *Dissenting knowledges, open futures: The multiple selves and strange destinations of Ashis Nandy.* New Delhi: Oxford University Press.

McMichael, P. (1996). *Development and social change: A global perspective.* Thousand Oaks, CA: Pine Forge Press.

Nandy, A. (1983). *The intimate enemy: Loss and recovery of self under colonialism.* Delhi: Oxford University Press.

Nandy, A. (2004). *Bonfire of creeds: The essential Ashis Nandy.* New Delhi: Oxford University Press.

Nederveen Pieterse, J. (Ed.). (1992). *Emancipations, modern and postmodern.* London: Sage.

Nederveen Pieterse, J. (2004). *Globalization or empire?* New York: Routledge.

Passavant, P. A., & Dean, J. (Eds.). (2004). *Empire's new clothes: Reading Hardt and Negri.* New York: Routledge.

Robertson, R. (1992). *Globalization: Social theory and global culture.* London: Sage Publications.

Shiva, V. (1998a) *Biopiracy: The plunder of nature and knowledge.* Totnes: Green Books. (Original work published 1997).

Shiva, V. (1998b). Rebuilding an earth democracy: A 50th anniversary perspective. In R. Sekhar (Ed.), *Making a difference: A collection of essays* (pp. 161-177). New Delhi: Spic-Macay.

Venn, C. (2006). *The postcolonial challenge: Towards alternative worlds.* London: Sage.

Waters, M. (1995). *Globalization.* London: Routledge.

West, C. (1990). The new cultural politics of difference. In R. Ferguson, M. Gever, T. M-H. Trinh, & C. West (Eds.), *Out there: Marginalization and contemporary cultures* (pp. 19-36). New York: New Museum of Contemporary Art; Cambridge, MA: MIT Press.

Williams, M., & Ford, L. (1999). The World Trade Organisation, social movements and global environmental management. *Environmental Politics, 8* (1), 268-289.

DOES GLOBALISATION MAKE FAMINES MORE OR LESS LIKELY?

David Hall-Matthews

Introduction

Famines are not new. Indeed, they are often associated with a lack of modernity; they were frequent in "biblical" times (Edkins, 2000, p. 1). Their persistence since the eighteenth-century Enlightenment has perplexed administrators and commentators alike; the failure of man to conquer the climate in so dramatic a way is seen as shocking and even scandalous. It seems obvious that they should not be allowed to happen, and local political leaders must take their share of blame when they do. Yet with their frequency, if anything, increasing in the twenty-first century, there is also a common feeling that something must be wrong globally. International relief agencies, the United Nations, the international trade system – all intended, among other things, to prevent anybody anywhere from suffering humanitarian crises – have fallen short.

Globalisation is not new either, except perhaps as a rather ill-defined concept. However, its most significant constituent part – the phenomenal increase in the speed and reach of global communications in the last decade – means that contemporary famines cannot go unnoticed, no matter how remote or inaccessible their location. Yet for all their potential shock value, famines are notoriously poorly reported in the Western news media. This is partly *because* they are not new; their continuing frequency makes them dull as well as depressing (Moeller, 1999). There is a universal humanitarian desire for famines to stop happening, but their occurrence is not necessarily a high

111

priority, especially when the communication revolution has also created an information overload. The much-hyped phenomenon of globalisation makes people feel that they can find out anything about anywhere; that they have become citizens of the world. Yet this feeling can be uncomfortable.

Part of the reaction to globalisation has been, in all parts of the world, to re-emphasise local concerns (Hines, 2000). On the one hand, this means that greater awareness of far-off problems can seem oppressive; many in the West wish that poorer parts of the world would just stay quiet and not impinge on their busy lives. There is only so much that people want to know, and famines do not make enjoyable viewing. They do not lend themselves to simple explanations or solutions. On the other hand, it is natural to feel that, in spite of globalisation – or even because of it – local problems should be solved locally. Local politicians should be given more control over their own destiny, not rely on the global community to improve it for them. Famine may seem like a global responsibility, but it can be hard to care about complex and intractable problems, affecting the lives of people about whom little is still known. The Internet has made immediate communication possible with any country – even a famine-prone one – but only with those people who also have access to it, which is unlikely to include famine victims. How can globalisation help to prevent or mitigate famines, when they seem to take place beyond its reach?

The issues of famine and globalisation are both highly complex and contested. This chapter will attempt to address them in a way that is accessible to students, without becoming involved in too many of the academic debates surrounding them. It will start by discussing what famines are – how they are caused and understood – arguing that the factors that shape them are actually part of the same global processes that affect all our lives. The potential difference that specific aspects of globalisation can make to famines – both positive and negative – will then be considered.

What are famines, and how are they caused?

It may seem obvious what famines are, but scholars have argued inconclusively for decades over how exactly they should be defined. Taylor, cited famously by M. K. Bennett in the *International Encyclopaedia of Social Sciences* in 1968, wrote: "Famine is like insanity: hard to define but glaring enough when recognised" (Bennett, 1968, p. 322). There is some insight in this deliberate refusal to provide a precise definition, but sadly it cannot be guaranteed that every famine will be recognised, or still less responded to. In many cases, governments or other interested parties – including relief agencies and donors – would prefer food scarcity and hunger not to be labelled as famine, for a variety of reasons. Costs of relief and embarrassment at failure to prevent crisis can be exacerbated by local and global political concerns. It would therefore be useful to have universal agreement on what famine is, in order to depoliticise the question of when – and by whom – famine should be declared. It is difficult, however, to address the complex issue of what causes famines without straying into political issues and attaching blame (De Waal, 1997; Edkins, 2000).

One way round this problem is to concentrate on the common association of famines with droughts, or other climatic disasters like floods. This would at once give them a clear start and end point and obviate the need to blame local authorities, except perhaps for failure to anticipate the problem. Even then, though, the problem of causation would not go away. Globalisation is associated with increased industrial production, which has in turn contributed to global warming and climate change, and it has therefore been argued that famines are becoming more likely – as deserts grow and snow melts faster in mountains, causing landslides and floods – because of our collective failure to reduce emissions of carbon dioxide and to replenish forests (Downing, Olsthoorn & Tol, 1998). There is certainly some validity in this view, and this chapter could focus solely on environmental issues and give a reasonable answer to the question in its title. It will not do so, however, for two reasons. Firstly, debates over global warming are not helped by being limited to its potential effects in specific areas. If the aim was to explore the relationship between globalisation and the environment, there would be no reason to look exclusively at famines. Secondly – and more importantly – the relationship between famines and natural disasters is highly disputed. While droughts can trigger famines, it has long ago been proved that not every drought will – and also that not every famine has taken place in the context of climatic problems (Sen, 1981).

Even where drought has been the primary cause of famine, it is simplistic to say that it is the only one. It is also too convenient both for governments and researchers. Kenneth Hewitt has pointed out that there is a natural tendency to categorise phenomena by their visibility, leading to the misleading desire to treat famines as the equivalent of other natural disasters like hurricanes – or even unnatural ones, such as aeroplane crashes (Hewitt, 1983). The focus, both in the media and among policy-makers, is on responding to the sudden human tragedy. In a technocratic age, he argues, we can comprehend accidental technical failures and acknowledge the power of forces that we have not yet developed the technical capacity to control. What we cannot so easily come to terms with are the longer-term, less dramatic and harder to understand forces – be they environmental, economic, social or political – without which famines would not happen (Hewitt).

To illustrate this, it is worth considering where famines usually take place. Most do occur in naturally dry areas, where drought is more likely, but there are plenty of dry areas in the world where we cannot imagine famines happening: parts of Australia, Saudi Arabia or Texas, for example. This is partly because relatively low numbers of people live off the land in these places, but also because, in the event of a shortfall in crop production in a given year, farmers could afford to buy food instead. This is the same reason that famines never happen in cities, despite high population density and limited food production. Therefore, in order to understand why and how people are affected by famines, we need to pay less attention to the production of food and more to their capacity to get hold of it. In economic terms, we need to look for demand-side rather than supply-side explanations. The Nobel prize-winning economist Amartya Sen has done this by analysing what he calls people's "entitlements" to food (Sen, 1981). A reduction in the amount of food available in a given region, he declares, is neither necessary nor sufficient to cause a famine. The problem arises when large numbers of people cannot afford whatever food is available.

Sen (1981) describes four types of entitlements to food: production entitlements (food you produce yourself); exchange entitlements (food you buy or barter); labour entitlements (food you earn by working); and endowments (food you are given by people who have a social obligation to you – this could be friends or family, or the government, or a relief agency that feels responsible for your welfare, or it could be a landlord or village leader whose power and wealth have been strengthened by your loyalty to him). These categories help to show why the relationship between drought and famine is complex. Drought will not cause famine just because people cannot grow food themselves, but only if they also cannot buy, borrow or demand it. However, it can be argued that, in this respect, Sen is not really explaining why famines happen so much as describing how they work (Devereux, 1993). In rural areas, most job opportunities are agricultural, so it is likely that there will be fewer available during a drought, when little is growing. Friends, family and feudal lords will only provide for others for as long as they are fully confident of their own survival (Reddy, 1993). Even shopkeepers may refuse to sell their grain if they fear it may run out before they can purchase new stocks (Hall-Matthews, 1999).

This brings us to the most important aspect of what Sen has called the Exchange Entitlements Collapse theory of famine (Sen, 1981). Simple supply and demand economics ensures that when food becomes scarce and the number of people wanting it remains constant, the price will go up. In all famines, one of the first signs of crisis is an exponential rise in the cost of foodgrains, to a level where the majority of the population in famine-prone regions cannot afford to buy them. This is not the same as saying that food scarcity inevitably leads to entitlement failure and therefore famine, however, because the existence of high prices ought logically to attract grain traders in other regions. By bringing their own stocks to the famine area, they could simultaneously make a large profit and reduce prices to affordable levels by increasing the local supply. This would prevent famine from emerging. If traders do not export grain to a drought-affected area, famine is much more likely.

It is important to note here how Sen's entitlements theory can also be used to show how famines can happen when there has not been a drought, but a different form of economic shock. Conflict situations, for example, can disrupt production, trade and social relationships in an equally devastating fashion, and indeed more famines in recent decades have been associated with wars than with drought (Macrae & Zwi, 1994). Even a sudden change in the global price of commodities that peasants are seeking to sell, like coffee, can trigger an exchange entitlements collapse. Most recently, the prevalence of HIV and AIDS in sub-Saharan Africa has drastically affected families' ability to command food, and there is a real danger of famine becoming more frequent – or even semi-permanent – in some countries (Hope, 1999; De Waal, 2002). The increasing phenomenon of family members having to travel long distances for work, sometimes across borders, has in turn played its part in exacerbating the threat of conflict and the spread of disease. However, this does not mean that what have been described as "new famines" (Devereux, Howe & Deng, 2002) can be blamed simply on globalisation. Many other complicated issues are involved in the rise of both conflict and HIV/AIDS.

Sen's entitlements theory is essentially an economic one. Many other authors have contended that famines are better analysed politically (Keen, 1994; De Waal, 1997; Edkins, 2000). This allows them to reach a more sophisticated understanding of famine causation, but makes it harder to agree on a universally applicable definition. Sen provides the simplest possible definition by arguing that a famine takes place where large numbers of people die of starvation. This seems logical, but is open to manipulation in cases where a government seeks to deny that a famine has taken place. Firstly, even in the worst famines, relatively few people die of starvation, which is primarily a condition, like old age, that increases the likelihood of catching fatal diseases. Cholera, measles, dysentery and malaria kill more people than starvation itself (De Waal, 1989a; Dyson, 1989). Moreover, the symptoms of starvation, cholera and dysentery are difficult to distinguish from each other. There are rarely enough trained medical staff in famine situations and, in some cases, no proper death records are kept. Conversely, the presence of relief agencies sometimes means that deaths are recorded very accurately during famines; but this also makes comparison with the norm difficult in areas where the death rate in ordinary years is not known, or highly variable (Sen, 1980). Thus, it becomes possible for a government to claim that mortality levels have been exaggerated by political opponents or that an apparent crisis was just normal poverty in a region with chronically low life expectancy (Rangasami, 1993).

The most important danger of defining famine by mass mortality concerns the timing of relief. Many international donors are wary of intervening before they are sure a famine is really happening, for fear of wasting money (Clay & Stokke, 2000). If they cannot be sure until thousands of people have already died, they will inevitably provide aid too late. It is therefore necessary to find a definition of famine that includes the period when people start to suffer before they die, so that those providing relief suitably early will not be accused of crying wolf. In colonial India, a provincial governor who anticipated a famine and ensured that the whole population survived was widely criticised for spending public resources un-necessarily, leaving him to complain in his autobiography that, "… by an irony of fate it was actually argued that the danger of famine could not have been extremely urgent because it had been successfully overcome" (Temple, 1882, p. 405). He insisted that anyone who had been in the area would have known that there was a famine, but this leaves us back where we started, relying on government or donor representatives being present to recognise the glaringly obvious. Too often, they arrive too late.

Part of the problem is that, in searching for a definition that will explain both how and why famines happen, the international community does not trust the people affected themselves, partly because of the unfair assumption that they will exaggerate in order to attract relief. Yet research in Sudan by Alex de Waal revealed that many famine sufferers did not seek food aid. They would rather go hungry than risk losing their land, which would make them destitute for the rest of their lives (De Waal, 1989b). Secondly, when they talked about famines they had experienced, villagers drew a distinction between famines that everyone survived and those that killed people. Asked to describe what distinguished famines that did not kill from ordinary poverty, they offered words like "oppression" and even "land theft," suggesting that they saw the problem as primarily man-made (Jackson, 1976; De Waal, 1989b) and perhaps even deliberate (Keen, 1994).

Every famine is different, and it is unlikely that there will ever be a definition on which everyone agrees. The best consensus would perhaps be that famines occur in the midst of complex, long-term processes that include chronic poverty and often disease, the failure of market forces to make affordable food available, social breakdown, and the lack of either the will or the capacity (or both) of the government responsible to prevent them. This means that, in order to understand any famine, it is necessary to look at a lot of different factors. We need to research potential famine victims' individual wealth and household assets, but also the whole of the local market in food, labour, credit and other commodities, and then all the forces that affect that local market, including international markets and the role of the state. Next, we have to look at their political situation – whether people are supported and protected by local and national authorities, or perhaps seen as enemies, or simply unimportant, by their governments. Do they have any kind of voice or rights that would help them to demand a response when famine is on its way? How well equipped are governments to respond if they want to? Similarly, what is the social situation? Do people have friends, neighbours or relatives who are able and willing to help, or a local landlord who could protect them in a crisis? In summary, do people have ways to minimise the risk of famine, making it less likely to occur, and easier to survive and recover from if it does, thereby maintaining their food security?

With so much to take into account, it is little wonder that, for all the information that globalisation has brought to our doorsteps, most people have no better knowledge of why famines still occur. All the world's experts have not succeeded in solving the problem. Yet it is also obvious why we should care more about the existence of famines than ever before, and not only because it represents a humanitarian failure that shames the whole world. It is striking that many of the issues listed above are closely linked to people's general concerns about globalisation itself: how, and to what extent, markets work and how local markets relate to global ones; how and to what extent states work and how poor states relate to richer ones and to global institutions; how societies work and whether people still feel part of local, traditional communities or whether these have been undermined by people's participation in larger global networks associated with professions or personal interests.

This suggests that famines are not exceptional disastrous events that stand out from the modern world that we live in or contradict our understanding of it. The processes that cause famines are actually the same processes – economic, political and social – that shape all of our lives. Taken to its logical extent, any study of the risks generated by markets, the failure of markets, marginalisation of groups for political reasons, state failure, social exclusion, or breakdown of societies will have to consider the risk of famine. Famines are not abnormal, but part of normal, global processes of competition, conflict, exploitation and marginalisation, and also of growth and development.

Before the causal relationship between famines and globalisation can be explored, it is necessary to clarify which aspects of globalisation are being considered. It can refer to many things, including abstract concepts and ideological positions. For the purposes of this discussion, four material aspects are relevant. Firstly, globalisation suggests a significant increase in the volume and value of international trade. Secondly, as discussed in the introduction, globalisation implies improved communication facilities. This allows not only for quicker dissemination of information, but also for easier movement of goods and people. Thirdly, related to this, globalisation has resulted in an increase in migration between rural and urban areas and across borders, some of the consequences of which have been considered. The final aspect of globalisation that may affect the impact of famines in the future is the power of global institutions, be they political or economic international bodies or private multinational corporations. The following discussion of the potential of globalisation -for good or ill - will focus on these issues.

How does globalisation make famines more likely?

Globalisation makes the world seem smaller. It also, however, makes local communities and markets seem smaller and less significant in comparison to ever more powerful international ones. Many developing countries' governments seek to gain from globalisation by opening themselves up to international trade and focusing their production on exports (Dasgupta, 1998; Khor, 2001). From the point of view of countries with food-insecure populations, this means that there is, in theory, a greater potential for profitable export, particularly of agricultural products, which will be discussed in the next section. The negative effect of this has been a steady shift away from the production of cheap foodgrains, which have never been very profitable, and towards marketable cash crops like tobacco, cotton, coffee or vegetables. At the same time, increased imports have reduced prices in domestic markets. This is good for consumers, who have to pay lower prices, but could have a negative effect on peasant producers, if they are unable – because of production costs – to compete with those prices (Madeley, 2000). Many smallholders have been encouraged – or forced – to give way to larger commercial estate managers, in order to ensure economies of scale and efficient production (Hoogvelt, 2001). While this creates opportunities for paid labour, it is rarely permanent and usually only seasonal. In the long term, losing land – even at a good price – always reduces food security and almost all areas in the world that are still vulnerable to famines are characterised by highly unequal local land distribution (Bernstein, Crow & Johnson, 1992).

Organising agricultural production in order to compete internationally also makes countries vulnerable to the vagaries of global commodity markets. Prices of commodities like cotton and coffee are highly variable and subject to dramatic falls that make it impossible to continue to produce at a profit. This creates trade traps, in which both small and large producers can end up spending more on the costs of production than they earn for years at a time (Coote, 1992). This risk is not new – it happened in the case of cotton in India in the 1860s, when the end of the American Civil War brought more competitive cotton producers in the USA back into global markets (Hall-Matthews, 1999) and it is happening now in poor countries like Burkina Faso as a result of excessive subsidies to American cotton production, which have pushed global prices down (House of Commons, 2003). What has changed is the increasing tendency of independent governments to take such risks, in the hope of higher gains. Some have even failed to ensure that sufficient food is grown domestically to feed the whole population in ordinary years (Bookstein & Lawson, 2002). Where this has happened, food prices have risen steadily at the expense of consumers, except where governments provide subsidies, which are opposed as inefficient and market-distorting by international institutions (Jodha, 1975; Chossudovsky, 1997). If droughts are widespread, as in Southern Africa in 2001-02, it can be difficult for governments to import enough food (Devereux et al., 2002).

As suggested earlier, poor farmers themselves would usually prefer to spread risk, even if it means remaining poor or being exploited. Obviously, chronic poverty and exploitation are not desirable, but they are preferable to famine. Yet feudal landlords are being replaced in many areas by capitalist investors, and paternalistic headmen or politicians by developmental states. When social or political leaders remove farmers' capacity to prioritise their food security and anticipate shocks, and instead force them to take risks, some will do well and become less poor. Others, however, will do less well and suffer the threat of starvation. Globalisation will make famines more frequent if market risks are introduced too quickly, before poverty reduction strategies have been effectively implemented.

Increasing the likelihood of famine might be a reasonable risk to take where sufficiently robust safety nets exist to ensure that they are dealt with before they result in mass mortality or permanent deprivation. However, those states, especially in sub-Saharan Africa, to whom primary responsibility for famine prevention and relief must always fall, have also had their capacity to respond effectively reduced by globalisation (Williams, 1994). Of course, it can be argued that several states were never very effective, or even committed to famine prevention as a priority (Van de Walle, 2001). But, even if we assume their good intentions only as a heuristic device, it is clear that many are not well enough equipped, technically, administratively or financially, to take the steps necessary to protect their populations. All they can do is call on the World Food Programme, other UN agencies or bilateral donors for assistance; which may or may not be heeded. In turn, this very weakness may further reduce the political desire to declare famine at all.

The reduced capacity of states to make appropriate economic and welfare decisions and to raise the resources to back them through taxation or other means has been exacerbated by international bodies. International economic institutions – the World Bank, the International Monetary Fund and the World Trade Organisation – have between them a unique ability to invest in poverty reduction and state capacity building and, above all, to ensure that globalisation continues in a more fair and even way for everybody (Williams, 1994; Wilkinson, 2000). Yet the question remains of whether such institutions have the political will to focus their efforts on famine prevention. They rely on rich countries for funding and are not designed to ensure that the concerns of less powerful nations – or powerless people – are prioritised (Cavanagh, Wysham & Arruda, 1994; Dunkley, 2000). The International Monetary Fund and World Bank responded to the chronic indebtedness of most African states by introducing Structural Adjustment Programmes and Poverty Reduction Strategy Papers that are designed to reduce the role of the state in economic affairs (Dasgupta, 1998; Booth, 2003). Governments have been pressured to play a smaller role in their own economies and, as a result, have become less inclined – and less able – to take account of the needs and desires of vulnerable local groups. Decisions that affect people's lives in crucial ways are decreasingly likely to be taken at close quarters.

Crucially, reduced economic management by states even undermines the capacity of domestic markets to ensure food security. High food prices during crises will only attract external traders once communications, in the sense of both rapid information flows and ease of transportation, are good enough. Where they are particularly bad, information about local high prices may never reach the places where stocks are plentiful (Hall-Matthews, 1999). Building transport infrastructure has never been especially profitable. In fact, Britain is the only country in the world where a railway network was developed entirely through private enterprise (Kenwood & Lougheed, 1992) and recent experiences here illustrate the continuing need for public subsidy to ensure the viability of both road and rail systems. Thus, state investment in infrastructure, with financial support from development agencies such as the World Bank, is essential in order to make globalisation work for everybody. However, this argument goes against the central tenet of modern globalisation advocates, that state investment is undesirable and inefficient whereas, if demand is sufficiently strong, the private sector will respond. This brings us back, however, to the difference between demand, as classically understood, and need, which often cannot attract private investment because of entitlement failure. The critical question of transport facilities in poor areas epitomises the inherent weakness of profit-driven globalisation when confronted with chronic poverty and welfare needs (Cavanagh et al., 1994).

The influence of states over the direction of their economies has also been eroded by multinational corporations, which are necessarily focused on profitable production and bear no responsibility for the welfare of those that lose out as a result of capitalist competition. It is well documented that they rarely make a direct contribution to government coffers because of concessional tax deals, that they produce primarily for export and that they repatriate profits to their countries of origin, thus failing to strengthen domestic markets (Helleiner, 1989). They can, however, create important labour opportunities which, when they are accessible and permanent, help rural workers to earn additional income. This potential advantage will be examined in the next section, but the risk is that, as on large domestically-owned estates, jobs in foreign-owned factories will not provide an adequate substitute for land ownership and can leave people more vulnerable than ever if they are withdrawn. The impact of multinational corporations on work patterns has so far tended to reduce security and sustainability, with temporary contracts offered selectively to young workers in urban areas (Wright, 2002). Food security can only be bolstered by the creation of permanent off-farm employment opportunities for men and women of all ages within famine-prone districts themselves.

As discussed more fully in other chapters in this volume by Anne Boran and Giles Mohan, another key aspect of globalisation has been an increase in the movement of people between nations. The phenomenon of economic migration – whether in search of a better life or merely to escape poverty – has existed for centuries and its benefits have been contested for almost as long. In recent decades, family members' remittances of their overseas earnings have exceeded the volume of international aid to many poor countries, and can therefore be said to have played their part in both development and the maintenance of food security (Libercier & Schneider, 1996). However, this strategy comes at a human cost, with families split up for extended periods. The most common form of individual migration is between villages and cities in the same country, much of it seasonal. However, there have also been huge rises in the number of entire families who migrate longer distances as refugees from wars, civil conflicts or other hardships (Duffield, 2001). While these people are rarely considered within debates about globalisation, except when they move into other continents, they matter – and not only to this discussion – because their migration is a manifestation of increasing global inequality. So far, globalisation has failed to offer any realistic prospect of reversing this trend. It is predictable that both poverty and migration will create an increase in political and social tension and further reduce food security. The consequences will be worrying if globalisation continues to encourage and facilitate greater movements of people without addressing inequality.

The case that globalisation has made – and will continue to make – famines more likely, then, is essentially that it has introduced new forms of economic, political and social risks and undermined existing risk-avoidance or mitigation strategies. Rational peasant caution has been discouraged or disallowed; equally rational, but dangerous, strategies like migration and reliance on commodity production have been encouraged; and the capacity of states, societies and households to anticipate or respond effectively to crises has been reduced.

Implications of Globalisation

How does globalisation make famines less likely?

The argument that globalisation reduces the likelihood of famine revolves around similar issues. The key point is that, at both economic and political levels, new opportunities have arisen for wealth creation and efficient management of problems that outweigh any increase in short-term vulnerability. Poverty, it is argued, is primarily associated with inefficiency in both states and markets (Ravallion, 1987). By reducing this, people will be freed to improve their living conditions to a point where famines are inconceivable. While it is conceded that the process of transition may involve increased risks for some, better information and responsiveness at the global level will ensure that the threat of famine is dealt with better than it has been in the past.

The first aspect of this argument requires us to look again at the global economy and the question of growth and trade. Ever since Adam Smith wrote *The Wealth of Nations* in 1776, it has been believed that increased international trade will be good for every country, including poor ones, because it creates an incentive to efficient production (Griesgraber & Gunter, 1997). As a result, even when developing countries have balance of payments deficits - because they import more in value than they export - they will still benefit from cheaper prices, better quality goods, economic growth, job creation, increased inward investment and opportunities for individuals to make healthy profits. The last two centuries have seen persistent efforts to increase free trade in order to achieve this, and globalisation implies an acceleration of both the actual volume of international trade and the political commitment by many governments to play their part by opening up their markets (Woods, 2000).

For people threatened by food insecurity, this can help in several ways. Firstly, the opportunity to export to wealthy areas can generate higher prices and more consistent demand for their agricultural products than could ever be achieved locally. Thus they could, for the first time, accumulate wealth that would both act as an insurance against bad seasons and enable them to expand. In order to achieve this, however, they need to be able to get access to those lucrative markets – so local transport facilities need to be improved as much as international ones. People also need to be able to produce competitively and efficiently, with production costs sufficiently low to ensure continued profits if global prices decline. Alternatively, they need to diversify their production so that, if the price of one commodity falls, they can switch the emphasis to another. This may require them to invest in expanded production at the start, before the profit has been realised (Hall-Matthews, 1999). The other way to avoid over-dependence on volatile single commodity prices is to combine farming with working in industry, either on a seasonal basis, or by dividing household members into income earners and farmers; the effect would similarly be to spread economic risk. This strategy has always been used by poor farmers, and is more realistic than trying to compete directly in international markets. Where globalisation increases off-farm employment opportunities – through increased foreign direct investment in factories, or in infrastructural improvements – it therefore supports peasants' own survival strategies.

More importantly, if local markets work better as a consequence of their engagement with international ones, the prices of basic foodgrains will also be stabilised. The key danger of local shortages leading to exponentially increased prices that people cannot afford will therefore be reduced, because external traders can respond by exporting to those local areas. Perhaps the most important question in seeking to analyse the impact of globalisation upon the risk of famine is whether increased international free trade will have this effect on local food markets. This depends primarily on how traders weigh up the risk of transporting bulky foodgrains to poor remote areas with which they are not familiar, and which may not have good transport facilities, against the opportunity to profit from famine prices. Given the inevitability of condemnation for doing the latter, there is a danger that traders with sufficient resources to sell large quantities of food will prefer to retain their focus on regular urban markets or export opportunities (Hall-Matthews, 1999). Indeed, they may prefer to deal in more expensive foods like mange-tout – or non-food items such as sunflowers – that regularly bring in a decent profit, instead of basic grains which are only valuable during famines. In that case, the benefits of global opportunities for traders will actually reduce the effectiveness of the market response to food crises. However, if well-informed and funded private trade networks develop as a result of export profits, it is likely that they will also improve domestic food market distribution eventually, as well as creating better opportunities for poor farmers to sell their own produce.

Although famines are complex, it is reasonable to believe that there is now sufficient experience and expertise in famine prevention and relief to ensure that even the worst crises can be responded to effectively before people die. By strengthening the capacity of international institutions, globalisation can therefore rid the world of famine, even if it has so far proved unable to reduce chronic food insecurity. While weak states in sub-Saharan Africa may be less effective at dealing with famine, United Nations organisations are potentially much better. As recently as the 1950s, the biggest famine ever recorded took place in China without the outside world – or even many political leaders in Beijing – knowing that it was happening (Becker, 1996). Even in 1975, the Ethiopian emperor Haile Selassie successfully hid an on-going famine for so long that donor responses arrived far too late (Human Rights Watch, 1991). It is now inconceivable, as discussed at the start, that famine anywhere should not be noticed by the international community. Moreover, since the Band Aid phenomenon during the Ethiopian famine of 1984, it has become impossible for international donors to choose not to respond – as they had done, for political reasons, before that famine was featured on the BBC News (Philo, 1993).

Politically neutral UN bodies like the World Food Programme and Food and Agriculture Organisation also now have the capacity to do their job more effectively, through better managed food distribution, more sensitive early warning systems and broader recognition of famine as a question of people's human rights to food, rather than just a technical problem (Wood, Apthorpe & Borton, 2001). Again, however, the extent to which international awareness has held such organizations to account for their performance in preventing or relieving famine depends on the reach and nature of globalisation (De Waal, 1997). Has it made the disgrace of famine in the modern world a sufficiently important priority, or has the concern with greater profits, increased trade and global communities at the elite level actually taken attention away from the chronic suffering of the distant poor? Has it marginalised them even further? Does the international media cover issues in rural Africa better now, because it can, than it ever did before? African conflicts are well reported, but the less dramatic slide into starvation is rarely seen until famine is glaring enough to be recognised by its mass mortality (Benthall, 1993). Even local African journalists tend to focus on urban issues. Neither they nor Western correspondents find it easy to criticise relief agencies, and blaming governments can sometimes both miss the point in the context of globalisation and make donors less willing to respond.

Many take the view that the on-going crisis in Zimbabwe, for example, has been caused by Robert Mugabe and cannot be solved until he is removed. While there is some logic in seeing international food aid as a potential prop to his harmful regime, if globalisation is going to help address famines at the political level, it will require a more developed sense of global humanitarian responsibility (De Waal, 1997). The weakening of states and concomitant strengthening of international institutions only creates a potential advantage for famine sufferers if global bodies can guarantee both their ability and the political will to help them directly. If they focus instead on battling with states on ideological, political or efficiency grounds, the overall capacity to respond may be reduced.

Conclusion

The relationship between such complex phenomena as famines and globalisation cannot be wholly negative or positive. Attempts to prevent famines have been helped by the proliferation of media outlets and the spread of the Internet, which have created the opportunity to exchange ideas, knowledge and experiences, giving new impetus to attempts to solve complex problems, both global and local. Improved physical communication infrastructure can also help to facilitate both trade and mutual understanding. However, it is essential that decent road, rail and air links are extended to all regions and people before we can talk seriously about the effects of globalisation on remote famine-prone territories. If globalisation does encourage investment in transport infrastructure in poor rural areas, its effects will be highly beneficial. If it does not, there is a risk that the negative effects of international imports that undercut local markets will not be offset by greater market access for poor farmers.

It is important to recognise that just because technical advances in media, transport and communications are possible, and could, where they are developed, make it easier for the international community to relieve and prevent famine, does not mean that they necessarily will. To date, globalisation has been driven by profit, and little has been done to ensure that it also addresses the quite different issue of welfare protection. In famine-prone areas, there are no more roads, computers or reporters. As a result, there are few new opportunities for either trade or democratic accountability, which could force local leaders or international donors to respond to crises. If anything, such areas are more marginalised, economically and politically, and more prone to conflict, increasing food insecurity.

Globalisation has reduced the effect of physical distances between people, and has brought the concerns of poor countries much higher up the international agenda. However, the difficulties faced by individual poor households are not necessarily reduced – and could be worsened – by export strategies pursued by ever weaker states. Globalisation has not reduced the gap in understanding between the rich and the poor, even though it does have the potential to make everyone richer and more secure. The problem is that globalisation, which seems to bring everyone closer together, only really affects the educated, informed, accessible elite. Real globalisation – which brings better communications, trade and political voice to everybody in the world, rather than leaving the poor and marginal behind – would be sure to make famines less likely. Rural people in Africa should therefore demand more globalisation, not less. At present, however, there is no logical reason to expect that globalisation based on the expansion of profitable trade will reach out into areas where famine remains as likely as ever.

References

Becker, J. (1996). *Hungry ghosts: China's secret famine.* London: John Murray.

Bennett, M. K. (1968). Famine. In D. L. Sills (Ed.), *International encyclopedia of the social sciences, vol. 5* (pp. 322-326). New York: Macmillan Company.

Benthall, J. (1993). *Disasters, relief and the media.* London: I. B. Tauris.

Bernstein, H., Crow, B., & Johnson, H. (Eds.). (1992). *Rural livelihoods: Crises and responses.* Oxford: Oxford University Press, in association with the Open University.

Bookstein, A., & Lawson, M. (2002). Briefing: Famine in Southern Africa. *African Affairs, 101,* 635-641.

Booth, D. (Ed.). (2003). *Fighting poverty in Africa: Are PRSPs making a difference?* London: Overseas Development Institute.

Cavanagh, J., Wysham, D., & Arruda, M. (Eds.). (1994). *Beyond Bretton Woods: Alternatives to the global economic order*. London: Pluto Press.

Chossudovsky, M. (1997). *The globalisation of poverty: Impacts of IMF and World Bank reforms*. London: Zed Books.

Clay, E., & Stokke, O. (Eds). (2000). *Food aid and human security*. London: Frank Cass.

Coote, B. (1992). *The trade trap: Poverty and the global commodity markets*. Oxford: Oxfam.

Dasgupta, B. (1998). *Structural adjustment, global trade and the new political economy of development*. London: Zed Books.

Devereux, S. (1993). *Theories of famine: [From Malthus to Sen]*. New York: Harvester Wheatsheaf.

Devereux, S., Howe, P., & Deng, L. B. (2002). The "new famines". *IDS Bulletin, 33 (4)*, 1-11.

De Waal, A. (1989a). Famine mortality: A case study of Darfur, Sudan, 1984-5. *Population Studies, 43*. 5-24.

De Waal, A. (1989b). *Famine that kills: Darfur, Sudan, 1984-1985*. Oxford: Clarendon Press.

De Waal, A. (1997). *Famine crimes: Politics and the disaster relief industry in Africa*. London: African Rights & the

International African Institute, in association with James Currey.

De Waal, A. (2002, November 19). What AIDS means in a famine: [Editorial]. *New York Times*.

Downing, T. E., Olsthoorn, A. A., & Tol, R. S. J. (Eds.). (1998). *Climate, change and risk*. New York: Routledge.

Duffield, M. (2001). *Global governance and the new wars: The merging of development and security*. London: Zed Books.

Dunkley, G. (2000). *The free trade adventure: The WTO, the Uruguay Round and globalism: A critique*. (New ed.). London: Zed Books.

Dyson, T. (Ed.). (1989). *India's historical demography: Studies in famine, disease and society*. London: Curzon Press.

Edkins, J. (2000). *Whose hunger?: Concepts of famine, practices of aid*. Minneapolis: University of Minnesota Press.

Griesgraber, J. M., & Gunter, B. G. (Eds.). (1997). *World trade: Toward fair and free trade in the twenty-first century*. London: Pluto Press.

Hall-Matthews, D. N. J. (1999). Colonial ideologies of the market and famine policy in Ahmednagar district, Bombay Presidency, c. 1870-1884. *The Indian Economic and Social History Review, 36 (3)*, 303-333.

Helleiner, G. K. (1989). Transnational corporations and direct foreign investment. In H. Chenery & T. N. Srinivasan (Eds.), *Handbook of development economics, Vol. 2* (pp. 1441-1480). Amsterdam: North-Holland.

Hewitt, K. (1983). The idea of calamity in a technocratic age. In K. Hewitt (Ed.), *Interpretations of calamity from the viewpoint of human ecology* (pp. 3-32). Boston, MA: Allen & Unwin.

Hines, C. (2000). *Localization: A global manifesto.* London: Earthscan.

Hoogvelt, A. (2001). *Globalization and the postcolonial world: The new political economy of development.* (2nd ed.). Basingstoke: Palgrave.

Hope, K. R. (Ed.). (1999). *AIDS and development in Africa: A social science perspective.* New York: Haworth Press.

House of Commons, Environment, Food and Rural Affairs Committee. (2003). *The WTO conference in Cancun: Minutes of evidence, Wednesday 16 July 2003.* London: Stationery Office.

Human Rights Watch. (1991). *Evil days: Thirty years of war and famine in Ethiopia.* New York: Author.

Jackson, K. A. (1976). The family entity and famine among the nineteenth-century Akamba of Kenya: Social responses to environmental stress. *Journal of family History, 2,* 193-216.

Jodha, N. S. (1975). Famine and famine policies: some empirical evidence. *Economic and Political Weekly, 10 (41),* 1609-1623.

Keen, D. (1994). *The benefits of famine: A political economy of famine and relief in southwestern Sudan, 1983-1989.* Princeton, NJ: Princeton University Press.

Kenwood, A. G., & Lougheed, A. L. (1992). *The growth of the international economy, 1820-1990: An introductory text.* (3rd ed.). London: Routledge.

Khor, M. (2001). *Rethinking globalization: Critical issues and policy choices.* (New ed.). London: Zed Books.

Libercier, M.-H., & Schneider, H. (1996). *Migrants: Partners in development co-operation.* Paris: Organisation for Economic Co-operation and Development, Development Centre.

Macrae, J., & Zwi, A. (Eds.). (1994). *War and hunger: Rethinking international responses to complex emergencies.* London: Zed Books, in association with Save the Children Fund (UK).

Madeley, J. (2000). *Hungry for trade: How the poor pay for free trade.* London: Zed Books.

Moeller, S. D. (1999). *Compassion fatigue: How the media sell disease, famine, war and death.* New York: Routledge.

Philo, G. (1993). From Buerk to Band Aid: The media and the 1984 Ethiopian famine. In J. Eldridge (ed.). *Getting the message: News, truth and power* (pp. 104-125). London: Routledge

Rangasami, A. (1993). The masking of famine: The role of the bureaucracy. In J. Floud & A. Rangasami (Eds.), *Famine and society* (pp. 51-64). New Delhi: Indian Law Institute.

Ravallion, M. (1987). *Markets and famines.* Oxford: Clarendon Press.

Reddy, G. P. (1993). Drought and famine: Study of a village in a semi-arid region of Andhra Pradesh. In J. Floud & A. Rangasami (Eds.), *Famine and society* (pp. 121-138). New Delhi: Indian Law Institute.

Sen, A. K. (1980). Famine mortality: A study of the Bengal famine of 1943. In E. J. Hobsbawm, W. Kula & A. Mitra (Eds.), *Peasants in history: Essays in honour of Daniel Thorner* (pp. 194-220). Calcutta: Oxford University Press, for the Sameeksha Trust.

Sen, A. K. (1981). *Poverty and famines: An essay on entitlement and deprivation.* Oxford: Clarendon Press.

Smith, A. (1776). *An inquiry into the nature and causes of the wealth of nations*. (2 vols.). London: printed for W. Strahan & T. Cadell.

Temple, R. (1882). *Men and events of my time in India*. London: John Murray.

Van de Walle, N. (2001). *African economies and the politics of permanent crisis, 1979-1999*. Cambridge: Cambridge University Press.

Wilkinson, R. (2000). *Multilateralism and the World Trade Organisation: The architecture and extension of international trade regulation*. London: Routledge.

Williams, M. (1994). *International economic organisations and the Third World*. New York: Harvester Wheatsheaf.

Wood, A., Apthorpe, R., & Borton, J. (Eds.). (2001). *Evaluating international humanitarian action: Reflections from practitioners*. London: Zed Books.

Woods, N. (Ed.). (2000). *The political economy of globalization*. Basingstoke: Macmillan.

Wright, R. (2002). Transnational corporations and global divisions of labor. In R. J. Johnston, P. J. Taylor, & M. J. Watts (Eds.), *Geographies of global change: Remapping the world* (pp. 68-77). (2nd ed.). Malden, MA: Blackwell.

VICIOUS OR VIRTUOUS CYCLES? A GENDER EQUITY PERSPECTIVE ON TUBERCULOSIS AND HIV IN THE CONTEXT OF GLOBALISATION

Sally Theobald and Rachel Tolhurst

Introduction

This paper explores the ways in which globalisation can accentuate the vulnerability of women and men to Tuberculosis [TB] and Human Immunodeficiency Virus [HIV], in terms of infection and impact. Concurrently, globalisation offers new windows of opportunity for women, men, health providers and policy makers to reshape the ways in which prevention and treatment of disease are managed and to campaign for the provision of vital drugs. This complex, and frequently contradictory, picture is illustrated in resource-poor contexts through insights from our research and the international literature.

This paper begins with a brief discussion of key debates on globalisation from the two critical perspectives that underpin this paper: health and gender. We then introduce the paper's core case study, of intertwined HIV/TB epidemics, to explore the complex effects of globalisation. This exploration is guided by Doyal's (2002) identification of four key facets of globalisation that need critical attention from a gender and health perspective, which provide the framework for the paper. These are:

- Changes in income and poverty distribution;
- Liberalisation of trade;
- Hollowing out of nation states;
- Globalisation of production.

Implications of Globalisation

Our analysis begins by documenting how global *changes in income and poverty distribution* are rendering more women, men, girls and boys vulnerable to becoming infected with HIV and TB and experiencing negative health outcomes. We then discuss the impact of the uneven *liberalisation of trade* on access to HIV treatment in resource-poor contexts, and the ways that globalisation has also contributed to efforts to dismantle gendered barriers to treatment opportunities and health outcomes. The impact of the *hollowing out of nation states* on the financial autonomy of the public health sector is then outlined, with a focus on the impact of these trends on the location of care for people suffering from HIV and TB. The fourth facet - *globalisation of production* - is not considered in detail, as there is little information available on how the globalising of workforces affects vulnerability to HIV and TB. However, we outline emerging concerns and directions for further research.

The paper moves on to argue that globalisation is creating new windows of opportunity for gendered health activism. For many, access to the Internet means access to new information networks and new channels for experience-sharing. This is triggering new partnerships and new areas for advocacy, which challenge the ways in which HIV and TB prevention and treatment for women and men are conceptualised and realised at global, national and local levels. We conclude with insights into how we can try to build on the opportunities created by globalisation to campaign for more equitable treatment outcomes for poorer women and men.

What is globalisation? – Applying health and gender lenses

Literature on the meaning and implications of globalisation has increased dramatically in the last decade. It is outside the remit of this paper to review the multiple theoretical and empirical strands that underpin these debates. For the purposes of the paper, we adopt Pearson's (2000, p. 10) definition of globalisation as "... the process in which economic, financial, technical, and cultural transactions between different countries and communities throughout the world are increasingly interconnected and embody common elements of experience, practice and understanding".

The media coverage of Severe Acute Respiratory Syndrome [SARS] provided some powerful images of the links between globalisation and health, by showing how global travel can contribute to the spread of disease. However, globalisation is affecting health in a myriad of less visible ways, which are complex and contested. For example, Dollar (2001) argues that economic globalisation has improved health on a global scale, through raising the incomes of poor people. Cornia (2001) counters this view by arguing that the benefits of globalisation, including health benefits, have been confined to a small number of countries. These differences in opinion reflect the wider debates about the meanings and experiences of globalisation. This contested terrain is partly due to the diverse political stances and methodological approaches informing opinion and empirical research. Ways to measure and prioritise health and well-being vary between different commentators through space and time, leading to varied conclusions. Finally, the shape and effects of globalisation may be complex, multi-directional, and often contradictory.

This paper focuses on the HIV and TB epidemics to explore how globalisation is triggering both negative and positive outcomes for women and men in resource-poor contexts. Gender analysis is integral to this exploration. The most basic definition of gender is that it refers to the socially constructed roles, responsibilities, characteristics and rights of women and men in a given cultural context, in contrast to sex, which describes the biological differences between women and men (Liverpool School of Tropical Medicine Gender and Health Group, 1999). This definition refers to the concept of "social constructionism": that is, that roles, expectations, identities, values and ideals that may appear to be "natural" come about through social processes and are underpinned by social institutions. The construction of gender roles and relations varies between different social and cultural contexts and changes over time. A feminist perspective further stresses that gender roles and relations are hierarchical and unequal.

Gender has rarely been taken seriously in the broader analysis of globalisation (Doyal, 2002). However, important strides have been made in work that provides a gender analysis of global restructuring, structural adjustment and reforms (Elson, 1995, 1999), and shows how gender shapes industrialisation, new working patterns and processes (Pearson, 1995; Loewenson, 2000). As with globalisation and health, research on the ways in which gender shapes the globalising industrial workforce and the implications of this has seen heated debate and diverse views from different commentators. For example, Pearson (1992) delineates three main groups of literature within gender and development discourses: namely, "industrialization marginalizes women", "industrialization is based on the employment of women", and "the end of a consensus: diversity and difference".

"The end of consensus" view argues that we cannot automatically predict the effect of globalising industries on women's and men's employment, because it varies through space and time. We believe that this is also a useful way of conceptualising the effect of globalisation on women's and men's vulnerabilities and responses to HIV and TB. Although we can argue that broad global patterns can be delineated, how these are experienced individually can vary and are shaped by the ways in which gender roles and relations are constructed in different contexts. The next section briefly presents the current epidemiology of HIV and TB.

HIV and TB: Increasingly intertwined global epidemics

HIV prevalence rates are increasing in all of the world's major regions. The total number of deaths from Acquired Immune Deficiency Syndrome [AIDS] in 2001 was estimated at 3.1 million (UNAIDS/World Health Organization, 2002). The majority (95%) of People Living with HIV and AIDS [PLWHA] live in resource-poor countries and, in particular, in sub-Saharan Africa (UNAIDS/ World Health Organization, 2002).

In the early years of the epidemic, AIDS was conceived of as a largely male disease, but recent figures show that male: female ratios have been changing. Globally, almost 50% of people living with HIV/AIDS are women, and women living with HIV/AIDS now outnumber men in sub-Saharan Africa, at 58% of cases amongst adults (UNAIDS, 2002). An analysis of global prevalence data shows a fairly consistent epidemiological pattern by age and sex: in women, the prevalence of HIV infection is highest at the ages 15 to 25, and peaks in men between five to ten years later. The dominant risk factor is heterosexual sex. Table 1 illustrates the differentials in prevalence rates between young women and men.

TB is the world's second most common cause of death from infectious disease after HIV/AIDS, killing nearly two million people each year (Frieden, Sterling, Munsiff, Watt, & Dye, 2003). TB is increasing rapidly on a global

Table 1: HIV prevalence rate (%) among young people (15-24)

	High estimate		Low estimate	
	Female	Male	Female	Male
Global	1.78	1.05	1.00	0.59
Sub-Saharan Africa	11.39	5.56	6.41	3.13

Source: (UNAIDS, 2002)

scale, with an estimated 8-9 million new cases worldwide in 2000 (Frieden et al.). Many new infections are attributed to HIV: in 2000, 11% of all new TB cases in adults (612, 000) occurred in persons infected with HIV, and 9% of all new TB cases were directly attributable to HIV (World Health Organization, 2001). Over 10 million people are estimated to be co-infected with TB and HIV: the presence of HIV infection and immuno-suppression is a strong risk factor for the progression of latent TB infection to active disease (DeCock, Grant, & Porter, 1995). This has contributed to the number of TB cases doubling or even trebling in some African countries over the past decade (World Health Organization, 2002a). Thirty-five percent of HIV positive sub-Saharan Africans have been estimated to be co-infected with M. tuberculosis (Corbett et al., 2002). Tuberculosis is the leading cause of death for PLWHA in Africa (Grant, Djomand, & DeCock, 1997; Rana et al., 2000).

In virtually all countries, historically reported rates of TB have been higher among males than among females (Holmes, Hausler, & Nunn, 1998), as illustrated by Table 2.

Table 2. Smear-positive TB notification rates[1] (per 100,000 population) by age and sex for each WHO region[2], 2002.

Age	0-14		15-24		25-34		35-44	
Sex	M	F	M	F	M	F	M	F
AFRO	6	7	58	63	158	122	180	101
WPRO	1	1	17	15	24	16	28	16
SEARO	1	2	38	30	64	42	82	38
EMRO	1	2	17	14	26	18	24	17
EURO	0	0	10	7	19	9	22	7

Age	45-54		55-64		65+	
Sex	M	F	M	F	M	F
AFRO	148	71	106	51	90	35
WPRO	36	17	47	22	65	23
SEARO	97	37	101	33	75	22
EMRO	25	18	29	21	33	22
EURO	23	5	14	3	9	4

Whether or not this reflects a true disparity in the incidence of TB has been disputed, owing to confounding factors such as access to treatment, particularly in countries of the South (Holmes et al., 1998; Thorson & Diwan, 2001). However, the disproportionate number of new infections of HIV/AIDS occurring in women is beginning to alter the sex distribution of TB prevalence (Hanson, 2002; World Health Organization, 2002b). In Kenya, the male-female TB ratio is steadily moving towards 1:1, owing to the

---

[1] TB notification rates means TB cases reported to National TB Control Programmes – this usually means only those detected by the public health system.

[2] AFRO = Africa Region; WPRO = Western Pacific Region; SEARO = South East Asian Region; EMRO = Eastern Mediterranean Region; and EURO = European Region.

increasing incidence of HIV/AIDS in the female population (UNAIDS/World Health Organization, 2000).

The next section turns to the first facet of globalisation outlined by Doyal (2002) and explores what the implications are for women and men's vulnerability to, and experience of, HIV and TB.

Facet 1: Changes in income and poverty distribution - A gender analysis of vulnerability to, and experiences of, HIV and TB

It is clear that globalisation is changing income and poverty distribution, although exactly how is subject to debate that is fractured along ideological and political, as well as methodological, lines. On one side of the spectrum are neo-liberal arguments that claim that globalisation creates wealth that will "trickle down" and lead to greater wealth for all. On the other side are those (largely from a dependency theory tradition) who argue that globalisation is leading to increasing inequalities both within and between communities, as well as an increase in the overall numbers in poverty (Navarro, 1998, as cited in Doyal, 2002). Our sympathies lie more with the latter position, although we recognise that globalisation has produced opportunities for improved living standards for some previously poor and marginalized groups. Individuals experience poverty in highly gendered ways that have both direct and indirect implications for health (Oxaal & Cook, 1998). It is therefore important to employ a gender lens in any analysis of the relationship between globalisation, income distribution and health. So how do poverty and gender shape vulnerability to HIV and TB?

Poorer individuals and communities may be particularly vulnerable to HIV, although this is subject to debate (UNAIDS, 1999). Farmer (1999, p. 91) argues: "In many settings, HIV risks are enhanced not so much by poverty in and of itself, but by inequality ... what [people with HIV/AIDS] share is a *social position* – the bottom rung of the ladder[3]". Gender identities, norms, roles and relations are central to shaping such inequality through influencing women's and men's access to and control over resources and their negotiation of sexual relationships and practices, and thus their vulnerability to sexually transmitted infections and HIV. In much of the world, women's independent income earning possibilities are less than their male counterparts and their socio-economic status is generally lower (UNAIDS, 1999). Social and economic dependence on men means that many girls and women lack their own autonomy and resources and therefore fear abandonment by their partners (UNIFEM, 2002). This creates unequal power relations, which make it difficult for women to negotiate safer sex, such as condom use (Mill & Anarfi, 2002).

Absolute poverty can also directly increase people's exposure to the risk of infection. For example, multiple partnerships and sex in direct or indirect exchange for money, goods or administrative "favours" are, in some circumstances, one of few "livelihood strategies" available to women (Bruyn, 1992). The possibilities for many women to desist from such relationships or insist on protective measures are therefore limited. This may be particularly true for poor young women and girls, and examples of girls taking a "sugar daddy" to support their education costs have been well documented in different contexts (Beldsoe, 1990; UNIFEM, 2002). This trend can in

---

[3] Farmer argues that in Haiti, HIV followed a path of transmission from relatively rich to relatively poor groups, because of the way that these socio-economic inequalities shaped sexual relationships.

part help to explain the higher prevalence rates amongst younger women in particular[4].

While TB is not exclusively a disease of the poor, the association between poverty and TB infection rates is well established and widespread. The prevalence of TB is higher in poor countries. Of the 22 highest TB burdened countries, 78% have GNP per capita of less than $760 (low income) and none are high income countries (Hanson, 2002). At the regional level, a positive relationship has been observed between the estimated positive incidence rate and the percentage of the population living below the poverty line (Hanson). A study conducted in the Philippines found that the urban poor have higher rates of smear positive TB (5.61 per 1000) than both national rates (3.1) and urban non-poor (3.47): (Tupasi, 2000, as cited in Hanson).

There is also evidence that poverty and gender intertwine in the shaping of responses to symptoms indicative of TB. Even where anti-tuberculosis drugs are free, patients still incur costs in seeking diagnosis and completing therapy. Poor people have fewer resources to use for the direct costs of seeking care, such as transport to health facilities and consultation fees, and the indirect costs, such as childcare. In a Chinese Ministry of Health TB prevalence survey (2000), 45.3% of people diagnosed with TB cited financial problems as their reason for delaying getting treatment. Women often have lower access to household resources to seek care for TB. Qualitative studies in Bangladesh (Fair, Islam, & Chowdhury, 1997)

---

[4] This is also shaped by numerous other factors, such as male preference for younger sexual partners, partly in the belief that they are more likely to be HIV negative (Schoepf, 1993), and the higher biological risk of exposure to the virus for young women during heterosexual intercourse (Zierler & Krieger, 1997).

and Pakistan (Khan, Walley, Newell, & Imdad, 2000) found that households would generally prioritise TB treatment for men because, as the main income earners, their health was perceived as more important. Poor women in China said that they delayed longer in seeking care because they did not want to use limited family money for themselves (Wang, L. X., Wang, X., Fu, Tang, & Squire, 2002). Clearly, the longer individuals delay seeking treatment, the more severe their experiences of the disease are likely to be. Thus, gender roles and relations shape experiences of poverty and this can lead to vulnerability to HIV infection and delayed treatment-seeking for TB.

At the same time, being infected with either HIV or TB can be an impoverishing experience for individuals, households and states (Gwatkin, 2002), in ways that are also mediated by gender roles and relations. HIV is a particularly impoverishing disease, because it especially affects sexually active age groups, which are also the most economically active groups in society. HIV/AIDS can trigger negative effects on both household expenditure and income. Expenditure is increased, owing to the costs of illness and death, such as medical care and funerals, which often require that households sell assets. Income is reduced through the loss of productive working time, because of sickness or diversion of time from work to care. The gendered implications of the loss of productive working time through caring are discussed under Facet 3. A study in Chiangmai, Northern Thailand, found that HIV/AIDS caused a drop of 83% in the income of those households affected by the disease (Pitayanon, Rerks-Ngarm, Kongsin, & Janjaroen, 1994). Similar findings are reported across varied geographical contexts. For example, in Rwanda, a study of 348 HIV affected households found that 73% were either unable to meet, or met with difficulty, the food needs of the households (UNAIDS/World Health Organization, 2006).

There is also evidence that TB impoverishes individuals and households. The costs of seeking TB treatment are particularly high for the poor. A study in Thailand found that, for those adult TB patients living below the poverty line, out-of-pocket expenditure for the diagnosis and treatment of disease amounted to more than 15% of annual income (Kamolratanakul et al., 1999). Fifteen percent of these patients had to sell some of their property and more than 10% had to take out loans to cover the cost of treatment. No analysis by gender, age or ethnicity was conducted but, in the context of the feminisation of poverty in Thailand, it is likely that these costs are particularly high for poor women and female-headed households (World Bank, 2000). Evidence from Malawi shows that girls have been taken out of school to do household tasks while parents undergo TB treatment, with likely long-term effects on their wealth and well-being, because of reduced educational attainment (Nhlema et al., 2003).

Fig. 1 (opposite) illustrates the vicious cycle of poverty, gender inequality and HIV/TB infection.

Thus, globalisation affects the ways that poverty is experienced and this in turn shapes women's and men's vulnerability to HIV and their ability to seek TB treatment. At the same time, being infected with either TB or HIV or both can have an impoverishing effect, with particularly devastating effects for poorer women and men. The next section applies a gender lens to Doyal's (2002) second facet, by exploring what the liberalisation of trade means for responses to treatment for HIV and TB.

Vicious or Virtuous Cycles?

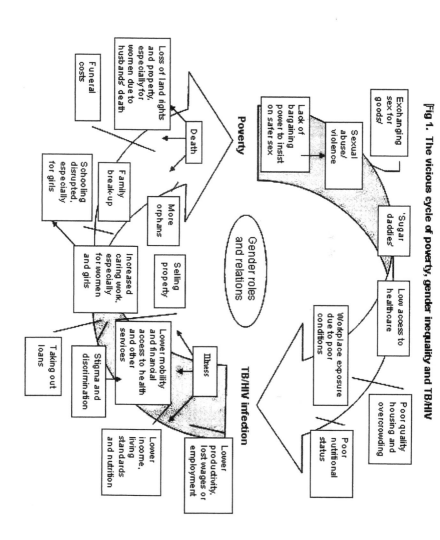

Fig 1. The vicious cycle of poverty, gender inequality and TB/HIV

Facet 2: The liberalisation of trade – A gender analysis of responses to HIV and TB treatment

Trade liberalisation is a commonly identified facet of globalisation that is highly visible to consumers in the industrialised countries, where supermarket shelves are increasingly filled with products from all over the world. The World Trade Organization [WTO] is in theory currently overseeing a global process of reducing, and ultimately eliminating, barriers to multilateral trade (Barris & McLeod, 2000). However, which markets are open, and to whom, is the subject of intense controversy. Many argue that trade liberalisation has to date been uneven in direction and impact, and has mainly benefited the industrialised countries. The increasing global market domination of transnational corporations, symbolised by the worldwide availability of products such as Coca-Cola, has been dubbed *coca-colanisation*. The politics of the global production and sales of Antiretroviral Drugs [ARVs] for HIV treatment provides an illustration of how global power structures shape the distribution of the benefits of transnational trade.

ARVs are drugs used to inhibit the replication of the HIV virus. Whilst they are not a cure, they can radically improve the quality of life for PLWHA. HIV disease in the North is now largely managed in outpatient clinics, with mortality rates and inpatient stays plummeting in the last decade. However, the large majority of PLWHA in the developing world do not have access to life-enhancing ARVs. Of the nearly 30 million PLWHA in sub-Saharan Africa, fewer than 30,000 were estimated to have benefited from ARVs by the end of 2001 (Gill, 2003), which equates to 0.1% of the population. One of the major reasons for this is the high price of patented ARVs, which are beyond the reach of health services and individuals in most countries of the South. The pharmaceutical companies producing ARVs have argued that the prices they charge are necessary to offset the costs of research and development. The WTO Trade Related International Property Rights Agreement [TRIPS] has been used by governments of the industrial North, such as the USA, to prevent many developing countries from either producing their own cheaper "generic" versions of ARVs, or buying them from other countries with the capacity to do so.[5]

The TRIPS agreement to a great extent reflects the interests of multinational pharmaceutical companies, often dubbed "Big Pharma", which have enormous lobbying power with governments of the industrialised North, because of their profitability. In turn, the ability of governments of the North to influence the content of agreements such as TRIPS, and to ensure that countries of the South adhere to and even go beyond them, reflects their global hegemony, which is underpinned by economic and military dominance.

However, there are also inspiring examples of national and transnational resistance to this hegemony. Significant resistance has come from transnational alliances of HIV activists, who have mounted high profile mass campaigns for access to ARVs for all, targeting the World AIDS conferences in Durban (2000), Barcelona (2002) and

---

[5] Thomas (2002) argues that, under TRIPS, countries of the South are legally entitled to "adopt measures necessary to protect public health and nutrition and to promote the public interest in sectors important to their socio-economic and technological development" (Article 8.1) and to pursue parallel importing and compulsory licensing (which would enable them to manufacture or buy generic ARVs), under certain circumstances. However, the USA argues that TRIPS is the minimum standard acceptable for patent rights and puts pressure on countries in its bilateral relations to go beyond the agreement by passing more restrictive patent and trade laws.

Bangkok (2004). These campaigns have significantly influenced international health policy. Since 2003, there has been increasing interest in this area from global bodies and funding agencies. For example the World Health Organization has launched the 3 x 5 initiative, which aims to have 3 million people in resource-poor contexts on ARVs by 2005.

At the national level, some resource-poor countries have managed to resist the power of Big Pharma to provide ARVs to their citizens. One such example is Brazil, where free ARVs were provided to 110,000 HIV patients in 2001 (Flynn, 2002). This was made possible because Brazilian scientists working within Brazil started to manufacture their own ARV drugs before TRIPS was signed in 1996. Despite this, the United States, pressurised by Big Pharma, threatened an investigation into Brazil's right to continue producing ARVs (Flynn). With the support of the United National High Commission for Refugees and the World Health Organisation, Brazil was able to resist the investigation by using the argument that access to life-saving drugs is a basic human right. Currently, Brazil saves $250 million a year by not paying for the high-priced, patent-protected, imported drugs and through reducing the additional expenses of hospital care for untreated patients (Flynn). Brazilians with access to ARVs account for half of all PLWHA accessing the therapy in countries of the South (World Health Organization/UNAIDS, 2002).

However, even in Brazil, an estimated half a million infected people do not benefit from free ARVs (Flynn, 2002) and proportionally fewer women than men with HIV access treatment (Segurado, 2002). In the majority of resource-poor countries, the very low availability of ARVs has meant that there is very little information on the sex or socio-economic characteristics of those who are able to access this therapy. However, it is very likely that, as discussed in relation to TB treatment above, the ability to access treatment, along with the direct costs, opportunity costs and stigma associated with doing so, are influenced by poverty and gender relations (Kemp, Aitken, LeGrand, & Mwale, 2003). Anecdotal evidence from those working within health systems in resource-poor contexts suggests that this is the case. For example, Thika District Hospital in Kenya has had a specialist HIV care clinic since 2001, and started providing ARVs at the District Hospital outpatient service at cost, on a cost recovery basis of $12 a month in 2003. However, few regular attendees can afford transport to their appointments, let alone the drugs themselves. This has effectively created a two-tier system, whereby only the richer Kenyans are able to access the ARVs (M. Taegtmeyer, personal communication, 2004). In neighbouring Uganda, there is anecdotal evidence that some men are accessing ARVs whilst keeping their HIV diagnosis from their wives, as there is not enough money available for both husband and wife to have ARVs (D. Logie, personal communication, 2003).

As global bodies show an increasing willingness to explore ways of supplying ARVs in countries of the South, there is a need to reflect on some very tough questions. If there are not enough drugs or facilities or human resources available to provide the drugs for everyone that needs them, should they be provided at all? If so, who should be targeted? Should differential mechanisms be developed for ensuring access for the most poor and vulnerable? How should these groups be identified? If these questions are not addressed, there is a risk that initiatives aimed at promoting global equity in access to health care will serve only the richest and most powerful in resource-poor contexts.

This section has shown how hegemonic institutions and prevailing power structures shape the impacts of globalisation in terms of the uneven liberalisation of trade (restricting access to ARVs). However, it has also illustrated how these forces can be resisted through the agency and action of (virtual) communities, often in the form of transnational alliances between activists from the North and South. However, the gender equity challenges in the provision of HIV and TB treatment do not disappear with the provision of drugs. We need constantly to evaluate and address the barriers faced by poor women and men in accessing treatment, if we are to develop equitable and sustainable treatment programmes. The next section raises some particular challenges to this aim, by exploring what the hollowing out of the public sector means for HIV and TB treatment.

Facet 3: The hollowing out of the public health sector: Gender equity implications for HIV and TB care

In the 1980s, volatile world commodity prices and worsening terms of trade reduced the ability of low-income governments to repay loans from international financial institutions, such as the World Bank and International Monetary Fund [IMF] (Bangser, 2002). These two institutions developed sweeping economic reform packages designed to enable low-income governments to repay rescheduled loans, known as Structural Adjustment Programmes [SAPs] (Bangser). All new lending became conditional on these programmes, which included policies of privatisation, liberalisation, deregulation and a reduction in the role of the state. Investment was commonly shifted from the so-called "non-productive sectors", such as health and education, to the productive or profit-making sectors, such as export orientated agriculture or industry[6]. The negative effects of SAPs and their effects on access to welfare services have been widely documented (Christian Aid, 1999) and it has been shown that they frequently led to a decline in the availability of care and a shift in responsibility to the household and the individual (Moser, 1992; Kim, Millen, Irwin, & Gershman, 2000). The shifting of responsibility from the state to the household has been an area of interest for feminist economists (Beneria & Feldman, 1992; Elson, 1995), who have shown that the success of such shifts is dependent on women's unpaid labour.

SAPs and the broader economic crisis resulted in severely under-funded health sectors in low income countries. The introduction of cost-recovery, usually through user-fees, was a central plank of a commonly adopted set of so-called "health sector reforms", which were heavily influenced by the practice of the New Right in industrialised countries such as the UK and the USA under Thatcher and Reagan (Wilkinson, Gouws, Sach, & Karim, 2001). Proponents of user fees argue that the increased revenue can lead to improved quality of services and that equity challenges, such as reducing the ability of poorer groups to access care, can be met through exemptions and waivers (Nanda, 2002). However, a number of empirical

---

[6] In 1999, Poverty Reduction Strategy Papers (PRSPs) replaced Structural Adjustment Programmes as the pre-conditions for loans and debt relief by the World Bank and the IMF. In theory, PRSPs involve national governments designing their own development strategy, which should be focused on poverty relief. However, a recent assessment of the content of PRSPs found that "... the strategies still focus on economic growth, without, on the most part, addressing how this growth is to be redistributed to the poor. The core macro-economic elements have changed little from the old Structural Adjustment Programmes, with a continued adherence to privatization, liberalization and a reduced role for the state" (World Development Movement, 2001, p. 1).

field studies have shown that, despite the implementation of exemptions, user fees have led to delays in seeking care amongst vulnerable groups, such as poor women, children and the elderly (Kutzin, 1995, as cited in Standing, 1997; Malama, Chen, De Vigli, & Birbeck, 2002). Thus, user fees contribute to the barriers to accessing care for poor women and men discussed under Facets 2 and 3.

At the same time, in the context of over-stretched, under-resourced health services and exploding HIV and TB epidemics, we are increasingly witnessing a continuing transfer of health care burdens and responsibilities from the government to the community and the household. This trend is embodied in home-based care programmes for PLWHA, in which families and volunteers look after a PLWHA's basic health needs (Abrahamsen, 1997). Similar trends are emerging in relation to TB treatment. The treatment for TB involves taking many drugs, for a minimum of 6 months, even when the patient no longer feels sick. The drugs can have a number of difficult side effects. In order to promote adherence to tuberculosis treatment, increase cure rates and reduce the threat of multi-drug resistance, the World Health Organization recommends a standardised global approach to the management of TB treatment: which is, that TB patients *everywhere* must be observed swallowing their TB drugs every day (World Health Organization, 1995). This is referred to as Directly Observed Treatment [DOT]. This "one size fits all" approach has triggered much debate (Macq, Theobald, Dick, & Dembele, 2003). Proponents have argued that the prevention of multi-drug resistance requires daily observation (World Health Organization, 1995; Brown, 2000), whereas opponents have used either ethical arguments (Grange & Festenstein, 1993) or lack of evidence of the efficacy of DOT, to argue against its necessity (Garner & Volmink, 2003).

Vicious or Virtuous Cycles?

What is clear is that increasing rates of TB and the hollowing out of the public sector are resulting in increasing strains for over-stretched health service providers and that in many resource-poor contexts it would be impossible for all TB patients to be observed swallowing their drugs daily by health staff. At the annual International Union Against Tuberculosis and Lung Disease Conference in Paris in 2001, we interviewed TB service providers from all over the world to understand the problems faced in delivering the standard DOT approach and how they are trying to adapt to meet these challenges. The analysis showed a remodelling of DOT, often through decentralisation processes, so that the essence remained the same: i.e. patients should be watched whilst swallowing their drugs, but that this could be done by different people, such as family members or shopkeepers, and not necessarily at the health centre (Macq et al., 2003).

There are many advantages to such an approach for those suffering from HIV/AIDS or TB. For example, PLWHA may get more personal and loving care in their household than in overstretched health facilities, and TB patients may have more chance of adhering to treatment if they do not have to go to the health centre every day.

However, from a gender equity perspective, it is also important to explore the impact of ill health on those who care for the sick. Caring is socially constructed as a female responsibility in most contexts (World Health Organization, 1994). Women and girls bear the main responsibility for the physical, emotional and psychosocial needs of PLWHA at the household and community level (Panos Institute, 1990). Studies in India and many sub-Saharan African countries have found that the burden of caring for the sick and dying at household and community levels is seen as a female role, although women are not assured of the same level of care when they are sick (Macwan'gi, Sichone & Kamanaga, 1995; Taylor, Seeley & Kajura, 1996; Woelk et al., 1997; Bharat & Aggleton, 1999; Olenja, 1999; Ndaba-Mbata & Seloilwe, 2000). There is also evidence that, in DOT provision, the vast majority of observers are women. In South Africa, for example, it is estimated that over 90% of observers are female (Macq et al., 2003). In Nepal, both men and women provide DOT, but from different working positions: the men as Village Health Workers and the women as Female Community Health Volunteers (FCHV). The Village Health Workers get financially remunerated for their work, whereas the FCHVs do not (Macq. et al.).

Figure 2 illustrates the common structure of health care provision for PLWHA and TB patients.

Fig 2. Different levels of care for PLWHA and TB patients

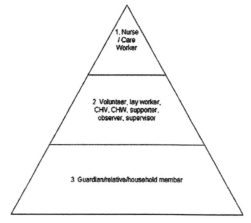

Vicious or Virtuous Cycles?

Whereas nurses and care workers are normally remunerated for their work, volunteers are not, although they may receive incentives such as free health care, T-shirts and educational materials for themselves and their families (Bali, 2003). Guardians, relatives and family members are very rarely remunerated for their work, which is often construed by policy makers as an extension of family responsibilities. However, caring has significant impacts on carers' lives and on their households. These can include:

- Reduction in time spent on income generation and productive activities (Macwan'gi et al., 1995; Abrahamsen, 1997);
- Increased working hours (Abrahamsen, 1997);
- Emotional stress (Ndaba-Mbata & Seloilwe, 2000);
- Disruption of families, because of psychological and economic pressures (Anderson & Kaleeba, 1994);
- Reduced assets due to costs of medicinal supplies (UNAIDS/World Health Organization, 2000);
- Children (especially girls) being withdrawn from school to help with caring (Ankrah, 1993);
- Increased vulnerability to HIV and TB infection (Ngamvithayapong, 2001).

Carers at the household and community level make a significant contribution to health care. From an equity and sustainability perspective, this critical role needs to be recognised and supported. The next section considers the fourth and final facet: the globalisation of production.

Implications of Globalisation

Facet 4: Globalisation of production: The workplace as a site of both infection and prevention

Much research on the gender and health impacts of the globalisation of production has focused on experiences of and responses to occupational health hazards, rather than communicable disease (Chavalitsakulchai & Shahnavaz, 1993; Chant & McIlwaine, 1995; Theobald, 2002). However, there is some (limited) evidence that the development of new gendered workforces in diverse parts of the globe is creating new gendered vulnerabilities to TB infection. For example, TB appears to be more prevalent among female factory workers than among other populations of women in Bangladesh (Zohir & Paul-Majumder, 1996). Concurrently, there is growing interest in the workplace as a site for TB and HIV treatment. In South Africa (Bechan, Connolly, Short, Standing & Wilkinson, 1997) and Senegal (Ndiaye et al., 2000), treatment for tuberculosis in the workplace has had a positive impact on workers' health experiences. Some multinational companies have been active in HIV awareness. For example, Heineken has had an AIDS prevention programme in the Central African Republic for 10 years and started to introduce ARVs into its health services for employees, their partners and children in 2001 (International HIV Treatment Access Coalition, 2002). The UK Department for International Development's consultation strategy on HIV/AIDS advocates supporting "... efforts to further increase awareness among businesses of the impacts of HIV/AIDS as well as dissemination of emerging best practice in workplace policies and broader company response strategies" (2004, p. 15). Further research on appropriate approaches is needed, to ensure that workplaces do not enhance workers' vulnerability to HIV/TB and that the possibilities of workplaces as sites for prevention and treatment are explored in ways that meet workers' own gendered needs and priorities.

Seizing the opportunities offered by globalisation: Towards a gendered health activism

We have given a range of examples of how the various facets of globalisation offer new threats and new challenges to promoting gender and equity concerns in HIV/TB prevention and treatment. However, globalisation also offers new opportunities for resisting the current political and economic hegemony and its gendered impacts on health. As Doyal (2002) discusses, gender and health advocates have made strides in developing global alliances to promote better health for women (and men). Much of this activism has been focused on sexual and reproductive rights and Violence Against Women. The most visible achievements have been made at the international conferences in Cairo (1994)[7], Beijing (1995), which led to the Beijing Platform for Action[8], and New York (1999)[9].

Globalisation has also provided some conditions that are conducive to the development of new advocacy and campaigns for the promotion of gender equity in relation to TB and HIV. Most of the clearest activism for gender equity has historically been focused on HIV-related policy. This may be partly because the operation of gender inequities is more clearly visible in relation to issues of

---

[7] International Conference on Population and Development [ICPD].
[8] The Fourth World Conference on Women in Beijing produced a platform for action, which is an agenda for women's empowerment, available at:
http://www.un.org/womenwatch/daw/beijing/platform/plat1.htm.
[9] This marked the end of the five-year Review of Progress on the ICPD agenda.

sexuality, and because such issues have traditionally been a key feminist concern. It may also be because, from its outset, HIV has raised issues of discrimination and marginalisation that have galvanised activism from a rights-based perspective, and focused attention as much on the "social" as on the "medical" aspects of societal responses.

Examples of activism include the Society for Women Against AIDS in Africa (SWAA), which has worked tirelessly since the beginning of the epidemic to promote exchange and dialogue between its members across the continent, and to campaign for strategies to address women's vulnerability to HIV, as well as supporting PLWHA.[10] There are also examples of activism that targets the hegemonic influence of US policy in relation to HIV. The US-based Center for Health and Gender Equity [CHANGE] spearheaded a campaign by Non Governmental Organisations and Networks of PLWHA worldwide against the appointment by George W. Bush of Randall Tobias as Head of the US Emergency Plan for AIDS Relief, using the Internet and e-mail petitioning. The objections to Tobias's appointment lay in his strong links with US Big Pharma, lack of public health experience and simplistic approaches to HIV prevention, which were not grounded in the realities of women's and men's lives, vulnerabilities and capabilities (CHANGE, 2003).

In relation to TB policy, new alliances for promoting equity are emerging. Efforts to "remodel" DOT in the face of the challenges created by rising TB prevalence in the context of weakened health systems may be interpreted as resistance to the global standardisation of TB treatment. This has led to new working partnerships between health

---

[10] For further details see:
http://www.swaainternational.org/en/home.html.

providers, non-governmental organisations, communities, TB patients and their families. At the same time, some aspects of decentralised approaches to DOT raise new gender equity challenges, in the shape of increased burdens on carers, as discussed under Facet 3. Thus, both globalising trends and efforts to resist their negative effects can lead to complex and contradictory processes and outcomes, with new challenges constantly emerging.

However, an awareness of the need for gender sensitivity in TB care and treatment is also emerging in the research and policy arenas, as reflected by the increasing number of research articles, policy briefings and operational research projects that explore and attempt to address ways in which gender inequities affect vulnerability to TB and ability to access and adhere to quality care (Fair et al., 1997; Johansson, Long, Diwan, & Winkvist, 2000; Macq et al., 2003; Sanou, Dembele, Theobald, & Macq, 2004). The WHO has enabled a process of exchange, through funding a network of researchers to conduct research and share findings in this area[11].

As discussed under Facet 2, campaigns for the rights for PLWHA from resource-poor contexts offer another critical example of global advocacy. As global bodies move slowly towards making this more of a reality, advocacy to promote attention to gender and equity will be crucial. With some policy makers advocating the need for a DOT approach to the implementation and distribution of ARVs (Harries, Nyangulu, Hargreaves, Kaluwa, & Salaniponi, 2001), it is crucial that lessons are learnt from the TB world

---

[11] TDR [UNDP/World Bank/WHO Special Programme for Research and Training in Tropical Diseases] is currently supporting research projects in India, Bangladesh, Malawi and Colombia on gender and TB. For further details see: http://www.who.int/gtb/policyrd/Gender&TB.htm.

when promoting gender and equity concerns in relation to adherence to drugs policies in resource-poor countries.

Networking and dialogue amongst diverse communities, non-governmental organisations, activists and health policy makers and providers have been central to all the diverse campaigns discussed above. Access to the Internet has underpinned much of this activism and has enabled new partnerships and alliances to be formed. However, the equity challenge is still an issue, as most of the global poor do not have the skills or the facilities to use these new technologies.

Conclusion

This paper has taken forward the debate on globalisation, gender and health through applying Doyal's (2002) framework to current debates and challenges in HIV/TB.

The key arguments are summarised in Fig. 3 (opposite).

Globalising trends in the following areas have impacted on women and men's vulnerability and responses to the intertwined HIV and TB epidemics in a myriad of complex and contradictory ways:

(1) Changes in income and poverty distribution;
(2) Liberalisation of trade;
(3) Hollowing out of nation states;
(4) Globalisation of production.

The varied ways in which gender is constructed across time and space is central to these experiences and needs to be addressed in ongoing globalisation debates. As Doyal

Vicious or Virtuous Cycles?

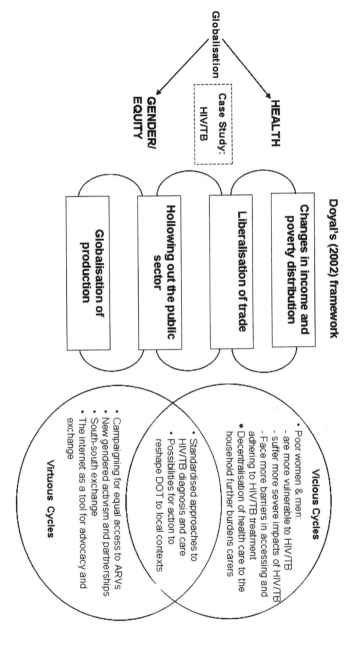

Fig 3: Conceptual map of the Chapter

(2002, p. 12) argues: "Existing models [of globalisation] will continue to be partial and unscientific unless they are based on a recognition of gender as a fundamental organizing principle in all areas of social and economic life". The various facets of globalisation have diverse repercussions that are shaped by global power structures and mediated at the local level by gender relations.

Globalising trends have created both vicious and virtuous cycles. On the one hand, they have intensified the vulnerability of poor women and men to HIV/TB and worsened the impact of these diseases on their lives and livelihoods. Concurrently, globalisation has been the platform for new gendered activism, partnerships and advocacy strategies that have shaped the ways in which TB and HIV treatment is provided. There are no easy victories, however, and consistent pressure must be brought to bear on the governments of the industrialised North and powerful transnational institutions. For example, the Global Women's Issues Scorecard on the current Bush Administration has been monitoring the delivery of commitments made to fund responses to HIV/AIDS, and highlighting where promises are broken and gender equity is neglected.[12]

Globalisation is clearly here to stay. The challenge is to build on the opportunities it offers to try to put in place strategies to resist the vicious cycles and trends it

---

[12] In 2004, this scorecard has highlighted that the administration has spent only $1.9 billion out of the promised $15 billion on the US Emergency Plan for AIDS Relief, and has failed to take any specific steps to address the growing vulnerability of women and girls to HIV infection, such as promotion of the female condom or programmes to tackle domestic violence.For further details see:
http://www.wglobalscorecard.org/Mar04AIDS.htm.

generates, and to create virtuous cycles to promote ongoing and responsive approaches, that reflect the needs and priorities of poor women and men. As Dr Joep Lange, the President of the International AIDS Society, put it in Barcelona in July 2002: "If we can get cold Coca Cola and beer to every remote corner of Africa, it should not be impossible to do the same with drugs" (International HIV Treatment Access Coalition, 2002). However, it is important to recognise that this is a political struggle, which ultimately involves nothing less than challenging the current global political economy.

References

Abrahamsen, R. (1997). Gender dimensions of AIDS in Zambia. *Journal of Gender Studies, 6* (2), 177-189.

Anderson, S., & Kaleeba, N., (1994). Women and AIDS care in the family. *World AIDS Day Newsletter, 3.*

Ankrah, E. M. (1993). The impact of HIV/AIDS on the family and other significant relationships: The African clan revisited. *AIDS Care, 5* (1), 5-22.

Bali, N. (2003). *The role of informal carer for HIV/AIDS patients in high prevalence sub-Saharan African countries: A literature review.* Unpublished master's dissertation, University of Liverpool.

Bangser, M. (2002). Policy environments: Macroeconomics, programming and participation. In G. Sen, A. George, & P. Östlin (Eds.), *Engendering international health: The challenge of equity* (pp. 256-280). Cambridge, MA: MIT Press.

Barris, E., & McLeod, K. (2000). Globalization and international trade in the twenty-first century: Opportunities for and threats to the health sector in the South. *International Journal of Health Services, 30* (1), 187-210.

Bechan, S., Connolly, C., Short, G. M., Standing, E., & Wilkinson, D. (1997). Directly observed therapy for tuberculosis given twice weekly in the workplace in urban South Africa. *Transactions of the Royal Society of Tropical Medicine and Hygiene, 91* (6), 704-707.

Beldsoe, C. (1990). The politics of AIDS, condoms and heterosexual relations in Africa: Recent evidence from the local print media. In W. P. Handwerker (Ed.), *Births and power: Social change and the politics of reproduction* (pp. 197-224). Boulder, CO: Westview Press.

Beneria, L., & Feldman, S. (Eds.). (1992). *Unequal burden: Economic crises, persistent poverty, and women's work.* Boulder, CO: Westview Press.

Bharat, S., & Aggleton, P. (1999). Facing the challenge: Household responses to HIV/AIDS in Mumbai, India. *AIDS Care, 11* (1), 31-44.

Brown, P. (2000, March 25). Drug resistant tuberculosis can be controlled, WHO says. *British Medical Journal, 320,* 821.

Bruyn, M. de. (1992). Women and AIDS in developing countries. *Social Science and Medicine, 34* (3), 249-262.

CHANGE. (2003, October 2). *Aids activists oppose Bush's global AIDS czar* [E-mail press release]. Retrieved May 23, 2006, from:

http://www.genderhealth.org/pubs/PR20031002.pdf.

Chant, S., & McIlwaine, C. (1995). *Women of a lesser cost: Female labour, foreign exchange, and Philippine development.* London: Pluto Press.

Chavalitsakulchai, P., & Shahnavaz, H. (1993). Musculoskeletal disorders of female workers and ergonomics problems in five different industries of a developing country. *Journal of Human Ergology, 22,* 29-43.

China Ministry of Health. (2000). *National tuberculosis epidemiological sample survey.* Beijing: Author.

Christian Aid. (1999). *Millennium lottery: Who lives and who dies in the age of Third World debt?* London: Author.

Corbett, E. L., Steketee, R. W., Kuile, F. O. ter, Latif, A. S., Kamali, A., & Hayes, R. J. (2002). HIV-1/AIDS and the control of other infectious diseases in Africa. *The Lancet 359*, 2177-2187.

Cornia, G. (2001). Globalisation and health: Results and options. *Bulletin of the World Health Organisation, 79* (9), 834-841.

DeCock, K. M., Grant, A. D., & Porter, J. D. H. (1995). Preventive therapy for tuberculosis in HIV-infected persons: International recommendations, research, and practice. *The Lancet, 345*, 833-836.

Dollar, D. (2001). Is globalisation good for your health? *Bulletin of the World Health Organisation, 70* (9), 827-833.

Doyal, L. (2002). Putting gender into health and globalization debates: New perspectives and old challenges. *Third Word Quarterly, 23* (2), 1-18.

Elson, D. (1995). Male bias in macro-economics: The case of structural adjustment. In D. Elson (Ed.), *Male bias in the development process* (pp. 164-190). Manchester: Manchester University Press.

Elson, D. (1999). Labor markets as gendered institutions: Equality, efficiency and empowerment issues. *World Development, 27* (3), 611-627.

Fair, E., Islam, M. A., & Chowdhury, S. A. (1997). *Tuberculosis and gender: Treatment seeking behavior and social beliefs of women with tuberculosis in rural Bangladesh.* Dhaka: BRAC.

Farmer, P. (1999). *Infections and inequalities: The modern plagues.* Berkeley: University of California Press.

Flynn, M. (2002). Cocktails and carnival. *New Internationalist, 346,* 1-3.

Frieden, T. R., Sterling, T. R., Munsiff, S. S., Watt, C. J., & Dye, C. (2003). Tuberculosis. *The Lancet, 362,* 887-99.

Garner P., & Volmink, J. (2003, October 11). Directly observed treatment for tuberculosis. *British Medical Journal, 327,* 823-824.

Gill, T. A. (2003). Patients versus patents. *New Internationalist, 362,* 22-23.

Grange, J., & Festenstein, F. (1993). The human dimension of tuberculosis control. *Tubercle Lung Disease, 74* (4), 219-222.

Grant, A. D., Djomand, G., & DeCock, K. M. (1997). Natural history and spectrum of disease in adults with HIV/AIDS in Africa. *AIDS, 11* (Suppl. B), S43-S54.

Gwatkin, D. R. (2002). *Vulnerability to HIV* [Discussion paper]. Washington, DC: World Bank.

Hanson, C. (2002). *Tuberculosis, poverty and equity: A review of literature and discussion of issues.* Washington, DC: World Bank.

Harries, A. D., Nyangulu, D. S., Hargreaves, N. J., Kaluwa, O., & Salaniponi, F. M. L. (2001). Preventing antiretroviral anarchy in sub-Saharan Africa. *The Lancet, 358,* 410-414.

Holmes, C. B., Hausler, H., & Nunn, P. (1998). A review of sex differences in the epidemiology of tuberculosis. *International Journal of Tubercolosis and Lung Disease, 2,* 96-104.

International HIV Treatment Access Coalition. (2002). *A commitment to action for expanded access to HIV/AIDS treatment.* Geneva: World Health Organization.

Johansson, E., Long, N. H., Diwan, V. K., & Winkvist, A. (2000). Gender and tuberculosis control: Perspectives on health seeking behaviour among men and women in Vietnam. *Health Policy, 52,* 33-51.

Kamolratanakul, P., Sawert, H., Kongsin, S., Lertmaharit, S., Sriwongsa, J., Na-Songkhla, S., Wangmanee, S., Jittimanee, S., & Payanandana, V. (1999). Economic impact of tuberculosis at the household level.

Vicious or Virtuous Cycles?

International Journal of Tuberculosis and Lung Disease, 3 (7), 596-602.

Kemp, J., Aitken, J.-M., LeGrand, S., & Mwale, B. (2003). *"Equity in ART?: But the whole health system is inequitable": Equity in access to ART in Malawi.* Based on a technical paper, *"Equity in health sector responses to HIV/AIDS in Malawi",* prepared for EQUINET/Oxfam GB. Retrieved May 19, 2006, from: http://www.globalforumhealth.org/forum7/CDRomF orum7/Wednesday/1.

Khan, A., Walley, J., Newell, J, & Imdad, N. (2000). Tuberculosis in Pakistan: Socio-cultural constraints and opportunities in treatment. *Social Science and Medicine, 50* (2), 247-254.

Kim, J. Y., Millen, J., Irwin, A., & Gershman, J. (Eds.). (2000). *Dying for growth: Global inequality and the health of the poor.* Monroe, ME: Common Courage Press.

Liverpool School of Tropical Medicine Gender and Health Group. (1999). *Guidelines for the analysis of gender and health.* Liverpool: Liverpool School of Tropical Medicine.

Loewenson, R. (2000). Occupational hazards in the informal sector: A global perspective. In K. Isaksson, C.

Hogstedt, C. Eriksson, & T. Theorell, (Eds.), *Health effects of the new labour market* (pp. 329-342). New York: Kluwer Academic/Plenum Publishers.

Macq, J. C. M., Theobald, S., Dick, J., & Dembele, M. (2003). An exploration of the concept of directly observed treatment (DOT) for tuberculosis patients: From a uniform to a customized approach. *International Journal of Tuberculosis and Lung Disease, 7* (2), pp. 103-109.

Macwan'gi, M., Sichone, M., & Kamanaga, P. (1995, May). *Women and AIDS: Challenges and dilemmas: Looking ahead (preliminary report).* Paper presented at the dissemination seminar on "Socio-economic Impact of HIV/AIDS in Zambia", Lusaka.

Malama, C., Chen, Q., De Vigli, R., & Birbeck, G. (2002). User fees impact access to health care for female children in rural Zambia. *Journal of Tropical Pediatrics, 48* (6), 371-372.

Mill, J. E., & Anarfi, J. K. (2002). HIV risk environment for Ghanaian women: Challenges to prevention. *Social Science and Medicine, 54,* 325-337.

Moser, C. (1992). Adjustment from below: Low-income women, time and the triple role in Guayaquil, Ecuador. In H. Afshar & C. Dennis (Eds.), *Women, Recession and*

Vicious or Virtuous Cycles?

Adjustment in the Third World (pp. 87-116). Basingstoke: Macmillan.

Nanda, P. (2002). Gender dimensions of user fees: Implications for women's utilisation of health care. *Reproductive Health Matters, 10* (20), 127-134.

Ndaba-Mbata, R. D., & Seloilwe, E. S. (2000). Home-based care of the terminally ill in Botswana: Knowledge and perceptions. *International Nursing Review, 47* (4), 218-223.

Ndiaye, M., Hane A. A., Ndir, M., Ba, O., Cissokho, S., Diop-Dia, D., Kandji, M., Ndiaye, S., Diatta, A., & Toure, N. O. (2000). Regulations on tuberculosis risk in workplaces in Senegal. *Revue de Pneumologie Clinique, 56* (6), 355-60.

Ngamvithayapong, J. (2001, December 17-20). *"Love and let it be: Challenges and opportunities for tuberculosis and HIV/AIDS control in Northern Thailand.* Abstract for presentation at the Fifth International Conference on Home and Community Care for Persons Living with HIV/AIDS, Chiang Mai, Thailand.

Nhlema, B., Kemp, J., Steenbergen, G., Theobald, S., Tang, S., & Squire, S. B. (2003). *A systematic analysis of TB and poverty.* Unpublished document, commissioned and funded by the STOP TB Partnership. Executive summary retrieved May 19, 2006, from: http://www.equitb.org.uk/uploads/executive_summary.pdf.

Olenja, J. M. (1999). Assessing community attitude towards home-based care for people with AIDS in Kenya. *Journal of Community Health, 24* (3), 187-199.

Oxaal, Z., & Cook, S. (1998). *Health and poverty gender analysis.* Briefing prepared for the Swedish International Development Co-operation. Brighton: Institute of Development Studies.

Panos Institute. (1990). *Triple jeopardy: Women and AIDS.* London: Author.

Pearson, R. (1992). Gender issues in industrialization. In T. Hewitt, H. Johnson, & D. Wield (Eds.), *Industrialisation and development* (pp. 222-247). Oxford: Oxford University Press.

Pearson, R. (1995). Male bias and women's work in the Mexico border industries. In D. Elson (Ed.), *Male bias in the development process* (pp. 133-163). (2nd ed,). Manchester: Manchester University Press.

Pearson, R. (2000). Moving the goalposts: Gender and globalisation in the twenty-first century. *Gender and Development, 8* (1), 10-19.

Pitayanon, S., Rerks-Ngarm, S., Kongsin, S., & Janjaroen, W. S. (1994). *Study on the economic impact of HIV/AIDS mortality on households in Thailand.* Bangkok: Chulalongkorn University/Thailand, Ministry of Public Health.

Rana, F. S., Hawken, M. P., Mwachari, C., Bhatt, S. M., Abdullah, F., Ng'ang'a, L. W., Power, C., Githui, W. A., Porter, J. D., & Lucas, S. B. (2000). Autopsy study of HIV-1-positive and HIV-1-negative adult medical patients in Nairobi, Kenya. *Journal of Acquired Immune Deficiency Syndromes, 24,* 23-29.

Sanou, A., Dembele, M., Theobald, S., & Macq, J. (2004). Access and adhering to tuberculosis treatment: Barriers faced by patients and communities in Burkina Faso. *The International Journal of Tuberculosis and Lung Disease, 8* (12), 1479-1483.

Schoepf, B. G. (1993). Gender, development, and AIDS: A political economy and culture framework. *The Women and International Development Annual, 3,* 53-85.

Segurado, A., (2002, June). Untitled presentation made at the Consultation on Integrating Gender Considerations into National HIV/AIDS Programmes, Geneva.

Standing, H. (1997). Gender and equity in health sector reform programmes: A review. *Health Policy and Planning, 12* (1), 1-18.

Taylor, L., Seeley, J., & Kajura, E. (1996). Informal care for illness in rural southwest Uganda: The central role that women play. *Health Transition Review, 6* (1), 49-56.

Theobald, S. (2002). Gendered bodies: Recruitment, management and occupational health in Northern Thailand's electronics factories. *Journal of Women's Health, 35* (4), 7-26.

Thomas, C. (2002). Trade policy and the politics of access to drugs. *Third World Quarterly (23)* 2, 251-264.

Thorson, A., & Diwan, V. (2001). Gender inequalities in tuberculosis: Aspects of infection, notification rates, and compliance. *Current Opinion on Pulmonary Medicine, 7* (3), 165-169.

UK Department for International Development. (2004). *Consultation document on the UK Government's new strategy on HIV/AIDS in the developing world.* London: Author.

UNAIDS (1999) *Gender and HIV/AIDS: Taking stock of research and programmes.* Geneva: Author.

UNAIDS (2002): *Report on the global HIV/AIDS epidemic.* Geneva: UNAIDS.

UNAIDS, & World Health Organization. (2000). *Epidemiological fact sheets on HIV/AIDS and sexually transmitted infections.* Geneva: Authors.

UNAIDS, & World Health Organization (2002). *AIDS epidemic update.* Geneva: Authors.

UNAIDS, & World Health Organization (2006). *Prepayment scheme for provision of health care for people living with HIV/AIDS [Rwanda].* Retrieved May 19, 2006, from: http://www.who.int/chronic_conditions/best_practic es/rwa/unaids/en/index.html.

UNIFEM. (2002). *Women, gender and HIV/AIDS in East and Southeast Asia: What is vulnerability to HIV?* Retrieved May 18, 2006, from: http://www.unifem.eseasia.org/resources/others/ge naids/genaid9.htm.

Wang, L. X., Wang, X., Fu, C., Tang, S., and Squire, S. B. (2002). Factors associated with failure to complete TB treatment in China [Abstract]. *International Journal of Tuberculosis and Lung Disease, 6* (10, Suppl. 1), S140.

Wilkinson, D., Gouws, E., Sach, M., & Abdool Karim, S. S. (2001). Effect of removing user fees on attendance for curative and preventive primary health care services in rural South Africa. *Bulletin of the World Health Organisation 79 (7)*, 665-671.

Woelk, G., Jackson, H., Kerkhoven, R., Hansen, K., Manjonjori, N., Maramba, P., Mutambirwa, J., Ndimande, W., & Vera, E. (1997). *The cost and quality of community home based care for HIV/AIDS patients and their communities in Zimbabwe.* Harare, University of Zimbabwe, Medical School.

World Bank. (2000). Thailand's response to AIDS: "Building on success, confronting the future" [Special issue]. *Thailand Social Monitor, 5,* 1-68.

World Development Movement. (2001). *Policies to roll-back the state and privatize?: Poverty reduction strategy papers investigated.* Helsinki: UNU World Institute for Development Economics Research.

World Health Organization. (1994). Caring for people with AIDS. In World Health Organization, *AIDS: Images of the epidemic.* Geneva: Author.

World Health Organization. (1995). *Stop TB at the source: WHO report on the tuberculosis epidemic.* Geneva: Author.

World Health Organization. (2001). *International Conference on Health Research for Development [COHRED]: Conference report, Bangkok, 10-13 October 2000.* Geneva: Author.

World Health Organization. (2002a). *World Health Organization report on infectious diseases: Scaling up the response to infectious diseases: A way out of poverty.* Retrieved May 5, 2004, from: http://www.who.int/infectious-disease report/index.html.

World Health Organization. (2002b). *Gender and tuberculosis* [Fact sheet]. Retrieved on May 3, 2004, from: http://www.who.int/gender/documents/en/TB.facts heet.pdf.

World Health Organization. (2004). *Global tuberculosis control: Surveillance, planning, financing.* Geneva: Author.

World Health Organization, & UNAIDS (2002) *Accelerating access initiative: Widening access to care and support for people living with HIV/AIDS* [Progress Report, June 2002]. Geneva: Authors.

Zierler, S., & Krieger, N. (1997). Reframing women's risk: Social inequalities and HIV infection. *Annual Review of Public Health, 18,* 401-436.

Zohir, S. C., & Paul-Majumder, P. (1996). *Garment workers in Bangladesh: Economic, social and health conditions.* Dhaka: Bangladesh Institute of Development Studies.

CROSS-BORDER MOVEMENT OF PEOPLE: BARRIERS, HAZARDS AND HEALTH

Anne Boran

Victims of the sands and the snakeheads

19 Chinese drown half a world away from home. The gangs behind the tragedy are on the run.

Rescuers pulled 19 bodies, including two women, from the waters and 16 survivors. Police said 14 were from mainland China, of whom nine were asylum seekers and five were unknown to the immigration service. Two were of white European appearance. (Lawrence et al., 2004, February 7).

Introduction

Headlines like this point to a "can of worms" at the heart of globalisation today. People on the move both generate, and suffer from, a series of problems related to the circumstances of these movements, whether voluntary or "forced", and whether the destinations are welcoming or not. This chapter explores cross-border movement of people, an aspect of globalisation which, although it has received insufficient attention to date, is forcing its way into the headlines and craving attention from international researchers and policymakers. Health is one of a multiplicity of interrelated problems faced by such migrants.

Globalisation, for the purpose of this chapter, is a term that describes a process by which nations, businesses and people become more dependent and interconnected across the globe, through increased economic integration, communication exchange, cultural diffusion (especially of Western culture) and travel (Labonte & Torgerson, 2002, p. 2). The current phase of globalisation, it is argued, involves an intensification of global flows of capital, information and people. Whereas the movement of capital and information tends to be viewed positively by analysts of globalisation because of its potential contribution to economic development, the movement of people generates ambiguous reactions. Governments are keen to compete against each other to provide incentives for capital and technological flows. They are less likely, except in times of severe labour shortages, to welcome transborder movement of people. On the one hand, global communications and travel enable financially secure global elites to have the world at their fingertips, to be visited, explored and consumed. Ease of travel and money provides a means to this end. This option is, on the other hand, only available for a minority of people, who for the most part, as Ritzer & Liska (2000, p. 153) point out, want a sanitised and "inauthentic" experience of other cultures. From the most optimistic perspective, tourism may expose the tourist to greater multicultural awareness and bring much needed resources to tourist destinations. It also poses potential risks, health risks included, both to the tourist and to recipient communities, around which "moral panics" are frequently constructed. Episodes like SARS and "bird flu" are cases in point. However interesting an analysis of tourism, its impacts and health risks might be as an aspect of cross-border movement of people, it is outside the scope of this chapter to pursue an analysis beyond these preliminary reflections.

For the majority of the world's poor – in 2000/2001, these amounted to 20% of the global population, living on less that 1$ a day (World Bank, 2000) – globalisation could present the attraction of a borderless world, offering either economic security in the form of potential employment or the security of a life free from threat and violence. Research suggests that low income countries are at great risk of conflict. Between 2001 and 2003, low income countries accounted for more than 50% of the countries and territories suffering violent conflicts, and nearly 40% of such places were in Africa (UNDP, 2005, p. 154). In reality, however, for this category of people, globalisation does not deliver a borderless world; borders are in fact policed with increasing vigilance, to prevent what represents a threat to the welfare of "legitimate" citizens or an economic burden on the nation state in question (Kesby, Fenton, Boyle & Power, 2003). In the UK, in February 2005, during the run up to the general election, Labour's Charles Clark announced a five-year strategy, centred on a points system, for the control of immigration and asylum, while the Conservatives promoted a quota system. A succession of measures, all aimed at control and regulation of the cross-border movement of immigrants and asylum seekers, have emerged over the past ten years (Fergusson, 2005, p. 46). Political discourse, especially during election campaigns, tends to radicalise opposition to incomers and to demonise immigrants and asylum seekers. An example of this was Michael Howard's plan to create a "border police force" to replace the 7,400 people employed to screen those coming into Britain at ports and airports, where "… we will have one face at the border, one police force, with one chief constable, with just one job: securing Britain's borders" (Howard, 2005, March 29). The Conservatives would, he claimed, withdraw from the United Nations *Convention Relating to the Status of Refugees* (1951) as a way to speed up the processing and deportation of failed asylum seekers and impose a range of other measures that would deter illegal immigrants from coming to Britain. Echoes of similar rhetoric can be found in fortress states throughout the world.

The events of 9/11 have brought an added dimension to, and justification for, the tightening of immigration policies in the USA and throughout Europe. The Universal Declaration of Human Rights (1948), formulated to create an international space for, and protection of, the oppressed and dispossessed fleeing their country of origin, can be circumvented and eroded as nation states find ways of avoiding and limiting their commitment to such rights. This paper raises concerns about the plight of people who feel compelled, for political or economic reasons, to abandon their country of origin and seek protection and survival elsewhere. It is concerned to look at the health implications of such forced movements, particularly for the displaced people. The chapter will examine the extent of the cross-border movements of people, the causes and health implications of such movements, the hazards of the migration process and the challenges of arrival in a host country. It will be argued that, although the nature of each forced migration may differ, underlying global, regional and national policies and practices could be standardised and tailored to minimise the degree of stress and trauma that the refugee, asylum seeker or undocumented migrant must endure to find a better and healthier life.

Health and globalisation

Health risks associated with global integration are nothing new. In the past, trade, colonial expansion, war and travel exposed participants to the risk of picking up exotic diseases or of imparting diseases to the native populations (Rodney, 1988, p. 78). European countries feared an outbreak of bubonic plague or contamination by lepers, so sufferers were isolated or alienated from the host community. "Quarantine" became established as a way of isolating the infected from the general population. The word "quarantine" (from the Medieval French *une quarantaine de jours*, a period of forty days) originates from a 40-day isolation of ships and people prior to entering the city of Dubrovnik. The isolation was a measure of disease prevention and merchandise protection, related to the plague or Black Death (Frati, 2000). In more recent centuries, vaccination has proven to be an effective means of contagious disease control, particularly in the developed world, and it assumes contemporary importance for official cross-border movement of people as a tool to control the resurgence of infectious disease, previously controlled by a nation state. For many travellers, vaccination is a requirement for movement across borders. For the undocumented migrant or refugee, pre-departure health care or vaccination is not likely to be an option, creating vulnerabilities for both the migrant and the destination state.

The public health implications of the movement of illegal and undocumented migrants are potentially serious. Asylum seekers are, by definition, documented, and their applications officially processed. Therefore, health services, however inadequate, should be able to pick up health problems like TB or AIDS. In fact, screening is likely to be a requirement. The issue of screening is hotly contested, because it can serve one of two purposes: either identification and treatment of disease, for the purpose of minimising the suffering of those infected; or identification only, for purposes of exclusion. The International Organisation for Migration [IOM] has been active since 1951 in transporting over 11 million migrants on behalf of recipient countries, and in places has managed both screening and treatment, increasingly through the informed consent of the migrant rather than the requirement of the recipient state. Infectious diseases, such as tuberculosis, leprosy and sexually transmitted diseases, and also parasitic diseases, have been screened in this way at reduced cost to the recipient nation (Keane & Gushulak, 2001).

Different types of migration

International migrants can be divided into several categories. These are not exclusive, and individuals or groups may be described under more than one heading. Movement between categories is also possible.

1. *Temporary Labour Migrants*. Those who travel for the purposes of employment, to return to a "home" state at a later date. This period may last anything from a few weeks, for seasonal work, to a period of several years.

2. *Global Economy Migrants*. Those who move within a global economy, as part of global production, being transferred to different countries as part of the internal market of Transnational Companies [TNCs]. These tend to be highly skilled managers or executives. Such skilled workers are also in demand in areas where there are skill shortages globally, causing a "brain drain" of professionals from the developing world (World Health Organisation, 2003, p. 11). Health workers are a case in point in the UK today.

3. *Undocumented Migrants*. Those who do not have legal status in the recipient country and who may or may not be tolerated, depending on the need for cheap labour.

4. *Refugee*. Those who are forced to flee their country of origin and are unable or unwilling to return because of "... well-founded fear of persecution on account of race,

religion, nationality, membership of a particular social group, or political opinion" (United Nations Convention Relating to the Status of Refugees, 1951, Art. 1, p. 18).

5. *Asylum Seekers.* These are related to the previous category, but they may not always fit the strict criteria laid down by the 1951 Convention.

6. *Forced Migrants.* This category includes both refugees and asylum seekers, and also those forced to move because of famine, drought or development projects.

7. *Family Members.* Migrants may be joined by other family members. This may or may not result in chain migration, and patterns are shaped by the policies of destination countries.

8. *Return migrants.* Those who, after extensive periods domiciled abroad, return to resettle in their former homeland.

The scope of this paper encompasses undocumented migrants, refugees and asylum seekers only: the type of people encountered in our headline story.

Approaches to asylum

According to Koser (2001, pp. 85-86) three main phases of migration are identifiable since World War II.

1. The 1950s were dominated by resettlement from Europe to North America, Australia and Israel. This period was characterised by idealism, as asylum protection was offered to victims of persecution and repression. It was also affected by Cold War ideology, which generated the migration of victims of the proxy wars between the superpowers in Central America, parts of Africa and

Vietnam, and the resettlement of mainly "White" skilled workers from Europe. Refugee policy was seen, to a large extent, as an instrument of foreign policy, at both international and domestic levels (Martin, 2002, p. 29).

2. The 1960s and 1970s featured a postcolonial outflow of refugees from poorer parts of the world, mainly to nearby and former coloniser nations like Britain and France. These helped fill labour market shortages in a period of global economic expansion.

3. The 1980s and 1990s were dominated by increasing restrictions on refugees, resulting from a contraction in the global economy. This coincided with an end to the Cold War and hence to the ideologically driven motive of saving people from communism. This phase was characterised by restrictions, not only in the developed world, but also in developing countries.

In the first two phases, Koser argues (2001, p. 88), there is an "interest convergence" between refugees and industrial states. No such convergence exists in the third phase, which helps explain the contraction of national quotas, the negative labelling of refugees as "bogus" (i.e. as economic migrants in disguise) and the subsequent imposition of restrictions. Health considerations presented an additional excuse for preventing undesirables from threatening the welfare of legitimate citizens. Few options were left open to real economic migrants - except for those with the required identified skills - to seek legitimate leave to work in a developed country, except through the "refugee" route.

Extent of the problem

Global migration figures demonstrate that migration numbers (in terms of foreigners born outside a country of residence) grew from 75 million in 1965 to 120 million in 1990; approximately 2% of the global population. It grew more rapidly in the 1990s, to approximately 140 million. Of these, some 13 million were UNHCR-recognised refugees. To put things in perspective, however, Skelton (1994) argues that internal migration is much more significant than international migration, since approximately one in six of the world's population (approximately 1 billion people) migrated, mostly internally, in the second half of the 1980s. UNAIDS & the International Organisation for Migration (1998) put the annual figure at approximately 40 million, of whom some 18 million are refugees outside their own countries; the rest are internally displaced. These figures raised concerns globally, especially in the more economically developed countries, not least because some 30 million people worldwide are estimated to be suffering from AIDS and 90% of the world's disease burden is carried by the developing world (Simbulan, 1999). This was seen to represent a significant risk from forced migrants to recipient countries.

In Africa, which is responsible for some two thirds of global refugees, there is a high level of HIV infection in the population as a whole. Therefore, refugees or undocumented migrants, particularly from rural low prevalence areas, may be exposed to a high risk of acquiring the infection in refugee camps or cities in the host country, and consequently of spreading the infection to low prevalence areas, should they return to their location of origin (Girdler-Brown, 1998). Given the levels of instability and conflict in many African countries in recent years, some recipient countries are faced with coping with large numbers of refugees and undocumented migrants with low levels of economic resources. An example is the Democratic Republic of Congo [DCR] which, in mid-1997, had refugees from Rwanda, Burundi, Uganda and Sudan. (Girdler-Brown, p. 521). By 2002, the level of refugees and asylum seekers reached some 400,000, despite the DRC's own serious internal problems, such as civil war, economic crisis, ethnic violence and the presence of foreign troops (*Factfile*, ca. 2002). The risk of acquiring disease can be increased during migration, especially when this process is lengthy or dangerous and where the status of the migrating person is illegal and, depending on the particular level of vulnerability (for example, in the case of trafficked persons), they are exposed to a considerable variety of health risks in the country of destination.

Whereas asylum applications impose visibility on this group of migrants, there is a growing problem of undocumented economic migrants, evident in all developed countries in the shape of informal market labourers, seasonal workers, and failed asylum seekers who have not returned to their country of origin. For most countries in Central and Eastern Europe, for example, it is likely that "irregular" immigration is characteristic and that most foreign workers are in some way illegal (Salt & Clarke, 2000, pp. 322-3). Undocumented economic migrants tend to fall short of official migration quotas or skills requirements for developed economies. These are, however, notoriously difficult to document, so statistics tend just to be estimates. It is claimed that there are approximately 11.5 million undocumented migrants in the USA, for whom Mexico is the leading country of origin. The number is estimated to increase by approximately 500,000 per year. This contrasts radically with the official asylum application figure of 52,650 in the year 2004. In the UK, the figure for undocumented migrants for the same year was rather unclear, but suggested to be approximately 400,000, whereas the official asylum applications figure was 40,200 (UNHCR, 2005). The lack of accurate data compounds the difficulties associated with the analysis of this complex aspect of globalisation.

Countries of origin

Contrary to what one might suppose, the major country of origin for European migrants in 2004 was the Russian Federation, followed by Serbia and Montenegro and China. Turkey became fourth in 2004, India fifth, Nigeria sixth, Pakistan seventh and Iraq ninth (down from fourth in 2003). In North America, Latin America and the Caribbean accounted for the largest number of asylum applications in 2004 (39%), followed by Asia (33%). In Australia and New Zealand, 68% of applicants originated from Asia, whereas in Japan and the Republic of South Korea, 82% of applicants originated from other parts of Asia (UNHCR, 2005, pp. 1-7). There are, therefore, "natural" regional targets for refugee and asylum groups. Reasons why these are targeted will depend on a number of factors, including ease of entry, facilitator knowledge and linkages, language, and policy towards refugees and asylum seekers.

Recipient countries

According to the UNHCR report *Asylum Levels and Trends in Industrial Countries* (2005), the number of asylum applications in 50 industrialised countries in 2004 was 396,400, down by 22% from the previous year. Since 2001, the drop is 40%. France has become the main destination for asylum seekers, replacing the USA, which is now the second major destination. The UK, the main destination in 2002, fell to third place in 2004. Germany, the leading destination for most of the 1980s and 90s, was fourth in 2004; Canada was fifth and Austria sixth. When compared to the total population of the country in question, however, Cyprus received the highest number of all destination countries (22 per 1000 of the population).

However, within the developing world, certain countries serve as a magnet to refugees and asylum seekers. In Africa, for example, the Democratic Republic of Congo in 2002 hosted 400,000 refugees and asylum seekers, mainly from Angola, Sudan, Burundi and Uganda; Sudan accommodated 330,000 refugees from Eritrea, Uganda and Ethiopia; and Tanzania some 690,000, mainly from Rwanda, the Democratic Republic of Congo and Burundi (*Factfile*, ca. 2002). Border proximity is a dominating factor guiding choice. In East Asia, China is a significant destination for refugees and asylum seekers, some 300,000 of them, mainly ethnic Chinese from Vietnam, as well as North Koreans and Burmese. Iran hosted 1,300,000 refugees and asylum seekers in 2002, mostly from Afghanistan and Iraq. Conflict in the region also provoked a movement of some 1,200,000 refugees into Pakistan. Such migrants regularly face hostility from host communities, and accommodation all too frequently involves refugee camps, where conditions often facilitate the spread of infectious disease and Sexually Transmitted Diseases [STDs].

The figures above suggest that it is a myth that the direction of flight is always towards Advanced Industrial Economies [AIEs]. Poorer nations sometimes face almost insurmountable difficulties catering for the needs of refugees and asylum seekers and depend heavily on the UNHCR for support. Political rhetoric in Advanced Industrial Countries [AICs] tends to underplay the imbalance between the burden borne by Less Developed Countries and overplay that borne by the industrialised world. This justifies regional border tightening and moral panics, suggesting that Europe risks invasion by Africans, the USA by Mexicans and Australasia by poorer Asian migrants. Given the level of propaganda, it is salient to recognise that the UK copes with only 2% of the worldwide refugee intake. Why the drive to cross such largely unwelcoming borders?

Pre-departure precipitating causes

Evidence suggests that threats to personal, family or ethnic security propel large numbers of people to abandon their homes and neighbourhoods to seek security and refuge elsewhere, most often within the same nation state. Most will seek out relatives, hide in obscure locations, move into urban centres or cross the border into a neighbouring country. As argued earlier, international migration is small in proportion to internal migration.

Precipitating causes of internal and cross-border migration are many and varied. Neo-classical theory claims that the movement of labour has to do with the maximisation of income, by movement from a low wage to a high wage economy. Free market economics may shed light on some internal movements of people, but is limited in explaining cross-border movements, not least because nation states are reluctant to allow a "free" labour market to dictate such movements. Poverty may be a powerful motivating force driving economic migrants who, through modern communication systems, are made aware of global disparities in income levels, differential employment levels and social well-being differences. That said, the very poor are unlikely to combine such awareness with sufficient capital to be able to travel or to access the necessary contacts and networks to engage successfully in the process.

Research shows that, as regards asylum seekers and indeed "economic migrants", it is generally not the poorest that migrate. It is predominantly middle-income groups in developing areas that are most likely to depart (UN Working Group on Migration, 1998; as cited in Castles, 2000). Considerable planning and capital is required to escape, the latter needed to use as bribes and to meet the normally extortionate journey costs. Families may sink all their resources into the escape project or depend on loan sharks to finance the migration. However, as studies of illegal trafficking are increasingly beginning to highlight, exploiters, such as unscrupulous brothel owners, are also seeking out the poor and vulnerable within the global system to feed illegal "demand". The most isolated, poor and uneducated are most at risk from this type of exploitation within the global system (Bain, 1998, p. 557).

Both "push" and "pull" factors can be seen as precipitant causes of national and international migration. Population pressures or demographic growth (Castles, 2000, p. 270) are likely to propel some economic migration, as they have done historically from, for example, Britain and other European countries. Industrialisation and advanced development are likely to attract such migration, as was the case with the USA, which received 30 million migrants between 1861 and 1920 (Castles, p. 272) and perhaps with locations like China today. It may even be an expressed desire of such destinations to attract migrants, to meet labour shortages or perceived demographic shortfalls.

Additionally, "push" factors, such as conflict, propel people to cross borders in search of safety, as they have done under colonial expansions, and during the formation of nation states. Conflicts continue to exert pressure today, because of unresolved struggles between contenders for control of a nation state or for secession from it. Evidence of this process is clearly identifiable in many African states, such as Ethiopia, the Sudan, Liberia and Zimbabwe, along with many others. "Forced migration is fuelled by conflicts, human rights abuses and political repression that displace people from their home communities" (Martin, 2002, p. 26) and seriously threaten their health and well-being. The UN Convention Relating to the Status of Refugees (1951) states that a refugee is one who has a "well-founded fear" and, owing to this fear, "… is unwilling to avail himself of the protection of that country." Unlike traditional conflicts, fought out between conventional armies, civilians more and more bear the brunt of modern conflicts, which expose them to war-related violence, exploitation and abuse. According to the World Health Organization, civilian casualties climbed from 5% at the turn of the century to 14% during World War I, to 65% by the end of World War II, and to more than 90% in the wars of the 1990s (World Health Organization, 2003, p. 10). In many cases, particularly where there is ongoing internal warfare, refugees suffer shock and trauma, and sometimes torture and abuse, including sexual abuse and loss of family members. This is likely to have both short- and long-term psychological effects, including Post-Traumatic Stress Disorder (World Health Organization, p. 16).

In Europe during the early 1990s, massive displacements of people were caused by civil wars in the former Yugoslavia, particularly in Bosnia Herzegovina and Kosovo. The fall of the Berlin Wall and the disintegration of the Soviet Union made Western Europe, and Germany in particular, a target for ethnic nationals and asylum seekers. In times of consolidation and redefinition, many of these Eastern European states are struggling to adjust to the demands of capitalism and democracy and their citizens are exploited by people traffickers for the undocumented economic migrant business.

Environmental catastrophes: for example, earthquakes, tsunamis, volcanic eruptions and hurricanes; environmental degradation: for example, desertification and pollution; man-made disasters: for example, large scale industrial accidents, nuclear or chemical; or development projects, such as large-scale dams,[1] force people to flee their communities of origin. As with refugees, communities are uprooted and cannot return to their homes. Most of the people affected, because such catastrophes are not usually accompanied by persecution, tend eventually to resettle internally, but some will cross borders, because of the trauma suffered and because they lack confidence in the coping abilities of the state in question to protect them and to help them rebuild their lives. These people will tend to be vulnerable, in economic and well-being terms, because of the stresses that loss of both livelihood and community brings.

Consequences of the migration process

Cross-border migrants face many hazards on the journey to safety and/or illegal economic security. Although poverty, or insufficient means to live in dignity, does not imply as severe a threat to life as does oppression and persecution, one could argue that "forced" migration appropriately reflects the reality of both conditions. Vulnerability exposes cross-border migrants, of both types, to health risks associated with the nature and length of the journey and the means of transport. The trafficking of migrants is now a big, probably multi-billion dollar,

---

[1] The Sardar Sarovar Dam in India displaced some 200,000 people and China's Three Gorges Dam was estimated to displace 1.3 million people.

business, involving a network of sophisticated, unscrupulous individuals and agencies. Research suggests that the growth of smuggling, as a means of cross-border migration, can be directly related to the growth of restrictive practices in the 1990s (Koser, 2001, p. 90). These practices have served to complicate the distinction between economic and political migrants and the issue of legal status, and have exposed vulnerable people to increased risks to their health and well-being. Koser argues that, because of the range of obstacles preventing access by asylum seekers to industrialised countries, they have become increasing dependent on smugglers to help them migrate. Consequently, by the end of the 1990s, an increasing proportion of asylum seekers were arriving illegally. People smugglers are likely to be using similar networks to those of drugs and arms smugglers. In fact, all those activities may be included in the portfolios of such operators, a factor that serves to expose refugees to increased risk. Traffickers can, however, simultaneously be viewed as entrepreneurs, operating within a global market, providing a niche service based on market demand. Thus they can be framed in either a positive light, as saviours, or in a negative one, as exploiters.

Eight of the dead pulled from the sea at Morecambe Bay were said to be from the Fujian province in South-Eastern China, where people pay up to £20,000 to snakehead gangsters to smuggle them out to Western Europe (Lawrence et al., 2004, February 7). Smugglers have varied levels of sophistication, ranging from the highly organised Chinese triads to the less organised Mexican operations. As with the drugs trade, the sophisticated operators are unlikely to be affected by crackdowns, either at nation state level or at international level. They are in business, and trafficking is their business, so continued recruitment is likely as long as there are potential migrants. Geographical proximity and migration networks are important migration facilitators (Neumayer, 2005). The journey may be fraught with risks, such as having documents (identity cards, passports or visas) and therefore identities stolen. Those smuggled may be then trapped into debt bondage or subjected to inhuman conditions on arrival (Salt & Clarke, 2000, p. 323).

Trafficked people, the vast majority of whom are women and children, face fraud, intimidation, the threat of physical force, debt bondage and coercion of all kinds (World Health Organization, 2003, p. 16). They may be subjected to physical abuse, resulting in trauma or death. Women, transported for the sex trade in developed countries, may suffer the most brutal and terrifying treatment to render them powerless and trapped within this "business". According to Bennett (1997, p. 9; as cited in Bain, 1998), the environment that migrants encounter on their travels may be of more significance to HIV risk factors than prior attitudes or habits. Unwanted pregnancies, abortions, and sexually transmitted diseases may result in poor reproductive and sexual health, as well as emotional and mental health problems. The trafficking of women into prostitution is a demand-led business that is beginning to be taken very seriously at the international level by Interpol and by the Home Office in the UK. The scale is difficult to determine and is likely to be many times the number (71) that was identified in the UK in 1998 (Kelly & Regan, 2000).

Evidence suggests that, whatever the circumstances, where refugees and asylum seekers are concerned, control of the process is ceded to the trafficker, who will have knowledge of asylum policies, will decide travel routes, sometimes provide documentation and even choose the final destination of refugees (Koser, 2001). Koser's research on Iranian refugees in the Netherlands illustrated that, not only does the process criminalise refugees through the use of false documents or none, but it also increases their vulnerability throughout the journey, from being trapped in a transit country, to running out of money, to being sent back to Iran and subsequent persecution. Very few succeeded in migrating to a country where they had family or social networks, thus increasing their sense of vulnerability and isolation. This vulnerability and isolation frequently leads to depression. Evidence from Beiser, Simich & Pandalangat's (2003) study of Tamil migrants and refugees in Canada suggests a catalogue of negative experiences suffered by refugees; 43% of the sample had lost their homes and lived as internally displaced persons, 7.5% spent time in refugee camps, 35% were separated from family members during the immigration period, 8% experienced harassment, 7% were cheated by travel agents and 25% shouldered large debts as a result of their migration. It is of little surprise that 12% suffered from Post-Traumatic Stress Disorder. One third of the respondents reported experiencing traumatic events, such as witnessing combat, physical assault or rape (Beiser et al., p. 239-240). It is not difficult to imagine a similar pattern for refuges from the many conflict areas throughout the world.

Risking life itself is frequently seen as the only option open to migrants in order to escape either political or economic oppression. African economic and political migrants continually put to sea in inadequate, overcrowded vessels to try to reach Europe and a better life. Loss of life is frequently the outcome of these expeditions, as Fortress Europe hardens its attitudes and entry conditions. The same is true across the world. An overcrowded boat sank off the coast of Indonesia in 2001, drowning the 356 migrants on board. Risk-taking behaviour is a common feature of cross-border migration, as migrants attempting to get to Britain from France demonstrate all too clearly in their attempts to board trains or lorries illicitly, frequently with fatal consequences.

Effects of conditions on arrival

Whereas countries of origin will tend to have some support services in place for official migrants and refugees to a host country, such services are unlikely to be available for undocumented migrants, who may face the most precarious of conditions. Even when the host country provides services for refugees and asylum seekers, the few studies that have been undertaken highlight serious flaws in addressing their well-being needs. Beiser et al. (2003, p. 241) claim that, despite 87% of their sample having family or friends to help them to adjust, isolation, unemployment and dependency, as well as previous experiences, created a high incidence of depression, for which there was a marked reluctance to seek treatment, because of cultural and linguistic problems. This was compounded by lack of mobility and a general mistrust of health services. Culturally and linguistically sensitive services need to be developed if this is to change.

In the UK, the health of refugees and asylum seekers typically worsens in the years following entry into Britain. This seems to be caused by a combination of factors, including social exclusion and negative stereotyping. This can be compounded by stressful and restrictive approaches to immigration, lack of a systematic health assessment system and degrading and miserly economic support. Added to this, dispersal policies, as a consequence of the UK's Immigration and Asylum Act 1999, leave refugees and asylum seekers without adequate support systems: cultural, legal or economic. Government policies, resulting in detention for long periods whilst applications for asylum are processed, increase alienation and stress. That a deterioration of health, particularly mental health, occurs is hardly surprising (Collin & Lee, 2003). Governments, for reasons suggested earlier in this chapter, regard refugees and asylum seekers as problems rather than potential assets, so detention centres appear to be about control (processing, screening, advising and deterring) rather than providing a haven where support, acculturation, diagnosis and treatment are proffered, together with a speedy and humane processing of applications for asylum. Accommodation centres with health and education facilities, introduced by the Nationality, Immigration and Asylum Act 2002, addressed a least a couple of those concerns, while tightening still more the conditions for granting asylum.

Başoğlu et al. (2005), in their study of the psychiatric and cognitive effects of war in the former Yugoslavia, found that, in addition to physical injury, refugees and asylum seekers are at high risk of chronic mental health disorders, because of the multiple stresses they experience before, during, and after their flight. They are at particularly high risk of Post-Traumatic Stress Disorder [PTSD], which involves persisting recurrent and disturbing memories and flashbacks of a witnessed or experienced trauma. Other symptoms include having difficulty sleeping, feeling detached from people and current experiences, exaggerated startle responses, depression, and somatization (emotional trauma or stress, experienced as physical symptoms). Some 33% had current PTSD and 10% suffered from current major depression more than one year after surviving the conflicts. Such responses are acerbated by unstable living arrangements and the lack of economic opportunity in the new living situation. The threat of forcible return to the country from which the refugees fled increases the feeling of vulnerability, as does the lack of resolution of the conflict there (Ringold, Burke & Glass, 2005). Because these are typical of the experiences faced by such migrants in the host nation, specialist services, sensitive to cultural needs, are required to help treat such conditions.

Where vulnerability exists, opportunists generally emerge to exploit it. Illegal status can provide economic opportunities for certain businesses in the developed world, indeed globally, to exploit illegal migrants. The Chinese illegal immigrants and refugees, highlighted in the headline opening this chapter, were employed to pick cockles in Morecambe Bay by an associate of a gang-master (UK-based labour provider) from the Fujian province in China. Lack of regulation and of any concern for their well-being resulted in the death of 19 people, caught by the fast moving tides, well known in the area to be highly dangerous. In an emergency statement to the House of Commons, Rural Affairs Minister Alun Michael said that criminal gangs could not be allowed to continue to put workers' lives at risk, and he later told *BBC News* that: "One of the problems in tackling the activities of gang-masters is that there is a conspiracy of silence - it is [in] nobody's interests to speak out" (*Seven held...*, 2004, February 10). A range of industries in the UK and in other Advanced Industrial Countries benefit hugely from trafficked people in search of economic opportunities. The catering industry, together with numerous farming sectors - poultry, vegetable and fruit – benefit through the existence of a pool of low-waged labour who are in no position to express concern about working conditions. In the USA, illegal immigrants work as farm labourers, maids, and manual labourers of all kinds. Estimates suggest that there are 12 million illegal immigrants in the USA. "Depending on who you listen to, 'illegals' either cost American tax payers $45 bn (£25.8 bn) each year in education, prison and health costs, or those 12 million are among the most productive net contributors to the national economy" (Wells, 2006, March 27).

Illegal immigrants are an attractive source of cheap labour, despite the legal risks involved in employing them. The consequences of illegal status, however, mean that undocumented workers may be forced to live in overcrowded and inhumane conditions, exploited by unscrupulous landlords because of their vulnerability. Gang-masters often charge each Chinese migrant a £150 registration fee and £20-£30 a week for accommodation (Lawrence et al., 2004, February 7). Both poor working conditions and below standard accommodation can impact negatively on health. Access to medical help may be denied or may expose illegal migrants to risk of arrest and return to their country of origin. They are, therefore, forced to depend on underground services and networks and face the constant risk of exploitation, along with poor wages and insecurity. On the positive side, from the perspective of the undocumented migrants, remittances may possibly be repatriated to provide support for their families in their country of origin, and investment opportunities may be exploited, which could enable the migrant to return home at some future date to a life of economic prosperity. Evidence suggests that, for most undocumented migrants, refugees and asylum seekers, this is their ultimate ambition for the future.

Policy responses to migration

Policies to deal with undocumented migrants and asylum seekers can be targeted either at state, international or supranational level. International policies demand co-operation between states to uphold state laws, whereas transnational crimes, such as the trafficking of persons, fall within the category of the United Nations *Convention against Transnational Organized Crime* (2000a), requiring signatory states to make it a criminal offence. The United Nations *Protocol to Prevent, Suppress and Punish Trafficking in Persons* (2000b) is an example of an attempt to address this problem of cross-border trafficking within the context of transnational organised crime. The focus centres on the criminals, like Chinese triads, without criminalising the victims of this crime. Not all states distinguish between criminals and migrants however; the UK being a case in point (McCreight, 2006).

The United Nations *Convention Relating to the Status of Refugees* (1951) should provide a framework within which nation states respond to refugees and asylum seekers. Indeed, the UN has a global role in monitoring peace and human rights in conflict-ridden areas to protect life and prevent refugee creation. The fact that the UN suffered some very high profile failures, for example in Srebrenica and Rwanda, points to serious fault lines in the system, in that its core message – protection against genocide, the ultimate threat to health – was flouted. The creation of safe havens within a conflict-ridden country, like that provided for the Kurds in Iraq, can provide protection for the threatened people. This solution, policed by NATO air power, lessened the risk of mass movement of refugees into neighbouring states. The idea, as piloted in Iraq, appeared to offer a creative solution to some refugee crises, a solution that would enable nation states to avoid domestic responsibilities for such refugees. Safe havens demand long-term commitment, however, together with heavy economic investment, and may well be seen to be destabilising in the longer term, because of the potential ambition to secede that may be fostered. They are unlikely to provide a solution to every conflict. The international community is unlikely to commit either the economic resources or the long-term military and political investment to such projects, as examples from Africa, such as Rwanda and Darfur, testify. The stakes have to be particularly high from the perspective of the dominant powers, as perhaps was perceived to be the case in relation to Eastern Europe and Iraq. It is unlikely, therefore, that the stream of refugees and asylum seekers will end.

Increasingly reluctant to commit generously to receiving refugees, nation states have turned to controls and disincentives of various kinds. There is pressure in Europe and the USA to define certain countries, such as Nigeria, Somalia and Algeria, as "safe" and to send asylum seekers back there on these grounds. In this way, countries can be seen as responding to the "letter" of the Convention, although not to its spirit. The terms of the UN *Convention Relating to the Status of Refugees* (1951), as applied to those with a "well founded fear of persecution", gives scope for states to deny protection to those who flee more generalised conflict conditions. Returning refugees and asylum seekers to conditions where torture is known to be a tool of the state is negligent in the extreme. Repatriation needs to be monitored and safe, something that is very difficult to guarantee in these circumstances. The return of rejected asylum seekers brings a host of problems in relation both to security and livelihoods; such problems include the reclaiming of property, abandoned or appropriated on flight, and political representation (Martin, 2002). The international community has a role in attempting to strengthen judicial processes that will protect returnees and prosecute the abuse of minorities.

Regional solutions may be of increasing importance in this regard. The creation of processing centres or temporary refugee centres at a regional level could protect refugees and manage the migration process. Martin (2002) cites an example from South-East Asia, where a processing centre was set up in Bataan to provide temporary asylum for refugees in Thailand, Malaysia, Singapore and Hong Kong while more permanent settlement was organised. Examples of negotiated shares of Kosovan refugees agreed by Eastern European states are also cited. It is difficult to distance such approaches from accusations of depersonalisation and functionalism, however, as the views of refugees can easily be negated as they become defined as the problem. The UK proposal, to create an international political solution to the refugee crisis by transporting asylum seekers hoping to come to the UK to a place outside Europe to process their claims, seemed more akin to arranging a dumping ground for refugees, out of sight and outside the comfort zones of UK and European citizens (Refugee Council, 2003). In Africa, some states, like the Democratic Republic of Congo, serve as a magnet for refugee populations from surrounding conflict situations. Stable African states perform an admirable role in accommodating refugees from surrounding strife-torn countries, despite limited financial resources. People are provided with a breathing space that enables them to monitor conditions in the area of conflict from close by, so that they can repatriate when conditions stabilise. Zimbabwean refugees who cross the border into the poorest regions of South Africa, however, cause a major trauma for the government as it tries to integrate its own socially excluded people economically.

The ultimate solution to forced cross-border movement of people would, in a perfect world, be a resolution of the precipitating causes of that flight. Solutions may incorporate the protection of minority rights, democratisation, political stability or economic development: all of which tend to create stability and a sense of security. To take the case of Darfur: a combination of protection for the refugees with pressure on, and sensitive negotiations with, the Sudanese Government, in dialogue with the African Union and the international community, could provide possibilities for a way forward. However, actual attempts at resolution demonstrate just how difficult such a task is, because of the conflict of interests within the Security Council, the African Union and between warring parties in the Sudan. Conflict situations like Darfur are notorious for exposing refugees to rape, killings, terror and flight for survival. Internal displacement, refugee camps protected by overstretched African Union forces, or cross-border migration to countries like Chad, are the inevitable outcomes, generating challenges at a range of levels. Humanitarian assistance that helps to minimise conflict and stabilise communities is called for, but not easily achieved. Again, the role of the African Union provides the possibility of a regional solution, in a context in which complexities can be understood and more sensitive solutions sought. Resources are needed, however, in the form of adequate financial, technological, and medical backup to support regional initiatives. Importantly, the treatment of the displaced needs to be managed in a humane way, perhaps by the visible presence of organisations such as UNHCR in every at risk country, to monitor or even manage refugee issues close to the ground, including issues of the safe return of refugees.

Political stability, respect for human rights and economic and social development are the ultimate conditions that minimise the flow of cross-border migration. Unless they are achieved, refugees and economic migrants will continue to flee adverse conditions that limit well-being and will seek safety and protection elsewhere. Legal routes that enable economic and political migrants to find safe havens, without further risk to life and health, need to be strengthened at the international level. Such routes will deny smugglers what some consider a "legitimate" role in facilitating cross-border migration and may also help to undermine the business of people trafficking. Robust international action is essential to protect women and children in particular from such criminal activities. It is also important to add that cross-border migration has always been a feature of nation states and not an aberrant side effect. The focus, therefore, needs to change, from one that contains or rejects the migrant to one that manages migration as a normal phenomenon, subject at times to intensification of flows, for reasons discussed above. The focus should shift as a consequence to protection and risk amelioration for migrants and host communities.

In relation to health, restrictive national laws are likely to drive problems like AIDS underground. Where screening is mandatory, as for example in Switzerland, it does not mean that the population is protected from AIDS. As the World Health Organization (2003) argues, all countries already live with the virus, and prohibiting the entry of HIV positive people will not safeguard the population in any significant way as a consequence. Discrimination on the basis of health is an issue of human rights law. Compliance with international and national guidelines in relation to infectious diseases curtails individual freedoms, including privacy (e.g. surveillance), bodily integrity (e.g. compulsory treatment), and liberty (e.g. travel restrictions and quarantine). At the same time, public health activities can stigmatize, stereotype, or discriminate against individuals or groups (Gostin, 2000). Yet, if a balance of rights and precautions is to be attained and reforms are to succeed, "... the world must relinquish important aspects of state sovereignty and insular self-interest to come together for a universal good" (Gostin, 2004). One of the most important issues that humankind must deal with today is how sovereign countries can join together to make global health work for everyone: not just the privileged.

International co-operation may involve regional decisions, and co-operation under World Health Organization direction could be a way forward, coupled with a strengthening of aid to regions that are less prosperous; Africa being a case in point. Joined-up thinking, which puts human rights and well-being at the core of policy making, is needed from the global to the local level. Focused research in a wide range of host nations could elucidate the particular dynamics operating in each location, taking account of the cultural mix, the causes precipitating the migration of incomers, the hazards endured during the process of migration, and related health problems faced by migrant and host populations. Such studies can enable targeted public and general health problems to be addressed in a coherent manner at local and national levels.

Miserly economic policies towards migrants within the nation state visit indignity on recipients of aid. In a national survey of 40 support organisations in the UK, 85% reported that their clients experienced hunger and 80% of the clients claimed that they were not able to maintain good health on the voucher system (Penrose, 2002). In the present climate, politicians compete to come up with harsher conditions for refugees and asylum seekers: conditions that will deter migrants and counter "soft touch" allegations from opponents. Insufficient financial support, increasingly exacting requirements for asylum application, racism, stereotyping to score political points, and shifting or denying responsibility places the burden of support on the voluntary sector. Opportunities and risks generated by cross-border movement of people through the globalisation process are not currently addressed generously, either through support for victims on arrival, co-operation with other nations in meeting responsibilities to forced migrants or adequate control of those who are only too ready to exploit the powerless within the global system.

It is clear that current policy is failing to address the reality of migration. The consequences of this failure are strongest for migrants themselves, in that the most vulnerable are exposed to the range of negative health impacts outlined above.

Conclusion

This chapter has explored some of the broad and complex issues that surround one of the less popular aspects of globalisation, namely that of the movement of people across borders. It highlights the sheer complexity of such movements in terms of precipitating "forces" and responses of various kinds. Refugees and undocumented migrants face hazards, together with health risks, at every stage of the migration process and, on successful arrival in a host nation, are frequently met with resentment, racism and ever tightening restrictions on asylum and employment. The most serious health hazards are likely to have mental health implications, as a result of the traumas and stresses suffered at each stage of the process. Refugee camps present particular risks in the developing world, in that they also expose migrants to many infectious diseases and health risks. Undocumented migrants face potential death, exploitation and lack of protection, and women and children in particular risk abuse and sexually transmitted diseases. In contrast, host communities have little to fear from migrant health problems.

Policymakers need to take account of the range of vulnerabilities faced by migrants across the world. Political and resource-heavy solutions are easy to avoid, as politicians put their own individual and party survival first. The story of the Chinese cockle pickers involves their own government, economic conditions in China, personal ambition backed by families willing to make great sacrifices for economic betterment, powerful traffickers and global networks. Governments mindful of internal tensions are reluctant to take any responsibility for the impact of increased restrictions and, consequently, for the narrow range of options open to economic migrants and refugees; the results of this expose them to risk, exploitation and even death. For the Chinese cockle pickers, what could have been done differently to produce a positive ending? The human rights and well-being of such people could be made the centre of policy concerns which regarded them less as "burdens" and more as potential assets that could contribute to and enrich society. This would demand a fine balancing act, of the sort that tends to be betrayed by short-term political goals.

References

Bain, I. (1998). South-East Asia. *International Migration, 36* (4), 553-585.

Başoğlu, M., Livanou, M., Crnobarić, C., Frančišković, T., Suljić, E., Đurić, D., et al. (2005). Psychiatric and cognitive effects of war in former Yugoslavia: Association of lack of redress for trauma and posttraumatic stress reactions. *Journal of the American Medical Association, 294* (5), 580-590.

Beiser, M., Simich, L., & Pandalangat, N. (2003). Community in distress: Mental health needs and help-seeking in the Tamil community in Toronto. *International Migration, 41* (5), 234-245.

Casciani, D. (2006, March 26). Battling the people smugglers. *BBC News.* Retrieved December 21, 2006, from: http://news.bbc.co.uk/1/hi/uk/4830988.stm.

Castles, S. (2000). International migration at the beginning of the twenty-first century: Global trends and issues. *International Social Science Journal, 52* (165), 269–281.

Collin, J., & Lee, K. (2003). *Globalisation and transborder health: risk in the UK: case studies in tobacco control and population mobility.* London: Nuffield Trust.

Factfile: Global migration: Refugees: Where they come from. (ca. 2002) *BBC News.* Retrieved January 23, 2007, from:

http://news.bbc.co.uk/1/shared/spl/hi/world/04/mi gration/html/refugees_from.stm

Fergusson, J. (2005, April). Britain's front line. *Prospect, 109.* Retrieved December 20, 2006, from:

http://www.prospect-magazine.co.uk/article_details.php?id=6833.

Frati. P. (2000). Quarantine, trade and health policies in Ragusa-Dubrovnik until the age of George Armmenius-Baglivi. *Medicina nei Secoli, 12* (1), 103-127.

Girdler-Brown, B. (1998). Eastern and Southern Africa. *International Migration, 31* (4), 513-551.

Gostin L. O. (2000). *Public health law: Power, duty, restraint.* Berkeley: University of California Press; New York: Milbank Memorial Fund.

Gostin, L. O. (2004). International infectious disease law: Revision of the World Health Organization's international health regulations. *Journal of the American Medical Association, 291* (21), 2623-2627.

Howard, M. (2005, March 29). *We can control our borders* [Speech at Conservative Campaign Headquarters]. Retrieved January 8, 2007, from: http://www.conservatives.com/tile.do?def=news.story .page&obj_id=121031&speeches=1

Keane, V. P., & Gushulak, B. D. (2001). The medical assessment of migrants: Current limitations and future potential. *International Migration, 39* (2), 29-42.

Kelly, L., & Regan, L. (2000). *Stopping traffic: Exploring the extent of, and responses to, trafficking in women for sexual exploitation in the UK.* London: Home Office, Policing and Reducing Crime Unit.

Kesby, M., Fenton, K., Boyle, P., & Power, R. (2003). An agenda for future research on HIV and sexual behaviour among African migrant communities in the UK. *Social Science and Medicine, 57* (9), 1573-1592.

Koser, K. (2000). Asylum policies, trafficking and vulnerability. *International Migration,* Special Issue 2000/1, 91-111.

Koser, K. (2001). New approaches to asylum. *International Migration, 39* (6), 85-101.

Labonte, R., & Togerson, R. (2002). *Frameworks for analysing the links between globalization and health: Draft report to the World Health Organization.* Saskatoon, University of Saskatchewan, SPHERU.

Lawrence, F., Pai, H-H., Dodd, V., Carter, H., Ward, D., & Watts, J. (2004, February 7). Victims of the sands and the snakeheads. *The Guardian.* Retrieved December 21, 2006, from:
http://www.guardian.co.uk/uk_news/story/0,3604,11 43060,00.html.

Martin, S. (2002). Averting forced migration in countries in transition. *International Migration, 40* (3), 25-40.

McCreight, M. V. (2006). Smuggling of migrants, trafficking in human beings and irregular migration on a comparative perspective. *European Law Journal, 12* (1), 106-129.

Neumayer, E. (2005). Bogus refugees?: The determinants of asylum migration to Western Europe. *International Studies Quarterly, 49* (4), 389-409.

Penrose, J. (2002). *Poverty and asylum in the UK.* London: Oxfam/Refugee Council.

Refugee Council. (2003). *Unsafe havens, unworkable solutions: Refugee Council position paper on the UK proposals for transit processing centres for refugees and regional management of asylums.* London: Author.

Ringold, S., Burke, A., & Glass, R. M. (2005). Refugee mental health. *Journal of the American Medical Association, 294* (5), 646.

Ritzer, G., & Lisca A. (2000). Postmodernism and tourism. In J. Beynon & D. Dunkerley (Eds.), *Globalisation: The reader* (pp. 152-155). London: Athlone Press.

Rodney, W. (1988). *How Europe underdeveloped Africa.* (Rev. ed.). London: Bogle-L'Ouverture Publications. (Originally published 1972).

Salt, J., & Clarke, J, (2000). International migration in the UNECE region: Patterns, trends, policies. *International Social Science Journal, 52* (165), 313-328.

Seven held in cockle inquiry. (2004, February 10). *BBC News*. Retrieved January 4, 2007, from: http://news.bbc.co.uk/1/hi/england/lancashire/3471 449.stm.

Simbulan, N. P. (1999). *The people's health in the era of globalization*. Paper presented during a forum conducted by the Medical Action Group on 6 December 1999 in celebration of Human Rights Week. Retrieved December 21, 2006, from: http://www.philsol.nl/A00a/MAG-Simbulan-dec99.htm.

Skelton, R. (1994). East Asian immigration and the changing world order. In W. T. S. Gould & A. M. Findlay (Eds.), *Population migration and the changing world order* (pp. 173-193). Chichester: John Wiley.

UK Statutes. (1999). *Immigration and Asylum Act: Elizabeth II, 1999, Chapter 33*. London: Stationery Office.

UK Statutes. (2002). *Nationality, Immigration and Asylum Act: Elizabeth II, 2002, Chapter 41*. London: Stationery Office.

UNAIDS, & International Organisation for Migration. (1998). Migration and AIDS. *International Migration, 36* (4), 445-468.

UNDP. (2005). *Human development report 2005: International cooperation at a crossroads: Aid, trade and security in an unequal world.* New York: United Nations.

UNHCR. (2005). *Asylum levels and trends in industrialized countries, 2004: Overview of asylum applications lodged in Europe and non-European industrialized countries in 2004.* Geneva: Author.

United Nations (1948). *Universal declaration of human rights.* New York: Author. Retrieved January 23, 2007, from: http://www.un.org/Overview/rights.html.

United Nations (1951). *Convention relating to the status of refugees.* Geneva: Office of the United Nations High Commissioner for Human Rights. Retrieved January 8, 2007, from:
http://www.ohchr.org/english/law/refugees.htm.

United Nations (2000a). *Convention against transnational organized crime and the protocols thereto.* New York: United Nations. Retrieved January 8, 2007, from: http://www.uncjin.org/Documents/Conventions/dcat oc/final_documents_2/convention_eng.pdf.

United Nations. (2000b). *Protocol to prevent, suppress and punish trafficking in persons, especially women and children: supplementing the United Nations Convention against transnational organized crime.* New York: United Nations. Retrieved January 8, 2007, from: http://www.uncjin.org/Documents/Conventions/dcat oc/final_documents_2/convention_%20traff_eng.pdf.

Wells, M. (2006, March 27). Immigration dominates southern US politics. *BBC News.* Retrieved 4 January, 2007, from: http://news.bbc.co.uk/1/hi/world/americas/4848588.stm.

World Bank. (2000). *World development report, 2000/2001: Attacking poverty.* New York: Oxford University Press.

World Health Organization. (2003). *International migration, health & human rights.* Geneva: Author.

INTERDEPENDENCIES AND DEVELOPMENT: THE AFRICAN DIASPORA AND ITS CONTESTED OBLIGATIONS TO HOME

Giles Mohan

Introduction: Globalisation from below?

There is a proverb in Ghana, which goes, "Whenever the trap is loosened, it will go back". The implication is that those who have migrated, whether within Ghana or abroad, will eventually come back. There is clearly a strong moral and social obligation amongst migrants to connect with and support "home". This chapter seeks to analyse the politics and geographies of these obligations and their implications for development, broadly defined. We can call this globalisation from below (Portes, 1997; Smith, 2001) to distinguish it from the more commonplace discussions of globalisation relating to big business and the cultural changes wrought by international capitalism.

But why is this globalisation from below worth studying from a developmental perspective? Is it socially, economically and political significant or simply the whim of a curious academic? There are at least two reasons why it is important to study this issue. Firstly, these connections between migrants and their homes is significant in terms of financial flows, political support and social welfare; everything that makes up "development". To take just the first of these: financial support. The data are poor, since much is transferred inter-personally, illegally, and maybe in the form of gifts. That said, figures suggest that, throughout the 1990s, remittances to developing countries were between $70 and $75 billion, which represents 50% more than Official Development Assistance (Suárez-Orozco, 2003; Koser,

2003). In absolute terms, remittances from Ghanaians outstripped Foreign Direct Investment for every year of the 1990s. Recently, President Kufuor of Ghana stated that, "Last year, the Bank of Ghana identified $1.3 billion as remittances from Ghanaians overseas into the banking system in Ghana. Two years ago, the total of such remittances was $400 million" ("Kufuor expresses gratitude", 2003).

Secondly, much of this diasporic development activity is "hidden", often by choice, so that the wider public, the policy-makers and academics do not know a lot about it. Much diaspora activity has remained hidden or invisible, with development focusing on the Northern Non-Governmental Organizations [NGOs] and donors. There are growing concerns within critical development studies about the ways in which the "development machine" generates stories about who or what are the agents of change. In public debates, Northern NGOs are seen as the key "humanitarian" agencies, albeit facing a growing legitimacy crisis, while the International Monetary Fund [IMF] and World Bank are either championed or pilloried as the agents of neo-liberal policy; and often the general public is treated to one-dimensional media stories that treat migrants as a drain on "our" economy. Such invisibility of African diasporas is also the product of academic divisions of labour. Within development studies and African studies, we see a focus on development "over there", with Africa treated as relatively self-contained. On the other hand, issues of racism and immigration "over here" tend to be the realm of sociology and social policy. In neither case are the actions of Africans outside of the continent, but linked to home, made visible, despite their significance. What this suggests from an ethical point of view is that we are all implicated in this, since migrants live here and we are directly or indirectly affected by their presence.

I begin by examining how diasporas are defined and how this forces us to think about development and territory in new ways. This leads to a consideration of debates about cosmopolitanism and the complex dynamics of diaspora as a form of transnational community, which sets the parameters for the range of obligations we find within them. These obligations centre on forms of citizenship, incorporating a variety of norms and values, which are (re)negotiated as circumstances change and may be backed by sanctions. Having established these general forms of obligation, I turn to the case study of Ghanaians in the UK and home-town associations in Ghana. Evidence suggests that diasporic support is important in development "back home", but that, not surprisingly, the understanding of these obligations and their impacts is neither static nor conflict free. One of the key findings was how the internationalised Ghanaian state seeks to capture the energies and resources of migrants for national development. I conclude by drawing out the implications of studying diasporas for political and development geography more generally.

Defining the African diaspora

The term diaspora is contested and dynamic and its usage varies between groups and over time, depending upon the ideological needs of these groups. One of the key problems is that the "paradigmatic" diasporic experience, namely that of the Jewish exile from Babylon, has come to dominate the discussion (Akyeampong, 2000). Additionally, for the sake of our discussion and with certain parallels, the African diaspora has been seen largely in terms of the horrific experiences of Atlantic slavery. These "victim" diasporas (Cohen, 1997) were clearly terrible events and their effects are still felt today. However, not all diasporic experiences are as traumatic, so we need to be simultaneously more flexible and precise in our theorisation.

Robin Cohen (1997) has developed a classification of diasporas (see Figure 1) which moves beyond the rather narrow use of diaspora as being essentially a victim experience. However, as with any classificatory typology, discrete categories can never really capture the complex realities of lived experience. Cohen's classification avoids the limitations of narrower definitions of diaspora in three basic ways.

Figure 1. **Common features of a diaspora**

---

1. Dispersal from an original homeland, often traumatically, to two or more foreign regions;
2. alternatively, the expansion from a homeland in search of work, in pursuit of trade or to further colonial ambitions;
3. a collective memory and myth about the homeland, including its location, history and achievements;
4. an idealization of the putative ancestral home and a collective commitment to its maintenance, restoration, safety and prosperity, even to its creation;
5. the development of a return movement that gains collective approbation;
6. a strong ethnic group consciousness sustained over a long time and based on a sense of distinctiveness, a common history and the belief in a common fate;
7. a troubled relationship with host societies, suggesting a lack of acceptance at the least or the possibility that another calamity might befall the group;

Interdependencies and Development

8. a sense of empathy and solidarity with co-ethnic members in other countries of settlement; and

9. the possibility of a distinctive creative, enriching life in host countries with a tolerance for pluralism.

Source: Cohen, 1997, p.26

Firstly, Cohen has added that not all diasporas are involuntary, which affects their composition, outlook and developmental potential. He observes that, "Being dragged off ... , being expelled, or being coerced to leave by force of arms appear qualitatively different phenomena from the general pressures of overpopulation, land hunger, poverty or an unsympathetic political regime" (Cohen, 1997, p. 27). So, people move and diasporas develop for more positive reasons than forced expulsion. Having said that, we must analyse all experiences contextually and empirically, so that we do not abstract these concepts " ... away from the situated practices of everyday life" (Mitchell, 1997, p. 535). For some, diaspora may be liberating, while for others their displacement is an ever-present trauma.

Secondly, Cohen includes characteristics that see both the imagining of home and its physical well-being and rejuvenation as crucial to defining diasporas. This develops Safran's (1991) argument that a diaspora exists once a people " ... regard their ancestral homeland as their true, ideal home and as the place to which they or their descendants would (or should) eventually return" (Safran, 1991, pp. 83-84). Hence, those with strong affinities with a homeland are more likely to support, either financially or politically, development efforts that seek to recreate or strengthen it.

Thirdly, in terms of the geographies of diaspora, Cohen helps us see how diffuse connections around the globe can be a developmental benefit for some diasporic communities. This means that, rather than viewing diasporas as comprising two points – either home, or exile from which the exiles simply want to return home - we need to think about multiple sites of exile and, crucially, the connections between them. As diasporas evolve over time, the members (or their subsequent generations) may move again, yet retain links to their home, to their original site of exile and to those places where other diasporic members have also relocated. This produces instead a geography of diaspora which is built around multiple localities connected by ever-changing networked relationships (MacGaffey & Bazenguissa-Ganga, 2000).

These observations suggest that different diasporic configurations operate in different ways and with different implications for development. Elsewhere, I proposed a three-fold classification (Mohan, 2002) for examining the positive linkages between diaspora and development. Firstly, *development in the diaspora*, when people within diasporic communities use their localised diasporic connections within the "host" country to secure economic and social well-being and, as a by-product, contribute to the development of their locality. Secondly, *development through the diaspora*, whereby diasporic communities utilise their diffuse global connections beyond the locality to facilitate economic and social well-being. Thirdly, *development by the diaspora*, in which diasporic flows and connections back "home" facilitate the development – and sometimes creation - of these "homelands". These categories, and the relationships between them, are fluid and blurred, reflecting the inherent tensions between de-territorialisation and fixity that characterise diasporas; for example, a Congolese trader in Paris, living with diasporic contacts, selling T-shirts sourced from a family member in Hong Kong and sending part of the profits back to his/her extended family, straddles all three categories.

Obligations and development

While this three-fold framework for linking diaspora and development can describe the types of connections and their geography, it does not really tell us what motivates people, beyond a rather mechanistic view that people from a place will automatically support that place. That is, we get no sense of human agency in these rather broad-brush classificatory frameworks. In this section, I look at how these long-distance obligations, which underpin developmental flows, are established. After that, we can examine the effects of these flows on development at home through a case study of Ghana.

Much of the work on obligations has focused on legalistic debates about obeyance of the law. These have tended to be state-centred and ignored the range of other, and usually multiple and overlapping, political communities to which people belong (Parekh, 1996). For Parekh, political community is " ... a territorially constituted human collectivity united in terms of its subscription to a system of rules and procedures concerning who is authorised to speak in its name and to take and enforce collectively binding decisions" (1996, p. 263). While the emphasis on social norms within a collective usefully defines legitimacy and action, political community need not be territorialised in this conventional sense.

More importantly, Parekh defines obligation as " ... social actions that the moral agent ought to undertake and his failure to do which reflects badly on him and renders him liable to social disapproval" (1996, p. 264). In this sense, they are inherently social and only gain meaning in the context of specific political communities. Moreover, unlike legalistic debates, obligations may not require sanctions and, even where they do, the existence of sanctions presupposes the existence of autonomous obligations.

Obligations, according to Parekh, are acquired in various ways. Firstly, they are acquired by engaging in specific practices, such as making a promise or entering a contractual arrangement. Such practices tend to make obligations relatively concrete and unambiguous. Secondly, obligations may be acquired by voluntary or involuntary membership of an organisation, group or community. These organisational obligations are more general, not easily catalogued, open to personal interpretation and subject to well-defined sanctions. Thirdly, obligations may be acquired by virtue of being human and are considered to be inherent in our humanity. Such obligations are necessarily vague, shaped by morality and easily overlooked.

Some cosmopolitan theories are useful in suggesting that different understandings and practices of citizenship exist beyond the confines of the nation-state. However, in rejecting the bounded territory of the state as the pre-eminent political community, they replace it with a non-geography of universalism; what MacIntyre terms "citizens of nowhere" (1988; cited in Erskine, 2002, p. 461). Although posited against defensive nationalism, this "impartialist" cosmopolitanism (Erskine, 2002) is problematic, because it can abdicate responsibility for specific care behind a discourse of abstract and universal love. As Parekh (2003, p. 12) argues:

> Cosmopolitanism ignores special ties and attachments to one's community, is too abstract to generate the emotional and moral

energy needed to live up to its austere imperatives, and can also easily become an excuse for ignoring the well-being of the community one knows and can directly influence in the name of an unrealistic pursuit of the abstract level of universal well-being.

O'Neill (1996) questions the legitimacy of political boundaries, but rather than following the impartialist cosmopolitan line of arguing for the irrelevance of boundaries, she calls for " ... a less exaggerated view both of boundaries and of (national) identities, which acknowledges that both can be permeable and variable" (1996, p. 301). This means that there may be a decoupling of membership of political community from territory, as well as the likelihood of belonging to a number of such communities. Erskine (2000, p. 575) calls this "embedded cosmopolitanism", which:

...offers an alternative to a strictly state-centric or spatially bounded interpretation of the morally constitutive community by combining an account of the moral agent as embedded in particular ties and loyalties with a powerful critique of the communitarian penchant for invoking associations with borders, set territories and given memberships.

These communities generously acknowledge the existence of other communities, are not territorialised in the "normal" way, yet are bound (however partially and temporarily) by a shared morality. It is within these political spaces that a variety of obligations exist. As Vertovec & Cohen (2002, p. 12) note:

Implications of Globalisation

> ... diasporic identifications and the rise of identity politics, have multiplied people's interests and affiliations.... A cosmopolitan politics, in this understanding, emphasizes that people have – and are encouraged to have – multiple affiliations. Political institutions catering to this would include civil and voluntary associations, networks and coalitions providing the expression of various interests and voices.

There is no co-ordinating mechanism to this process and, as Yeoh, Willis, & Fakhri (2003, pp. 212, 213) note, "Transnational identities, while fluid and flexible, are also at the same time grounded in particular places at particular times ... identities are constantly (re)worked, not in a freewheeling manner but through simultaneous embeddedness in more than one society". Given these proliferating and overlapping identities, it is crucial to conceptualise transnational migration as a long, multi-stepped, and often inter-generational social process. Migrants do not start with fixed ethnic identities. Rather, at each stage of the process of transnational migration, different elements or layers of the migrant's identity may become salient. Within these identities are embedded webs of affiliations, rights and obligations which are renegotiated to give meaning to each new environment.

It is within these political communities that a variety of obligations exist. In terms of obligations, I want to examine the specific moral community of diaspora, to flesh out the generic forms of obligation identified by Parekh (1996). Firstly, there has been a great deal of work on households and remittances. These theories situate the migrant within the decision-making unit of the household (Haan & Rogaly, 2002). From this, migration becomes a means of spreading risk, increasing income and investing in human capital. By this reasoning, the migrant is then strongly obliged to send money back, with a great pressure on them to "succeed".

Secondly, there are studies that utilise social capital and reciprocity. The lesson from these is that obligations are found in "... reputations, sanctions and moral norms" (Lyon, 2000, p. 665). This brings the focus on to questions of respect, gendered roles and relations, and civic pride, as well as the effect of sanctions, either actual or threatened, which bolster the obligations.

Thirdly, there has been some work on the role of kinship in transnational trade networks. These networks may be based around certain cultural affinities, but these are by no means static and are differentially exploited, depending on market and political opportunities; what Ong (1993) refers to as "flexible citizenship". These studies demonstrate how socialisation into family norms enables and constrains both men and women.

The fourth source of obligation relates to the "bonds" produced by racial oppression. Movements such as Garveyism have generally emerged from the diaspora and sought to link Black people on the basis of skin colour and racialised exploitation. Their contemporary relevance is that a common sense and/or experience of exploitation is an axis of solidarity and support.

Our framework starts with an understanding of obligation as a form of instrumental rationality, although it is impossible to separate out these motivations from more embedded cultural and political practices. These practices are not "traditions" in the sense of static and essential behaviours, but part of "civic virtue", defined as an idealised form of citizenship, consisting of a moral framework of rights and obligations and conceptions of justice and equality (Lonsdale, 1992). Crucially, understandings of what constitutes a "good" citizen are largely determined by the elites and are also continually contested and negotiated.

"When it spoils the town, it spoils us": Migration, obligation and development in the UK and Ghana

This section is based on findings from a project on Ghanaian diasporic communities. It needs stating at the outset that these networks are largely elite-based, reflecting both the higher level of involvement by elites in organisations and methodological problems concerning snowballing. Our methodology sought to let the members of the Ghanaian diaspora identify and "map" their diasporic networks. We traced connections from familiar sites in the UK back to organisations and individuals in Ghana. In the UK, we focused on Ghanaians in Milton Keynes, a new city in the South, and contrasted them with those in London; the reason for this being that, for many, movement to Milton Keynes, mainly from London, was relatively recent and we wanted to see whether this re-location, and the embourgeoisement that it potentially signalled, affected their relationship with the Ghanaian diaspora(s) and support of home. The Ghana fieldwork was largely with Kwahu organisations from rural Southern Ghana, as well as their Accra-based organisations. As far as possible, we tried to elicit how the people defined development by asking a series of open-ended questions about what "support" was provided to those at home, either individually or collectively.

Family, community and respect

The axes around which morality and obligation are constructed are kinship and community. In both cases, respect (Sennett, 2003) captures a constellation of emotions that define what it means to be a "good" citizen. Gaining respect within the kin group and community is not fixed, but key elements include securing the well-being of the extended family and contributing to the welfare of the community (Geest, 1998).

However, the key is visibility, insofar as private acts do not register with the wider social group.

> We all assist in the development project for fame. For instance, the person who built the school structure for us has named it after his own mother and he [the benefactor] is happy that his mother has such dignity in the town. (Chairman of Pepeaseman Nkoso Kuo)

The idea of respect and visibility is reflected in both housing and funerals.

Hence, while accumulating money is valued, the collective does not know how much one has, whereas a house is a public statement of success, whose value can be more easily acknowledged. Geest (1998) discusses house building in the Kwahu home-town as simultaneously providing shelter for matrilineal kin, demonstrating one's success and status, providing an asset, ensuring welfare support in old age, and acting as a reminder of your life after death.

For the Ghanaians in Milton Keynes, the main obligation was to support family (Arhinful, 2001) and, to a lesser extent, friends at home.

> Most of us have got it in mind that, one day, we'll be going home, and therefore we're building houses. We are sending money for the house to be built for us. We live in an extended family. The family doesn't stop at your wife and your children. It goes beyond that and

therefore most of us, like in my family, if they are able, will live in a big house. ("Grace", Milton Keynes)

It's [in] our culture that we have a saying: "Your parents look after you to grow your teeth, you look after them to lose their's". So it's our culture and you cannot do anything about it, it's like, it's a must, you have to do it. ("Elizabeth", Milton Keynes)

This hints at a contested obligation for them to allow members of the extended family to reside in these homes.

The home-town, its organisations and their activities

In terms of formal organisations, both the UK and Ghanaian organisations were largely elite-driven, which supports findings elsewhere (McNulty & Lawrence, 1996; Trager, 2001). In the Ghanaian towns, there is a rich associational life and in Accra most towns had a home-town association, although these varied in size and level of activity. The Accra organisations were pivotal in transnational activities, acting as a conduit both in and out. Given that the Accra-based leaders were generally professionals, they were well connected both socially and physically, so that requests and information flows to the diaspora generally passed through them. However, in all cases it was church-based connections that were the main channels for information and resources.

The growing importance of religion in African life is, contrary to Chabal & Daloz (1999), not a form of re-traditionalisation, involving a return to the "irrational", but relates to the relationship of societies with globalisation and modernity. For example, a study of Congolese traders in Paris found that one informant, Beatrice, utilises her religious contacts around the world to facilitate her business; that is, "To deal with the problems of doing business and finding her way in strange countries, cities, languages and cultures, she takes advantage in her membership of the Association for the Reunification in the Christian World" (MacGaffey & Bazenguissa-Ganga, 2000, p. 101). What is interesting is that many of these churches are internationally networked and link the diaspora both spiritually and materially. The rise of Pentecostalism in Ghana is emblematic of this. As Akyeampong (2000, p. 208) writes, "The Pentecostal experience has become crucial to the Ghanaian encounter with globalization and modernity .... The Pentecostal agenda is a modern one that celebrates the trans-national and the trans-cultural embodied in international mobility and the expression of emotion". Such networks permit the exchange of ideas, commodities and people.

In most cases, once a project had been agreed upon, then funding was sought. This usually involved an appeal to the local government, levies on local residents, and levies on Accra residents. Levies were collected at funerals, so there was a high degree of visibility and a strong social pressure, since failure to pay would result in any funeral in that family being held up until payment was received. This threat of stigmatisation provides a powerful onus to pay.

Most of the activities of the home-town association involve public goods and tend to fill the gap either never filled by the state or vacated by it following neo-liberal adjustment. The vast majority are infrastructure-related, including road building, hospital upgrading, construction of school buildings, sinking of boreholes, and market construction. In very few cases were there projects that sort to raise productivity, something which Latin American home-town associations seem more willing to engage in.

Other public activities were more cosmetic, focusing on beautification of the town. However, an important set of functions were welfare-oriented and covered such things as funeral expenses and loans during exceptional times of hardship.

From the UK end, we found a relatively limited number of development activities in Ghana facilitated by Ghanaians. The leadership of one organisation used its contacts with the local hospital to get access to unwanted medical equipment, which they shipped to Ghana. The association has also partnered church-based groups to send old clothes and school books to Ghana. What seemed more important was what could be termed "cultural capital", rather than "social capital" for advancement.

Renegotiating ethnicity, loosening the ties

For those who have gone abroad, each step can potentially weaken attachments to a single home. One migrant remarked, "Why have a home-town association when all you know is your family house and little more. We don't have an identifiable community, because we did not grow up there" ("Kwesi", Milton Keynes).

Indeed, the act of relocating to Milton Keynes from London involved renegotiating and loosening their relationships with the Ghanaian communities in the UK. They emphasised their desire to avoid pressure to participate in ethnic and clan-based associational and cultural life and to be not identified through their family or clan. One respondent said that his motivation for leaving London was to "... get away from the Ghana crowd" ("Kwame", Milton Keynes). Owing to their relatively small numbers and the recent influx, they tended to characterise the Milton Keynes Ghanaian community as nationally-based, in contrast to the London Ghanaian communities which they characterised as ethnically-based.

> So far as you are a Ghanaian, you know, it doesn't matter whether you come from the North or you are a Ga or Ashanti or .... You know .... No, it's not, no, there is no segregation in it. Every Ghanaian can join, which is good .... Yeah, the clans, yes, yes. The London one, yes, is always, like, the Ga Association, the Ewe Association. But no, in Milton Keynes, it doesn't matter whether you are Ashanti, Akan, we are all one. Which I love it that way. ("Grace", Milton Keynes)

So, the move saw a weakening of ethnic identity, although it is unclear whether their attachment to nation-state translates into concrete action, such as seeking to vote or fund national development.

Excessive obligations and renegotiating the family

The obligations to kin and home-town among migrants elicited mixed responses. While most were building houses in Ghana for family and/or to retire to, some also complained about the burden of obligations.

> How can you request this sort of money when you are leading this sort of life, you know. So we said, "Oh no, you are taking us for granted, you think that the money is just lying in the street". So we said, "No". ("Elizabeth", Milton Keynes)

> Did you ask me where am I going to get it from? Am I OK? Have I eaten? Have I clothed myself? But you just phone me, "Hi how are you, are you all right? Oh, it's only I need about £100". You didn't

even ask me, "Do you have it?" They think England is pot of gold.
You've been there, everything is easy, as soon as you walk in money
is everywhere. ("Mary", Milton Keynes)

What this meant was that the boundaries of the family
were being negotiated and redrawn, moving away from a
matrilineal extended family to a more nuclear one. Some
use this as an excuse to evade selectively their obligations,
and at the same time "educate" their poorer rural kin about
the changed definition of family.

Formal political processes: The state and civil society

Studies of the linkages between diasporic politics and the
state tend to focus on "long distance nationalism" and
support for the (re)construction of a homeland
(Østergaard-Nielsen, 2001). But this captures only some of
the linkages between diasporic politics and the
development of homes (Østergaard-Nielsen). Most
countries receiving migrant funds are waking up to this
potentially huge source of finance. West African states
seem only recently to have considered this potential, but
Ghana has instituted dual citizenship. Goldberg (1998)
terms these "extra-territorialised states", as they pursue
nation-building projects beyond the national borders.

In the past, many Ghanaian diaspora associations were
closely linked to opposition forces, as they were formed by
the various waves of migrants who left because of political
persecution or the linked economic uncertainty. Currently
in the Ghanaian diaspora, the state under the New
Patriotic Party (NPP) seems to have made a conscious
effort to strengthen and institutionalise its relationships
with diaspora communities and particularly with
associations. Indeed, it is widely rumoured that the latest

election victories were bankrolled by migrant Ghanaians. In his inaugural address of January 2001, President Kufuor stated:

> I must acknowledge the contributions made by our compatriots who live outside the country. Currently you contribute a third of the capital flow into the country. Many of you do more than send money home, many of you have kept up keen interest in the affairs at home and some of you have even been part of the struggle of the past twenty years. I salute your efforts and your hard work and I extend a warm invitation to you to come home and let us rebuild the country. Those of our compatriots who have made homes beyond our shores, I make a special plea for your help; we need your newly acquired skills and contacts, we need your perspective and we need your capital.

Officials at the High Commission forge links between itself and Ghanaian associations. The associations, such as the Ghana Union, disseminate information from the High Commission to the Ghanaian communities, via its affiliates. This approach may reflect both a political strategy on the part of the NPP, as it has established chapters in many localities in the UK, including Milton Keynes. The government recently implemented dual citizenship and a Non-Resident Ghanaians Secretariat, which are also clearly part of a strategy to harness the resources of the diaspora and help prevent a legitimacy crisis.

Conclusions

This paper has examined the question of obligations within

diasporic communities and sought to examine the implications of this for a broad understanding of "development". I argued that obligations were specific to a given socio-political community and were part of defining its civic virtue in terms of what a "good" member of that community should do. However, the identities of any political community, but particularly diasporic ones, are highly fluid, with multiple, overlapping and dynamic affiliations and obligations.

The role of migrants was significant for development in Ghana in terms of both household survival and public action, as well as for the longer-term "social security" of migrants. In these ways, these actions link quite clearly to understandings of "development". Less tangible was the importance of belonging and a "sense of place", however distant and mythical. While the idea of "embedded cosmopolitanism" captures the fluidity of these ties, the evidence shows that these are largely elite networks, possessing different degrees of obligation. So, while they are a part of a "community of communities", they are also riven internally with divisions, which undermine claims regarding citizenship for all. As Smith (1998, p. 226) observes, "... transnational communities create public spheres in which differences in status and class, especially upward mobility or educational success of children, can be displayed, and in which they have special meaning".

A further point is that many of the Ghanaian home-town associations view development in limited ways and fail to link underdevelopment to structural inequalities at a global scale. As a form of citizenship, the elite associational life we examined does not challenge power structures, and thereby depoliticizes development. In this sense, the associations are not "cosmopolitan" in the sense of pluralistic global governance and can, in Mamdani's

(1996) terms, cement customary forms of rule, as opposed to creating more liberal forms of citizenship.

So, this work suggests new avenues for understanding emergent geographies of citizenship. As I argued at the start of this paper, much analysis ties political community to some form of fixed and bounded territory or it argues that the fluidity of flows and networks enables subversion and resistance. The very dynamism of the latter is seen to be its strength, as de-territorialised flows create new forms of political space, but at the same time are continually recrafted to remain subversive, using the space of marginality to good effect. Much of this reflects a tendency amongst some intellectuals to project on to a set of social relations a political "anti-globalisation" agenda that they wish to see enacted. What the diasporic communities show is that flows can become sedimented and fixed. Diasporic networks can become institutionalised, while their embeddedness in a "home" suggests that the goal of such flows may be the securing/supporting of territories. Their very lack of territory is enabled because at root they have an attachment to place, however "imagined" it may be.

References

Akyeampong, E. (2000). Africans in the diaspora: The diaspora and Africa. *African Affairs, 99,* 183-215.

Arhinful, D. K. (2001). *We think of them: How Ghanaian migrants in Amsterdam assist relatives at home.* Leiden: African Studies Centre.

Chabal, P., & Daloz, J.-P. (1999). *Africa works: Disorder as a political instrument.* Oxford: James Currey.

Cohen, R. (1997). *Global diasporas: An introduction.* London: UCL Press.

Erskine, T. (2000). Embedded cosmopolitanism and the case of war: restraint, discrimination and overlapping communities. *Global Society, 14,* (4), 569-590.

Erskine, T. (2002). "Citizens of nowhere", or "The point where circles intersect?": Impartialist and embedded cosmopolitanisms. *Review of International Studies, 28,* 457-478.

Geest, S. van der (1997). Money and respect: The changing value of old age in rural Ghana. *Africa, 67,* (4), 534-559.

Geest, S. van der (1998). Yebisa Wo Fie: Growing old and building a house in the Akan culture of Ghana. *Journal of Cross-Cultural Gerontology, 13,* 333-359.

Goldberg, L. (1998). The power of status in transnational social fields. In M. P. Smith & L. E. Guarnizo (Eds.), *Transnationalism from below* (pp. 165-195). New Brunswick, NJ: Transaction Publishers.

Haan, A. de, & Rogaly, B. (2002). Introduction: Migrant workers and their role in rural change. *Journal of Development Studies, 38,* (5), 1-14.

Koser, K. (2003). New African diasporas: An introduction. In K. Koser (Ed.), *New African diasporas* (pp. 1-16) London: Routledge.

Kufuor, J. A. (2001, January 7). Inaugural speech delivered by H. E. John A. Kufuor on the 7th January, 2001. Retrieved April 13, 2007, from: http://www.ghanaweb.com/GhanaHomePage/republi c/prez-inug-adr.php.

Kufuor expresses gratitude to Ghanaians abroad and asks for more. (2003, February 25). *Accra Mail.*

Lonsdale, J. (1992). The moral economy of Mau Mau: Wealth, poverty & civic virtue in Kikiuyu political thought. In B. Berman & J. Lonsdale, *Unhappy valley: Conflict in Kenya and Africa. Book 2 – Violence and ethnicity* (pp. 315-468). London: James Currey.

Lyon, F. (2000). Trust, networks and norms: The creation of social capital in agricultural economies of Ghana. *World Development, 28,* (4), 663-681.

MacGaffey, J., & Bazenguissa-Ganga, R. (2000) *Congo-Paris: Transnational traders on the margins of the law.* London: International African Institute, in association with James Currey.

Mamdani, M. (1996). *Citizen and subject: Contemporary Africa and the legacy of late colonialism.* London: James Currey.

McNulty, M., & Lawrence, M. (1996). Hometown associations: Balancing local and extralocal interests in Nigerian communities. In P. Blunt & D. M. Warren (Eds.), *Indigenous organizations and development* (pp. 21-41). London: International Technology Publications.

Mitchell, K. (1997). Different diasporas and the hype of hybridity. *Environment and Planning D: Society and Space, 15,* 533-553.

Mohan, G. (2002). Diaspora and development: The Black Atlantic and African transformation. In J. Robinson (Ed.), *Development and displacement* (pp. 77-139). Milton Keynes: Open University, in association with Oxford University Press.

O'Neill, O. (1996). Transnational justice: Permeable boundaries and multiple identities. In P. King (Ed.), *Socialism and the common good: New Fabian essays* (pp. 291-301). London: Frank Cass.

Ong, A. (1993). On the edge of empires: Flexible citizenship among Chinese in diaspora. *Positions, 1,* (3), 745-778.

Interdependencies and Development

Østergaard-Nielsen, E. K. (2001). *The politics of migrants' transnational political practices*. Oxford: University of Oxford, Transnational Communities Project.

Parekh, B. (1996). Citizenship and political obligation. In P. King (Ed.), *Socialism and the common good: New Fabian essays* (pp. 259-289). London: Frank Cass.

Parekh, B. (2003). Cosmopolitanism and global citizenship. *Review of International Studies, 29*, 3-17.

Portes, A. (1997). *Globalization from below: The rise of transnational communities* [Electronic version]. Oxford: University of Oxford, Transnational Communities [Project]. Retrieved November 26, 2005, from www.transcomm.ox.ac.uk/working_papers.htm.

Safran, W. (1991). Diasporas in modern societies: Myths of homeland and return. *Diaspora, 1*, 83-99.

Sennett, R. (2003). *Respect: The formation of character in the age of security*. London: Allen Lane.

Smith, M. P. (2001). *Transnational urbanism: Locating globalization*. Oxford: Blackwell.

Smith, R. (1998). Transnational localities: Community, technology and the politics of membership within the context of Mexico and US migration. In M. P. Smith & L.

E. Guarnizo (Eds.), *Transnationalism from below* (pp. 196-238). New Brunswick, NJ: Transaction Publishers.

Suárez-Orozco, M. (2003.) *Hometown associations and their present and future partnerships: New development opportunities?* Washington, DC: Inter-American Dialogue.

Trager, L. (2001). *Yoruba hometowns: Community, identity, and development in Nigeria.* Boulder, CO: Lynne Rienner.

Vertovec, S. (1999). Conceiving and researching transnationalism. *Ethnic and Racial Studies, 22,* (2), 447-462.

Vertovec, S., & Cohen, R. (Eds.). (2002). *Conceiving cosmopolitanism: Theory, context and practice.* Oxford: Oxford University Press.

Yeoh, B., Willis, K., & Fakhri, S. (2003). Transnationalism and its edges. *Ethnic and Racial Studies, 26,* (2), 207-217.

THE SLOWLY SIMMERING FROG:
NOTES ON PRE-FASCISM AND GLOBALISATION

Mark Bendall

We don't seek Empires. We're not imperialists. We never have been. I can't imagine why you'd ever ask the question. (Rumsfeld, as cited in Empire Notes, *April 29, 2003; retrieved March 21, 2007, from: http://sopsy.com/rss/empireNotes)*

Since the atrocity of 2001, the British [and American] state, ... has remade itself to a remarkable degree. (Hennessy, 2007, April 27)

Globalisation does not mean the impotence of the state, but the rejection by the state of its social functions, in favour of repressive ones, and the [attempted erasure] of democratic freedoms. (Kagarlitsky, 2001)

Introduction

The business of Empire seemed alive and kicking. One could tell by the kicking. One could tell by the photographs of US soldiers, grinning, next to expired Iraqi prisoners of war in the Abu Ghraib morgue (Sontag, 2004). This chapter examines how and why the American hyper-power has attempted to manage globalisation as the fuel gauge flickers on empty. Using an interdisciplinary approach, it draws on communications studies, civil liberties aspects of criminology, and international relations; secondary sources are complemented by primary material from former intelligence officers. In short, the chapter uses the definition of fascism by Paxton (2004), some theories of Harvey (2003) about globalisation, and grounds this in evidence from documents, speeches and former agents to trace the contours of the state in the USA (and to a lesser extent the UK). How do those state contours interact with global forces? How and why do those state contours impact on their own civil societies and on other states?

Globalisation is examined through the lens of statecraft. Globalisation, amongst a plethora of possible definitions, is used here to indicate a process through which the existing world economic order is being renovated, so as to create optimal conditions for the free play of greed, class interest and profit-making (Petras & Veltmeyer, 2001). Empire can be defined, in essence, as the use of political and, ultimately, military power for economic domination.

The analysis will focus on strategic violence, such as the "War on Terror" and its representation. This "War" of uncertain end has been a natural product of the globalisation of capital, both in its substance – extending economic might abroad whilst being protectionist at home – and in its linguistic style and symbolic presentation. The "War" was framed as a product of the trauma of September 11th; this "hijacking" of the Twin Towers event initially, if not eventually, helped to justify liquidating those demonised by US adventurism. Repression, not only of these external enemies, but also of internal ones, has been a corollary of maintaining power. Laws have been reshaped, or flouted, to try to tighten the reins of civil society, as well as to restrain "undesirable aliens".

This article will assess whether US habits, in an era of globalisation, have become fascistic. The planning of key US advisors will be studied and the intellectual roots of any inchoate fascistic ideology will be traced to make this assessment. In order to proceed, a working definition of fascism as "ultranationalist populism" will be used. How do we establish more fully-fleshed criteria to justify the claim for fascism to have emerged? For Paxton (2004), fascism, as political pathology rather than single identifiable principle, contains "mobilising passions". On their own, they might seem harmless; in totality, they may become toxic. Some of these passions are of particular interest when studying early 21st century neoconservatism: the primacy of the group and the subordination of the individual; the belief that one's group is a victim, justifying action regardless of legality or morality against domestic and foreign enemies; dread of the group's fall from grace after being infected by alien influences; the need for a purer community, to be achieved by consent or, if necessary, violence; belief in a messianic leader and in gut instinct rather than abstract reason; a tendency to equate weakness with contemptability; an eliminationist rhetoric, in which enemies will be sought out "dead or alive", and some groups (such as immigrants) excluded. For full-blown fascism to occur, according to Paxton, there should be a revolutionary zeal from a mass movement, a one-party state, widespread physical intimidation of opponents and a systemic crisis that ushers in dictatorship. This chapter will therefore seek out evidence of these mobilising passions, and assess how mobile they have been.

Lastly, this chapter will show how US state protuberance has been as much symbolical as physical. It will adumbrate briefly how things done in the Empire's name are often framed in favourable terms, owing to the monopolistic consolidation of the mass media by profit maximising corporations.

In sum, do all these activities, spanning the militaristic, judicial and the symbolic, point to an intensified repression of part of humanity and an attempted compression of thought? Whilst vigorous counter-hegemonic resistance is acknowledged, the force of hegemony seemed distinctive in the first six years of the G. W. Bush Administration.

Therefore, it is upon this force and that high water-mark of neoconservativism that the chapter focuses.

The State

Discourse about globalisation sometimes can be about the sovereignty of multinational companies rather than nations. Global capital has taken the state prisoner, or so some thinking about globalisation insists. This paper, by contrast, underlines the persistence of the imperial state in navigating the choppy undercurrents of globalisation; it explores what the state can still *do*, rather than concentrating on what it cannot. John Pilger (2002, p. 5) argues that:

> The widely held belief among anti-globalisation campaigners that the state has "withered away" is misguided, along with the view that transnational corporate power has replaced the state and, by extension, imperialism ... the imperial state's enduring power is both as hidden hand and iron fist of rampant capital.

Pilger oversimplifies the debates; not everyone assumes the state is in retreat. It is, though, still right to emphasise the role of the repressive state in debates about globalisation. One has to be clear, temporally and spatially, about what one means by "the state", as the term is sometimes used sloppily, as in the quotation from Pilger, for there is palpably a huge difference between an African state heavily indebted to the International Monetary Fund [IMF] and, for example, a country like Sweden. The state may be defined here as the provider of order: law, procedure, safety and security, creating and where necessary regulating an ordered arena for markets to function. The state provides domestic public services and the repressive state apparatus, such as the military and the security services (Ignatieff, 2003, p. 124).

Whilst globalisation is obviously about more than one superpower, it is difficult to understand it without scrutinising its most muscular cheerleader: the USA. The muscle, in the form of the military-industrial complex, allows particular favoured Western corporations to penetrate global markets:

> The hidden hand of the market will never work without a hidden fist. McDonald's cannot flourish without McDonnell Douglas ... and the hidden fist that keeps the world safe for Silicon valley's technologies to flourish is called the US Army, Air Force, Navy, and Marine corps. (Friedman, as cited in Roy, 2004)

One may question quite how hidden that fist is, but the synergy of militarism and industry remains as pertinent and potent as it was when first flagged up by Eisenhower in his discussion of the military industrial complex at the end of his presidency.

Harvey (2003) tries to make complex links between US imperialism and global capital imperialism within a wider account of the empire of capital; this cannot just be laid at the door of the American regime (as writers such as Hardt & Negri [2000] point out). Harvey sees capitalist imperialism as a contradictory fusion of the politics of state and empire, and of the processes of capital accumulation in space and time. The postmodern empire of neo-liberal governance can appear too vague, he feels, if it appears to float above neat territorial boundaries. To counteract this, Harvey emphasises the tremendous resource transfer from the global South to the North, brought about by structural adjustment programmes sanctioned by the IMF. He points to the decimation of livelihoods and economies resulting from this rampant asset-stripping by financial capital. Economic violence has sown the seeds of anti-corporatism and especially anti-Americanism. His critique of this US-dominated international monetary system chimed with that of Roy (2004), who claimed that America uses its economic weaponry, as well as its military and ideological weaponry, to stave off the decline of hegemony where possible.

Harvey (2003) further notes the US administration's feverishly militarised efforts to squeeze the last drop of its own asymmetries of exchange. The idea of full spectrum dominance as having anything to do with revenge against al-Qaida (or Saddam Hussein) is discounted; nor, he asserts, is it anything to do with an *assumption* of imperial superiority. Instead, violent unilateralism is a response to US fragility. Here, Harvey's argument is in accordance with that of Todd (2003), who maintains, correctly, that America is already in irreversible relative decline. Its militarism is intimately connected with economic precariousness. The Empire can be injured if it is systematically challenged by states such as China, in which the accumulative logic of late capitalism is at its most ruthless, rendering America eventually a victim of global capital. With structures in place in Western Europe and elsewhere to maintain a new world order, an alternative to Pax Americana, the USA has to subdue contenders that could frustrate its exploitation of uneven fields of power (Harvey). However, Harvey does not deal thoroughly with the USA's inability to confront China, other than by establishing a militarised influence in key zones of raw materials that both of them will need in the long term.

There are important links between US domestic policy and its imperial foreign policy. Harvey (2003) points to the exacerbation of internal problems within the USA. Its power elite chose not to pass on the benefits of its global accumulation to its own impoverished communities; hence the "two Americas" that John Edwards, when running for the Vice-Presidency in 2004, played upon, to considerable popular support.

Harvey (2003) points alternatively to the culture of endemic corporate corruption – although this was an erroneous observation with regard to the Enron Case, as judicial intervention did then occur – and notes the lack of investment in vital infrastructural regeneration and the growth of "fictitious capital" in recent American history.[1] Crucially, the "War on Terror" functioned as a smokescreen to distract from the gravity of America's ungovernability, and from the outsourcing of US jobs from the rust-belt areas and elsewhere. At the same time, it is a pretext for the compulsory "democratisation" of the Middle East on Western terms.[2] This economic crusade had the intention of guaranteeing American influence (and, vitally, access to raw materials) for as long as possible (Harvey).

Context: The project of the old American century

To make sense of the US globalising mission that Harvey

---

[1] Certainly the lack of infrastructural support for the flood walls around New Orleans, in the wake of Hurricane Katrina in September 2005, confirms Harvey's point. Priority funding earmarked for the "levy" went towards payment for the "War on Terror" – a case of repression over social responsibility. Protecting the citizen is envisaged, not through health promotion, but more as a military crusade. The social dislocation that resulted when ethnic underclasses appeared to be temporarily abandoned by their own state were a classic example of the social retreat emphasised by Kagarlitsky (2001) – see the beginning of this chapter.

[2] The point that the Middle East is to be "democratised" is perhaps more problematic, in view of the USA's involvement in the security arrangements of, most obviously, Iraq.

(2003) articulated, one has to trace historical continuities with, and also the innovations of, the Bush regime. After World War Two, the USA became a global colossus in an uneven wrestle with the USSR. The thrust of American policy since then has been to maintain that dominance in the face of competitor nations and the logic of global capital.

The roots of this can be traced back at least to Kennan, the principal US Cold War strategist.

> We have about 50 percent of the world's wealth, but only 6.3 percent of its population ... we cannot fail to be the object of envy and resentment. Our real task in the coming period is to devise a pattern of relationships which will permit us to maintain this disparity without positive detriment to our national security. (Kennan, 1948).

Those who feel that the Bush administration has departed *in toto* from the historical trajectory of US policies forget Korea and the militarism of the Johnson and Nixon presidencies' attitude to Vietnam. The persecutions of the McCarthy era provide handy precedents for the early 21st century closing of the American mind in illiberal quarters.

The underlying structures of US global interventions, both militaristic and economic, have some shared continuities, regardless of the agents. For example, despite an apparent stark contrast of style and policy between Clinton and Bush, global inequality nonetheless intensified under Clinton, as he presided over the implementation of new GATS trade rules that consolidated the supremacy of some corporate rights over states. Hence, allegiance to capitalism, and willingness to use force to protect these allegiances, can be detected across Democrat and

Republican leaderships. Post-Cold War US administrations have pursued a grand strategy which, with undoubted modifications, would be recognised by leaders from Theodore ("carry a big stick") Roosevelt to the "House of Bush". Bacevich (2002, p. 3) clarified the planetary chess plan:

> ... to preserve and where both feasible and conducive to US interests, to expand an American imperium. Central to this strategy is a commitment to global openness – removing barriers that inhibit the movement of goods, capital, ideas, people. Its ultimate objective is the creation of an integrated international order based on the principles of democratic capitalism, with the United States as the ultimate guarantor of order and enforcer of norms.

New emperors and the neoconservative court

In contrast to Harvey's analysis (2003), what *has* distinguished the Bush regime is the adventurist arrogance with which the USA happily penetrated borders and incarcerated enemies. War was, as Trotsky suggested, always supposed to be the great accelerator. Neoconservatives sharpened America's globalising trajectory, being quite open in their policy of pre-emptive strikes to maintain hegemony. The caution induced by the shadow of the Soviet Union has given way and this new agenda has been articulated, quite brazenly, by key Bush advisers, such as Rice (2002, April 29):

> ... an earthquake of the magnitude of 9/11 can shift the tectonic plates of international politics. The international system has been in flux since the collapse of Soviet power. Now it is possible – indeed, probable – that that transition is coming to an end.

Implications of Globalisation

... if the collapse of the Soviet Union and 9/11 bookend a major shift in international politics, then this is a period not just of grave danger, but of enormous opportunity. Before the clay is dry again, America and our friends and our allies must move decisively to take advantage of these new opportunities.

Before China emerges as an irrepressible military rival, and not just an economic one, the USA has a chance to use its fading unipolarity to grab, and keep, the keys to the Empire's oil bank in the Persian Gulf and the Caspian Sea; which is especially important, as its own resources in the Gulf of Mexico are vulnerable to the global warming that, ironically, disproportionate US carbon emissions hasten. The USA, Harvey (2003) rightly emphasises, has been peculiarly dependent on external natural resources to sustain its global ambitions. This temporary dominance provided the window of opportunity to raid external resources. Initial popular domestic outrage after 9/11 provided Washington with a technique of mobilisation, so that such a raid on those resources was more politically acceptable.

The militarism of the House of Bush had its seeds in the policies of the first President Bush. In 1992, a Pentagon Defense Planning document was leaked. Its Kennan-like "first objective [was] ... to prevent any hostile power from dominating a region whose resources would, under consolidated control, be sufficient to generate global power"(US Department of Defense, 1992). This document was absorbed by neoconservatives from the then Defence Secretary Cheney to Wolfowitz (subsequently a major figure in the World Bank). The Defense Planning Guidance again affirmed that *proactive intervention* was needed to scare off contenders.

The Slowly Simmering Frog

An underlying continuity of key personnel in New Right administrations over the last thirty years has been discernible; as they have gained seniority, they have had some influence in radicalising geopolitical strategy. It is important to note these key actors. Whilst they have inherited structures from previous administrations, agents also, of course, themselves help to shape structures. Understanding the "War on Terror" requires analysis on this micro level, the level of agents and their ideologies, as well as the macro level.

The project for the New American Century, established in 1997 by Kristol, editor of the Murdoch-owned *Weekly Standard*, offered a neoconservative mouthpiece. Rather like fears about the missile gap with the Soviet Union in the Cold War, when the US elite exaggerated the notion that their country had a nuclear missile envy of the Soviet Union, the "War on Terror" was framed by orchestrated fear of US vulnerability to the arsenal of the "Axis of Evil" and assorted agents of terror. The solution presented was not just military build up, but its systemic deployment. This contrived fear of current and future weakness underlines Harvey's (2003) new imperialism thesis.

The neoconservative court and think tanks articulated a troubling methodology of global dominion. Some of these views glorify violence and fascistic methods, such as those of Mussolini. Neoconservative Michael Ledeen of the American Enterprise Institute called for a permanently bellicose policy for military, economic and cultural purposes:

> Creative destruction is our middle name, both within our own society and abroad. We tear down the old order everyday from business to science ... cinema, politics, law. Our enemies have always hated this whirlwind of energy and creativity, which

menaces their traditions (whatever they may be) and shames them
... we must destroy them to advance our historic mission. (Ledeen,
as cited in Hulet, 2003)

The American assumption of manifest destiny persists. Ledeen and other neoconservatives endorsed the Machiavellian doctrine that leaders have to "enter into evil", providing authoritarian leadership to harness mankind's essentially wayward desires: lying was "central to the survival of nations"; belief in God and a spectacular state were necessary to inspire soldiers to kill for the Empire (Ledeen, as cited in Hulet, 2003). This cannot be dismissed as ranting from the fringe; a number of these neoconservatives were members of power elites, or had access to them. Such geopolitics sought to justify the liquidation of "our enemies" (Ledeen, as cited in Hulet). This helps to explain G. W. Bush's presidential pronouncements about the "Axis of Evil" (a term that yokes together the symbols of the Nazi "Axis" with Reagan's Soviet "Evil Empire").

Claiming to be influenced by Professor Strauss of Chicago University, who endorsed Machiavellian ideas as necessary for 20th and 21st century socio-political realities, neoconservatives advocated permanent revolution, both intellectual and violent. All this corresponds to some of Paxton's (2004) "mobilising passions" of fascism, as listed on page 252 of this chapter, including the belief that, regardless of legality or morality, action against domestic and foreign "enemies" can be justified (Ledeen, as cited in Hulet, 2003)

Yet difficulties abound within this agenda. Admiration of (anti-Semitic) fascist revolutions is paralleled with ardent support for Israel. Worship of Jesus in God's own country is promoted, whilst enemies and non-combatants are cheerfully attacked with cluster bombs. Members of the administration were able to broker deals with the folk devil Saddam Hussein, then prosecute him for crimes against humanity committed with US-supplied weaponry. Ground supposedly liberated is irradiated with uranium-tipped, US-designed missiles. Despite some distancing from the neoconservatives in late 2006 by the White House, these paradoxical positions have not really been explored by all their holders; nor is the logic of the subsequent disavowal of them articulated convincingly.

These neoconservatives adopted selective readings of globalisation and global conflict that fitted their combative reading of history and of the New American Century. Huntington (1996), a *fin de siècle* Cassandra, famously saw the future as a series of clashes between the West and "the rest"; a notion that has become a clichéd conservative ideology. He rejected the realist model in which nation states are seen as primary players on the world scene, continuing to form alliances as they have always done and playing these out in conflicts. He rejected also a chaos model that can read no order in global patterns. Huntington claimed that the world is a forest of competing civilisations, rooted in immiscible cultures and religions, over which culture provides a canopy. Yet when cultures entwine, Huntington felt, the result is a struggle for life, as the ivy of one culture entangles and strangles the trunk of another. Endless entanglements were prophesised in a Nostradamus-like manner: between Islam and the West; the West and China; and also the West and Russia. This again corresponds to some of Paxton's (2004) definition of fascist "mobilising passions", such as the dread of infection from impurer cultures, and the need to corset together a sense of community distinct from rival communities.

There are links between Huntington's position and the more nuanced one of Barber (1995), who saw globalisation as a multifaceted phenomenon, spanning a homogenising neoliberal logic. Globalisation meant tension between corporations, nations, blocs and cultures. Barber tried to capture the centrifugal and centripetal aspects of globalisation. He split the world, on the one hand, into the modernising, Westernising and secular force of globalisation, shaped by multinational companies, and on the other, pre-modern, tribal and fundamental anti-Western forces locked in their own rivalries. The title of his book, *Jihad vs. McWorld*, seems to epitomise neatly the dichotomy between coca-colonisation on the one hand and the animosity of radical Islam in counterpoint .

However, to counter these writers, the idea of *jihad* has a complex history in Islam. It can be read as a struggle for spiritual expression or as a battle within oneself for spiritual equipoise. Osama bin Laden, so demonised by the neoconservatives around both Presidents Bush since he was no longer in the employ of the CIA, militarised the *jihad* in ways that do not cohere with the totality of Islam. Similarly, even the Right-leaning Fukuyama suggested that the parallel fundamentalism of the neoconservatives had become "over-militarised". Barber's readings of globalisation, like those of the neoconservatives influenced by Huntington, simplified the understanding of its processes and ambiguities. These interpretations assumed a world neatly bifurcated into homogenised blocs. The conflicts within them, the struggles between personnel and the spiritual articulations of globalisations' casualties, were glibly glossed over.

The flows of globalisation elude the comprehension of neoconservatives. If globalisation is a process of secularising change, it also generates a momentous reaction that propels religion from civil society and into public policy. Some religious reaction that is counter–

hegemonic to the US project is arguably more rational than neoconservative fundamentalism itself.

> Globalisation gives rise to a web of contradictions, tensions and anxieties.... It has led to the concentration of power, knowledge and wealth in institutions, at least those influenced by transnational corporations. ... But it also generated a decentralising dynamic as people and communities struggle to retain control over the forces that threaten their very existence.... In the midst of changes and severe pressure on livelihoods and cultures, people want to confirm their cultural and religious identities.... (World Council of Churches, 1988; as cited in Davidson & Harris, 2006, p. 46)

"Not knowing one's enemy", which was the result of this myopic neoconservatism, ensured perpetuation of conflict. Radicalising the more moderate aspects of Islam, which felt threatened by the imperial project, ironically meant that the American system generated more opposition by its own actions. The USA might appear to be at the pinnacle of its military *power*; yet it has reached its nadir of global *influence*. Hunter S. Thompson put this graphically and memorably: "We have become a Nazi monster in the eyes of the whole world – a nation of bullies and bastards who would rather kill than live peacefully. We are not just whores for power and oil, but killer whores with hate and fear in our hearts" (Thompson, as cited in Falk, 2003).

Globalisation and fascism

Neoconservative interest in fascism lent credence to the views of Falk, Visiting Professor of Global Studies at the University of California (2003). Falk argued that there are two types of fascism: an embryonic "global" fascism and an incipient traditional one. The United States is perceived as the dominant player in this global fascism, with its geo-political disciplining of other states being an attempt to impose costs and benefits for following its path of global regulation and order (Falk). Countries that fall into line with the "War on Terror" are publicly embraced and gain benefits; there is a marked avoidance, at the very least, of those resistant to American charms.

Falk (2003) asserts that there are clear links between economic globalisation and emerging global fascism: "Economic globalisation did create this sense of an integrated global order, and that this degree of integration could be achieved by economic means". With the Bush leadership and the outrage of 9/11, the trend toward integration and control has been decisively militarised and ideologised. It could be argued that the militarisation of the state has been a reaction to (or against) globalisation. Real power could be said to rest, not in Washington or Berlin, but with the World Economic Forum or the World Trade Organization [WTO]. However, Falk seems to reject this: "Now there's a new ascendancy of the security agenda.... The state has revived its control over politics" (Falk).

What is unclear from Falk's account is whether or not the power of global capital to flow independently of states has disappeared; it is neither clear how or if the European Union has become part of global fascism, nor how this concept would work in Far Eastern contexts. It may be more appropriate to talk of pre-fascist tendencies within some states. It seems decidedly premature to talk of a *global* fascism. Falk's talk of the state resuming control has a superficial ring; the state has always been militarised and active. The point this chapter asserts is that there is an *intensification* of that repression to exceptional levels in multiple arenas. It would be helpful, too, to clarify the notion of global fascism by distinguishing between different types of states, with vastly different levels of autonomy. Moving from his amorphous definition of "global fascism" to a more concrete one of traditional fascism, Falk (2003) points to disillusionment with democracy as a warning sign. Alternative, violent routes to change would then be sought, which would in turn lead the state to magnify its control over its newly mobilised citizenry.[3] On this point, a significant slice of the non-voting electorate could corroborate this crisis of legitimation in the US democratic regime; a crisis given a further twist by the questionable outcome of the Bush-Gore election, an election in which Gore obtained more votes, but lost.[4] The assiduous popular protests against the Vietnam War that brought the demise of Lyndon Johnson had no parallel around G. W. Bush's election; the lack of the same mass energy may indicate, if not apathy, then exhaustion or despair. Such lack of mobilisation, despite the dire opinion poll ratings for the President in 2006, may bear out part of Falk's thesis.

Globalisation, to add to Falk's argument, contributes to the crisis of legitimation. If the electorate perceive the state as being unable to counter the relocation abroad of transnational corporations (and hence jobs), they may fail to see its relevance. Hence, this chapter argues, the hyperstate must *appear* to be potent; it must counter threats from global capital to its autonomy with new laws and new militarism. The advanced Western states discussed

---

[3] Falk's view is shared in the UK by the *Power Inquiry* (2005), chaired by Helena Kennedy, QC, which warned that mass disaffection with formal party politics by UK youth, if combined with a chronic economic downturn, could lead to the re-imposition of authoritarianism.

[4] Yet Falk's notion of apathy, if applicable to the UK, must be tempered by the unusually high participation rates in the 2004 US presidential election.

here must appear to be doing things, to veil what they effectively cannot do.

Traditional fascism is defined by Falk (2003) as the convergence of military and economic power on behalf of an ultranationalist ideology that views enemies – internally and externally – as evil and thus subject to extermination or extreme punishment. Can this apply to the contemporary USA? Undoubtedly, the label "Evil" has tripped from the presidential lips. The discourse of terrorism seeks to validate extreme forms of violence and a warlike mentality (Falk). Falk argues that the language has taken on Orwellian contortions, with the search for peace meaning eternal war, etc.; he comes up with what might be called a Trojan horse theory:

> Certainly the people who are the architects of these policies would reject my analysis, and probably sincerely .... It will all be done in the name of democratization. It's a very deceptive and confusing style of political domination, because it pretends to be the opposite of what it is .... There is an ambiguity, because there is a concealed fascism that is occurring within the framework of a constitutional democracy.

This echoes the prediction of the 1930s Louisiana Governor, Huey Long: "When fascism comes to America it will be disguised as anti-fascism" (Davidson & Harris, 2006).

Falk does not discuss in detail the mass support for elite neo-fascism. If a pincer movement of fundamentalist Christians and the neoconservative elite encircled a representative democracy, it would strengthen the thesis of imperilled pluralism:

The Slowly Simmering Frog

Today's fascist threat in the US may be more serious than previous threats in one important manner; its mass ideological base, despite its populism, is openly confrontational with constitutional democracy.... The theocratic right is far more ideological and organised in terms of forming a counter hegemonic bloc to democracy.... Its base is deeply situated within civil society and is creating a powerful and lasting challenge. (Davidson & Harris, 2006, p. 50)

With a 2004 exit poll indicating that nearly 80% of White evangelicals, comprising nearly a quarter of the overall electorate, voted for G. W. Bush, they have become its single most powerful bloc. This, then, is an authoritarian impulse *from below* that could reverberate long after the House of Bush has subsided.

Repression in the era of globalisation: Downgrading the human?

Falk (2003) talked of a fascist ideology that views enemies as evil and subject to extermination or extreme punishment. There is some evidence of Orwellian manipulation of language to facilitate this punishment. Strategic use of language is not merely semantic. It aims to avoid international sanction, and seeks to justify detaining opponents of the ostensible agenda of democracy. Strategic language creates an environment for this "extreme punishment". For example, Rumsfeld said that Americans had been charged with "abuse" in Abu Ghraib, "... which I believe is technically different from torture" (as quoted in Sontag, 2004, p. 3). The claim did not appear to be coherent. As Sontag stated: "... words alter, words add, words subtract". To call what happened there torture would have led to more extensive public investigations, court martials, and resignations of senior military and cabinet officials, as well as reparation to victims. Whilst, after Sontag's death, there have been disciplinary procedures, predictably these have targeted individuals lower down the pecking order than the elite, and only belatedly reached Rumsfeld himself.

The linguistic turn of "endless war" that the neoconservative Ledeen (as cited in Hulet, 2003) lobbied for earlier implies endless incarceration of victims.

> The torture of prisoners is not an aberration.... It is a direct consequence of the doctrines of world struggle with which the Bush administration has fundamentally changed the domestic and foreign policy of the US. The Bush administration has committed ... to a new, pseudo-religious doctrine of war, endless war – for the war on terror is nothing less than that.... The new, international carceral empire run by the US military goes beyond even the notorious procedures enshrined in France's Devil's Island and Soviet Russia's gulag system (for, unlike these other systems, those incarcerated by the US had, for two years, neither been charged nor tried with anything specific). (Sontag, 2004)

The Hague Invasion Act 2002, passed by the US Senate before the war in Iraq, illustrates the double standard of American exceptionalism. If an American soldier is brought before the International Criminal Court in The Hague, then US law enables the military authorities to extract their colleague, in direct contravention of international law. At the same time as the neoconservative USA was ready to end the liberty of those it labelled a threat, any attempt by non-Americans, including, apparently, Western allies in Europe, to arrest an American for a military crime might be met with state terrorism. In view of the continuities established earlier, Sontag may be going too far in claiming a *complete* change in US policy; nonetheless, the invasiveness of the Bush regime, its readiness to incarcerate enemies and potentially exonerate its own, did seem to represent a new ruthlessness of means toward global ends.

Imperial punishments are clearly not just restricted to Guantanamo Bay or Abu Ghraib. They have implications for those citizens living *within* the Empire. McCulloch (2002, p. 58) emphasises that state repression is not really a response nor a solution to terrorism, if it is really about terrorism at all. Significantly, "*The escalation of state repression is associated with globalisation* [italics added], the waning of a nationally defined capitalist class and the ascendancy of a new internationalist class with global interests". Turning the military capacity of the Empire both outward and inward suits the interests of transnational capital.

Conflict within the Empire has become both inevitable and trenchant as the power elite moves away from the idea of social and employment equality; the priority is getting and keeping mobile international capital. The Empire and those who resist it, from both inside and outside, are brought into bitter conflict over systemic inequities: conflict over attitudes toward the sanctity of the natural environment; conflict over the lower living standards for those outside the comfortable middle classes (McCulloch, p. 58).

As McCulloch (2002, p. 58) writes,

> ... citizens responding to and resisting the negative impacts of globalisation are the enemy within, which states seek to put down by the use of force. While many understand that globalisation

involves a "race to the bottom" in terms of labour and environmental standards, it is less widely understood that it involves *a similar downward race in terms of the value states put on the lives of citizens* [italics added]. The blurring of the line between the police and military, common in emerging democracies and militarised states, is a growing feature of established democracies where paramilitary policing is on the rise and the military is taking a greater role in internal security.

Certainly, there is evidence of greater state intrusion over citizens' lives. A range of agencies police the physical and mental environment of the USA and the repressive state apparatus has intensified with the Patriot Act 2001, which gave the Empire powers to access any individuals' financial, medical, and library records for evidence of "thought crimes". Blatant examples of the Empire repressing anti-globalisation campaigners include the batoning and spraying of citizens in mass anti-globalisation meetings. In Britain, the closest ally of the USA in its adventurist imperial policy, the closeness of the Prime Minister and the police in jointly pushing for greater rights to detain suspects, with the police lobbying Parliament whilst the Terrorism Bill 2005-06, leading to the Terrorism Act 2006, was actively being debated in the House of Commons, may well be regarded as unprecedented.

Other examples of intrusion indicate the microscopic gaze of the panoptic state. There is evidence of state and civil society surveillance intruding into educational zones and self-expression, into the private sphere as well as the public. A website called *Campus Watch* attempted to name and vilify US university staff who are perceived as insufficiently enthusiastic about American adventurism or its embrace of Israel. One professor at Columbia, New York, is reported as having received a voicemail: "Listen, you Muslim terrorist bastard; we are watching you. We know you are an enemy of this country, and we are going to get you" (Dabashi, 2003, p. 10). This gives credence to rumours that a list (or lists) of "suspicious" professors with "un-American" views has been drawn up in neoconservative circles. However sporadic these threats may be, if intellectual freedom is one hallmark of a mature democracy, they represent a shadow over it. Less random, more planned, covert state surveillance was evident in "... moves by the US intelligence agency to place trainee spies secretly in university anthropology departments", to the outrage of UK academics (Brechter, 2005). More concerted campaigns are evidenced by a consortia of US universities who developed software to monitor negative opinion (about US adventurism), with the aim of notifying the authorities (Sardar, 2006).

Surveillance has targeted the vulnerable, whether young or old. In the worst cases, this suggests either gratuitous intimidation or organised paranoia. George Monbiot (2004) detailed how secret service agents interrogated a schoolgirl who had been suspended for wearing a T-shirt that proclaimed she was "Against Bush, Against bin Laden". Michael Moore's *Fahrenheit 9/11* (2004) delineated how innocuous peace groups in Fresno, California, comprised largely of more innocuous pensioners, had been infiltrated by covert state operators. A sophisticated listening device was even (reportedly) found in that most revolutionary of cells, the Church Hall Meeting Place of the Women's Institute. A culture of suspicion has included not only vertical state surveillance, but also horizontal citizen surveillance. An elderly gentleman expressing doubt about the "War on Terror" was reported by his gym colleagues, then interrogated by state agencies (Moore, 2004). This informing on neighbours recalls, in a milder, more sporadic form, the Nazi state, in which members of the Reich were encouraged to report anything suspicious to their local SS officers. Clearly there are significantly more freedoms in American democracy than under a National Socialist regime, yet the paradox of pre-fascist practices within a constitutional democracy is an uneasy one. The private sphere has become encroached upon, in places, by the state; at times, the long, sinewy arm of a neoconservative regime seems to reach into civil society.

These processes are not just restricted to the USA. The period of new repression spanned other established democracies that sought to control their populations more tightly in the era of globalisation. The European Union attempted to reclassify activists travelling to its meetings as terrorists. In Britain, repressive anti–terror legislation has curbed the right to protest; new laws (i.e. the Anti-Terrorism, Crime and Security Act 2001 and the Prevention of Terrorism Act 2005) suggested that protestors appearing outside premises could be charged with stalking under the 1997 Protection from Harassment Act. Websites deemed to "… cause concern or needless anxiety to others" could potentially be closed down under new laws, threatening anti-globalisation protests that were being mobilised electronically (Monbiot, 2004).

Peaceful demonstrators have been amongst the first to be arrested following a battery of legislation, including the Terrorism Act of 2000, despite promises that the democratic right to protest would not be harmed. Even a protestor simply reciting the names of UK servicemen killed in Iraq was taken into custody. A Civil Contingencies Bill allows the British government to suspend Parliament and ban all rights to assembly when it decides it is facing an emergency (Monbiot, 2004). In 2005, the British Home Secretary openly admitted increasing markedly the power of the state over its citizens, with draconian new powers that allowed the house arrest of citizens deemed to be a threat to the life of the nation. Campaigning groups like Liberty warned that this could be abused by future governments wishing to detain groups deemed difficult or deviant. These processes have accelerated following the tube bombings in London of July 7th, 2005. Insidiously, Anglo-American democracies have witnessed the whittling away of long established freedoms, whilst popular protests, after the mass march before the Second Gulf War, have seemed to lack stamina and decisive policy-changing consequences. The installation of identity cards will represent a fundamental change in the relationship between the citizen and the state. As George Monbiot (2004) rightly points out:

> This is the contract the powerful have struck with each other: to agree to a single set of neoliberal policies, and to criminalise all those who seek to challenge them. We are often told that the passage of laws like this is dangerous because one day it might facilitate the seizure of power by an undemocratic government. But that is to miss the point. Their passage *is* [italics added] the seizure of power. Protest is inseparable from democracy: every time it is restricted, the state becomes less democratic. Democracies such as ours will come to an end not with the stamping of boots and the hoisting of flags, but through the slow accretion of a thousand dusty codicils.

Helena Kennedy, QC, argues that "… by removing trial by jury and seeking to detain people on civil ASBO orders as a pre-emptive strike, by introducing identity cards, the government is creating new paradigms of state power" (Porter, 2006). As she told this author, "... we really do have to be careful about globalisation" (H. Kennedy, personal communication, June 3, 2006).

Yet where is the sustained mass public outcry that there was in 1968?

If terrorism is in part the "dark side" of globalisation, then so too is the use of the fear of terrorism by governments to repress resistance to the discreet charms of globalisation. Even some British law lords would support this interpretation. Some have argued that the true threat to the life of the nation rests not necessarily with terrorism, but with these anti-terror laws (Monbiot, 2004).

Power elite pressure upon the judiciary has been recognised as a problem on both sides of the Atlantic. Sandra Day O'Connor, a Republican-appointed and, from 2006, retired Supreme Court judge, pointed out that attacks on the judiciary "... pose a direct threat to our constitutional freedoms.... I want you to tune your ears to these attacks. You have an obligation to speak up" (Borger, 2006). That concerns about dents in democracy are echoed at the highest level of the American judicial system (and not only by grass roots activists) indicates that the threats to national vitality may arguably have come as much from neoconservatives as from al-Qaida. Gore Vidal (2002) laid out the consequences clearly: "... it is fairly plain to many civil-libertarians that 9/11 ... [put pay] not only to much of our fragile Bill of Rights but also to our once-envied system of government ...". It is premature to read the last rites for the US Constitution; it is perceptive to illuminate the deep wounds it has endured.

Former members of the UK security services have confirmed this authoritarian turn taken by Anglo-American governments of the early 21st century. Former agents interviewed by this author claimed that we are "creeping toward totalitarianism", as one ex-MI5 agent (A. Machon, personal communication, November 6, 2006) states. With the mass of the public failing to demonstrate about this abrasion of liberty, it could seem as if mature democratic states, very possibly, "… are sleepwalking into it" (D. Shayler, personal communication, November 6, 2006). The connection between the incremental loss of civil freedom and lack of mass popular concern about it can be understood with reference to frogs. If a frog is placed in a pan and the pan is heated quickly, the frog will jump out equally quickly, and save itself; but if the heat is increased gently, centigrade by centigrade, the frog will eventually boil to death (D. Shayler, personal communication, November 6, 2006).

Authoritarian syndrome and mass media

The ability of a state to manipulate some of its populace using mass communication has been well established by leading fascists:

> Why of course the people don't want a war, but after all it is the leaders of the country who determine the policy, and it's always a simple matter to drag the people along, whether it's a democracy or a fascist dictatorship. Voice or no voice, the people can always be brought to the bidding of the leaders. That is easy. All you have to do is tell them they're being attacked, and denounce the pacifists for lack of patriotism and exposing the country to danger. (Goering, as cited in Gilbert, 1947, pp. 278-279 – see: http://www.snopes.com/quotes/goering.htm, 2002)

This ability of any industrialised society to carry a fascist potentiality within it was picked up early by the

Frankfurt School. In *The Authoritarian Personality*, Adorno and his collaborators (as cited in Jay, 1973, pp. 240-3) produced a profile of a fascist personality type, drawn largely from White, native-born, Gentile, middle-class Americans. They noted key characteristics:

> A mechanical surrender to conventional values; blind submission to authority together with blind hatred of all opponents and outsiders; anti-introspectiveness; rigid stereotyped thinking; a penchant for superstition; vilification, half-moralistic and half cynical, of human nature; projectivity (the disposition to believe that wild and dangerous things go on in the world; the projection outwards of unconscious emotional impulses).

The outcome was an authoritarian syndrome. This syndrome was framed in uncritically Freudian terms as a sado-masochistic resolution of the Oedipal complex. It resulted in unconscious hatred of the father, which was transformed into love for those perceived as strong and then directed against the vulnerable. This also overlaps with the "strong father" thesis (Lakoff, 2004).

This authoritarianism is most relevant when related to the mass media. Adorno (as cited in Jay, 1973) argues that mass communication reinforces proto-fascist qualities; note a link between Adorno's definition and Falk's earlier reading of contemporary fascist activities. Individuals of this type are susceptible to stereotypes and taken in by facile "personalising" of public sphere rhetoric communicated through corporate media, whether in politics or advertising. For Adorno, the culture industries essentially deceive people and distract them from the agenda of Empire.

Whilst we do not have to accept the totality of Adorno's thesis, reductionist as it is about multifaceted audiences, there have clearly been some deferential attitudes to the *office* of the presidency, regardless of floating popularity polls. These deferential postures toward power feed into an "authoritarian syndrome".[5] Britney Spears, once a master signifier of US popular culture and, for a time, a role model for some American children, expressed this most chillingly in *Fahrenheit 9/11* (Moore, 2004), when she commented that we should '"just trust our president" in *whatever* he does. By late 2006, the nadir in G. W. Bush's personal approval ratings eclipsed the deference to the presidential office in some quarters. Nonetheless, the precedent had again been confirmed, as in the moment of McCarthyism, of the ability of the agenda-setting corporate media to amplify patriotism, a sense of national danger and the charisma of office, to play upon, periodically, an authoritarian syndrome.

The propagandistic and proto-fascist potential of some global corporate media, of which Britney Spears is a product, is evidenced by the media baron Murdoch's declaration of strong support for the war on Iraq, followed by 175 of his editors around the world, in "blind submission" (cf. Adorno, as cited in Jay, 1973). This was a classic case of news filtering and of the dangers, of which Herman and Chomsky (1994) have warned, of the over-concentration of ownership, as shown repeatedly by events from the Vietnam War to the Eurasian misadventure. These filters in the global media include: the business interests of the owner; the need to please current and potential advertisers; the reliance on press organisations

---

[5] This chapter focuses on hegemonic processes, and therefore debates about audience reception are beyond its scope, as it is a relatively brief study.

with commercial interests in media influence; the threat that "rogue" journalists face the sack or litigation; and finally, the fact that the global media is filtered, generally, and in the USA, markedly, by its taken-for-granted acceptance of neo-liberal ideology (Herman & Chomsky).

Miller (2004) explained how Right Wing influence has moved the corporate media away from news reportage to the attempted design of our consciousness. The Age of Information has turned into an Age of Ignorance. In particular, Miller highlights how CNN and Fox News destroyed the credibility of Scott Ritter, a former weapons inspector for the UN. Ritter opposed the neoconservative invasion of Iraq. In response, CNN's Miles O'Brien and Fox News's David Asman, Miller argues, portrayed this expert as un-American, a stooge of Saddam Hussein, the equivalent of Jane Fonda in North Vietnam.

There is evidence to underline Miller's argument, which took the Frankfurt School's thesis about the deception of mass *culture*, expanded it, and applied it to the deceptive nature of *news* media. A University of Maryland study (as cited in Bendall & Bendall, 2004) found that the more commercial television news people watched, the more incorrect they were likely to be about basic facts concerning the invasion of Iraq; an invasion deemed illegal by the Secretary General of the United Nations. Those who watched the Fox News Channel, the study found, were most likely to be misinformed about the incursions of the American Empire and, by implication, about the processes of globalisation. Most strikingly, Saddam Hussein and Osama bin Laden were fused and confused in some of the popular mentality analysed. As Chomsky (2002, pp. 27-28) put it:

> The bewildered herd is a problem…. They should be watching the
>
> Superbowl or sitcoms or violent movies. Every once in a while you

call on them to chant meaningless slogans like "Support our troops". You've got to keep them pretty scared, because unless they're properly scared and frightened of all kinds of devils that are going to destroy them from outside or inside or somewhere, they may start to think, which is very dangerous, because they're not competent to think. Therefore it's important to distract them and marginalize them.

One might add, from the evidence of the Maryland study, that it is as important to misinform them, too.

Chomsky could be accused of patronising and homogenising his audience. It is important to acknowledge those sophisticated viewers who find their own uses and gratifications and resistant readings, or just read something else entirely; it is equally important to recognise the power of some parts of the media to cloud and contort issues, as borne out by the studies mentioned.

Roy (2004, p. 86) has shown how, to add another filter to Chomsky's, the filter of the language used by the corporate media, whether public or private, can cater to the proto-fascist potentiality of the Empire's audience. Linguistic distortion occurs, not only in the misrepresentation of penal systems discussed earlier, but in the ideological apparatus of global media. Roy believes that this is a slaughter of language. Arab reporting and, by inference, French reporting, was depicted as emotional, with the implication that propaganda is foreign to the Anglo-American media. War reporting, to adapt Clausewitz, sometimes has been the conduct of political reporting by other means. Increasingly, the Anglo-American media referred to Iraqi soldiers as "militia", as "rabble". One BBC report called them "quasi-terrorists" (Roy). Use of the word "insurgents" suggested enemies stirring things up from outside, not patriotic or religious resistance from within. The politicisation (and hypocrisy) of media language is as abundant as the confusion of information with opinion. For example, the Iraqi military strategy was denigrated as "deceit"; in contrast, the bugging of the telephone lines of UN Security Council delegates was described by *The Observer* as "hard-headed pragmatism". These are examples of the conceptual language frames that elements of the dominant media and neoconservative elite both use to affect how some receivers think about social and political issues (Lakoff, 2004).

Although Roy (2004) points to elements of anti-Iraqi bias in BBC reporting, it is curious that, in counterpoint, the Hutton Report (2004) largely found the BBC rather too biased against the Government over the Kelly affair. One interpretation is that the government-licensed broadcaster was at times supportive of the Government's actions, but still not considered supportive enough. The punishment of reporters who stepped out of line casts doubt on the idea that we have a truly plural public service broadcasting or unlimited investigative reporting, with the power to effect change of Watergate's Woodward and Bernstein. (Note the culling of major media players from the BBC leadership and the editorship of *The Daily Mirror*: a warning to those who tread too hard on the toes of the neo-liberal power elite?).

Globalisation has seen the attempted dominance of the private corporation over the public broadcaster; a successful attempt in the United States, where the Public Broadcasting System is regularly reduced to begging for funds. Inevitably, corporate news will frame a reality that perpetuates corporate power. The propagandistic use of the corporate media essentially drives home an emotion: fear (Walker, 2002). The spectre of a Brown Scare (to replace the Soviet Red Scare) manipulated some of the electorate, *initially*, into accepting an illegal war, though with varying, and vastly diminishing, levels of success; and, in effect, into voting for sustained domestic inequalities[6] (Goldenberg, 2004). Evidence of the blue-collar electorate voting against its own economic interests and thus reinforcing inequalities came, for example, in the 2004 elections. The bogey of gay marriage, anxieties about the Right to Life and, of course, the ultimate folk devil of Osama bin Laden meant that some nervous Americans in swing states, such as Ohio, did not vote for the economic and welfare policies of the Democratic candidate. This is the deployment of moral politics, though, ironically, using immoral means (Lakoff, 2004).

Conclusions

Looked at *in toto*, "The American empire [may become] a military giant, a back-seat economic driver, a political schizophrenic.... The result is a disturbed, misshapen monster stumbling clumsily across the world" (Mann, 2003, p. 13).

The chapter has sketched out whether or not there has been a fascist turn in the US and UK states in response to globalisation. Whilst there have been troubling developments, the word fascist can be alarmist, as well as loose. "The possibility of fascist behaviour is now being discussed openly and with concern by even conservative Senators ... but Norman Mailer probably has it right when he said that America is in a pre-fascist state" (Pilger, as cited in Porter, 2006). The dialogic and disquieted response to neoconservativism indicated that the public sphere is,

---

[6] A young, olive-skinned, man was shown, with his eyes flickering around an airport, to signify Asiatic terrorism in an advertisement for the Bush electoral campaign in 2004.

though dented, still far from dead. Firstly, critiques of US foreign and domestic policy have become part of the narratives of some of the American corporate news channels, such as MSNBC. Secondly, Supreme Court reversals of key Bush policies, such as the indefinite detention of terrorist suspects, have seen an executive checked, if not balanced. The resurgence of the Democratic Party in late 2006 indicates that, if only at the level of party political participation, there was residual sceptical energy in US politics and culture, though it would be highly unlikely that such scepticism penetrated so far as to alter the system of capital accumulation. Hence, it would seem that the House of Bush represented the high tide of neoconservatism; this may have ebbed, though a change in the electoral tide or a high wind could well swell its chances again.

This chapter commenced with definitions of fascism from Paxton (2004). Using his criteria, it is clear that there have been necessary but *insufficient* elements in the neoconservative movement to qualify it as fully fascist. Firstly, its agenda is not openly revolutionary. Secondly, the USA, despite the extra-legal activities of the Bush Administration (such as wire-tapping, or the surveillance of banking transactions by the National Security Agency [NSA]) is very far from being a dictatorship. Thirdly, the questionable Republican tactics deployed against some African-Americans in Florida in 2000 notwithstanding, generally the conservative movement has not yet relied on nationwide physical violence and visible campaigns of gross intimidation to obtain power and suppress opposition. Finally, there has not been a full-scale crisis of the American polity (such as a nationwide Katrina) for fascism to mobilise adequately. Of Paxton's mobilising passions, certainly they may be passionately held by some conservatives. Conclusively, they have not yet the mass mobility to destabilise permanently the American polity.

It is possible that some leftist writers make as much of a folk devil of the USA as G. W. Bush did of Saddam Hussein. Critics of US intervention are faced with a paradox when confronting the benign interventions of the USA in other states' business – the constructive intervention in Bosnia and Kosovo, for example. The paradox of imperialism is that it may coerce, but it may also protect. US imperialism can step into a vacuum created by weak states. Ignatieff (2003, p. 125) makes the point: "Those who imagine a world beyond empire imagine rightly, but they have not seen how prostrate societies actually are when nation building fails, when civil war has torn it apart. Then and only then is there a case for temporary imperial rule, to provide the force and will necessary to bring order out of chaos". Ignatieff's judgements are a useful counter-argument to those who have no time at all for US entanglements. However, when imperialism helps destroy states and, accidentally or deliberately, sparks civil war, as in Iraq by 2006, then the myth of Uncle Sam as a sheltering patriarch of the family of nations is harder to swallow.

In the final analysis, therefore, the chapter has adumbrated *pre-fascist behaviours* in a post-9/11 USA: in its elite ideology and geopolitical strategy; in an attempted and contested erosion of civil liberties and the cold-shouldering of international law; and in its reliance on the frame of some corporate media. These have been the contours of a *neoconservative moment* that peaked over some six years of the Bush Administration.

As advanced Western states recognised the fundamental power (and threat) of global capital, repression has been projected against citizens and against materially useful, but otherwise inimical, sovereign states.

The USA has been perceived as the leading gamekeeper of the empire of global capital. It has been demonstrated that the idea of the state is, then, not a flaccid irrelevance in relation to globalisation; rather, the American state has helped sustain capitalist relations and penetrated enemies. These enemies have been constructed as Middle Eastern "others" by a media-industrial complex, yet the legal implications of the more intrusive state, ostensibly aimed at an "enemy within" or the "evil-doers" outside, directly encroach on the civil liberties of *all* citizens. Though subsequently contested by the Supreme Court, the category of the non-citizen enemy combatant, shorn of rights, was most worryingly invented at Guantanamo Bay. This invention of the expendable non-citizen, whose corpse was usually not even counted by the occupying powers (see Roberts, Lafta, Garfield, Khudhairi, & Burnham, 2004), is particularly regrettable, as the American Bill of Rights, when first envisaged, was such a beacon of individual freedom and guarantor of the right to pursue happiness. However long these state interventions remain, the very fact that they can evolve, sometimes with episodic popular enthusiasm, sets troubling precedents, especially if countervailing forces were ever to lose their capacity to check them.

Globalisation has generated, and has seemed to accentuate, inequality. Inequality generated reaction, whether of exhaustion or resistance. The drumbeat of war attempted to distract populations from inequalities, with diminishing degrees of success in the medium to longer term. The pre-fascist use of security services and new laws helped curb those who would not be distracted; those who did still actively resist have felt the state's steely fist. The oriental background to the war on terror let neoconservatives project the shadow side of the USA on to the repellent figures of Saddam Hussein and Osama bin

Laden (Said, 2003). Attempts to shore up the imagined community of nations have been generated by moral panics about Islam (Ahmed, 2005, p. 15), whilst other nations useful to the Empire have been selectively re-imagined and roughly re-ordered; they, in turn, have explosively resisted, and often internally combusted. Before the Bush Administration, and concertedly during it, the US Empire tried to manipulate through airwaves and armour; irrespective of changes in the political power elite, the logic of capital looks set to persist in its underlying systems.

Vigorous attempts to disrupt this hegemony will persist too. The role of citizen consumers in critical consciousness-raising and in striving to resist manipulation is vital for the survival of our species and other species in our shared and stressed ecosystem. If we are to have forced upon us a "War on Terror", do we not need an intellectual war against state terror as well, in the name of sustainability?

On a final note, the Right Wing Harvard historian Ferguson, who once presented a favourable reading of *Pax Americana*, has become disenchanted with neoconservative messianism. Ferguson recounts a story from Suskind, a journalist who spoke to a senior adviser to G. W. Bush, to explain this disenchantment.

> The aide [to Bush] said that guys like me were in what we call the reality based community, which he defined as "people who believe that solutions emerge from your judicious study of discernible reality". I nodded and murmured something about enlightenment principles and empiricism. He cut me off. "That's not the way the world works anymore", he continued. "We're an empire now, and when we act, we create our own realities. And while you're

studying that reality - judiciously, as you will - we'll act again, creating other new realities, which you can study too, and that's how things will sort out. We're history's actors and you, all of you, will be left to just study what we do". (Ferguson, 2004, p. 39)

"Just" being left to study a culture in an ideal type context can sometimes lead to critical consciousness of it (Freire, 2000). One must hope that, in however much of a bit-part, readers of this chapter might perhaps be history's actors too. If the insidious degradation of the citizen-state relationship under globalisation is, somehow, to be more widely questioned in some mature democracies, we need our own micro narratives to counter the meta narratives. To amend Marx, the point of such study is not to describe the world. Surely, and however stumblingly, it is to try to salvage it whilst there may still be time.

References

Ahmed, S. (2005, March). Be very afraid! *New Internationalist, 376*. Retrieved March 21, 2007, from: http://live.newint.org/issue376/be-very-afraid.htm.

Ali, T. (2002). *The clash of fundamentalisms: Crusades, jihads and modernity.* London: Verso.

Bacevich, A. J. (2002). *American empire: The realities and consequences of U.S. diplomacy.* Cambridge, MA: Harvard University Press.

Barber, B. R. (1995). *Jihad vs. McWorld.* New York: Times Books.

Bendall, J., & Bendall, M. (2004). World review [Electronic version]. *Journal of Corporate Citizenship, 15,* 5-18.

Borger, J. (2006, March 13). Former top judge says US risks edging nearer to dictatorship: Sandra Day O'Connor warns of rightwing attacks: Lawyers 'must speak up' to protect judiciary. *The Guardian,* p. 19.

Brechter, B. (2005, September 16). The power of the great big No. *The Times Higher Education Supplement.* Retrieved March 21, 2007, from:

http://www.thes.co.uk/search/story.aspx.

Chomsky, N. (2002). *Media control: The spectacular achievements of propaganda.* (2nd ed.). New York: Seven Stories Press. (Original work published 1991).

Dabashi, H. (2003, October 17). Forget reds under the bed, there's Arabs in the attic. *The Times Higher Education Supplement.*

Retrieved March 21, 2007, from:

http://www.thes.co.uk/search/story.aspx?story_id=2 005019

Davidson, C., & Harris, J. (2006). Globalisation, theocracy and the new fascism; the US Right's rise to power. *Race and Class, 47* (3), 46-66.

Falk, R. (2003). Early signs of fascism: [Interview, conducted by James MacKinnon]. *Adbusters, 11*, (4). Retrieved March 21, 2007, from:

http://blogs.salon.com/0002255/2003/06/23.html.

Ferguson, N. (2004, November 4). US Presidential Election: The depressing reality of this messianic President's new empire [Electronic version]. *The Independent,* 2004, p. 39.

Freire, P. (2000). *Pedagogy of the oppressed* (M. B. Ramos, Trans.). New York: Continuum. (Original work published 1970).

Fukuyama, F. (2006, February 19). After neoconservatism. *The New York Times.* Retrieved March 21, 2007, from: http://zfacts.com/metaPage/lib/Fukuyama-2006-After-Neoconservatism.pdf.

Giddens, A. (1991). *Modernity and self-identity: Self and society in the late modern age.* Stanford, CA: Stanford University Press.

Gilbert, G. M. (1947). *Nuremberg diary.* New York: Farrar, Straus and Company.

Goldenberg, S. (2004, March 13). Election ad plays on fear of Arabs [Electronic version]. *The Guardian,* p. 16.

Hardt, M., & Negri, A. (2000). *Empire.* Cambridge, MA: Harvard University Press.

Harvey, D. (2003). *The new imperialism.* Oxford: Oxford University Press.

Hennessy, P. (2007, April 27). Cold (war) comfort. *The Times Higher Education Supplement,* pp. 16-17.

Herman, E. S., & Chomsky, N. (1994). *Manufacturing consent: The political economy of the mass media.* London: Vintage. (Originally published 1988).

Hulet, C. B. (2003). *Universal fascism, freedom betrayed: What is Mr. Bush doing in your name?* Retrieved March 21, 2007, from: http://sandiego.indymedia.org/es/2003/10/101473.s html.

Huntington, S. P. (1996). *The clash of civilizations and the remaking of world order.* New York: Simon & Schuster.

Hutton, B. (2004). *Report of the inquiry into the circumstances surrounding the death of Dr David Kelly C.M.G .* London: Stationery Office.

Ignatieff, M. (2003). *Empire lite: Nation-building in Bosnia, Kosovo and Afghanistan.* London: Vintage.

Jay, M. (1973). *The dialectical imagination: A history of the Frankfurt School and the Institute of Social Research, 1923-1950*. London: Heinemann.

Kagarlitsky, B. (2001). Facing the crisis, *Links, 19,* 69-82.

Kennan, G. F. (1948). PPS/23: Review of current trends in U.S. foreign policy (R. Wvong, Transcriber). In *Foreign Relations of the United States*, vol. I (pp. 509-529). Retrieved March 21, 2007, from:

http://www.geocities.com/rwvong/future/kennan/pps23.html.

Lakoff, G. (2004). *Don't think of an elephant!: Know your values and frame the debate : The essential guide for progressives*. White River Junction, VT: Chelsea Green Pub. Co.

Mann, M. (2003). *Incoherent empire.* London: Verso.

McCulloch, J. (2002). 'Either you are with us or you are with the terrorists': The war's home front. In P. Scraton (Ed.), *Beyond September 11th: An anthology of dissent* (chap. 8). London: Pluto Press.

Miller, M. C. (2004). *Cruel and unusual: Bush/Cheney's new world order.* New York: W.W. Norton.

Monbiot, G. (2001, December 18). The end of the enlightenment. *The Guardian*. Retrieved March 21, 2007, from: http://www.monbiot.com/archives/2001/12/18/the-end-of-the-enlightenment/.

Monbiot, G. (2004, August 3). Comment & analysis: A threat to democracy [Electronic version]. *The Guardian*, p. 17.

Moore, M. (Writer/Director/Producer), Czarnecki, J. (Producer), & Glynn, K. (Producer). (2004). *Fahrenheit 9/11* [Motion picture]. United States: Lion Gate Films.

Paxton, R. (2004). *The anatomy of fascism*. New York: Knopf.

Petras, J., & Veltmeyer, H. (2001). *Globalisation unmasked: Imperialism in the 21st century*. London: Zed Books.

Pilger, J. (2002). *The new rulers of the world*. London: Verso.

Porter, H. (2006, July). Blair's big brother legacy. *Vanity Fair*. Retrieved March 21, 2007, from: http://www.vanityfair.com/politics/features/2006/07/blair200607.

Power Inquiry. (2006). *Power to the people: The report of Power: An independent inquiry into Britain's democracy*. London: Author.

Rice, C. (2002, April 29). *Remarks by National Security Adviser Condoleeza Rice on terrorism and foreign policy:* [Speech delivered at Paul H. Nitze School of Advanced International Studies, Johns Hopkins University]. Retrieved March 21, 2007, from: http://www.whitehouse.gov/news/releases/2002/04/20020429-9.html.

Roberts, L., Lafta, R., Garfield, R., Khudhairi, J., & Burnham, G. (2004, November 20-26). Mortality before and after the 2003 invasion of Iraq: Cluster sample survey. *The Lancet, 364,* 9448, 1857-1864.

Roy, A. (2004). *The ordinary Person's guide to empire.* London: Harper Perennial.

Said, E. W. (2003). *Orientalism.* (New ed.). London: Penguin. (Original work published 1978).

Sardar, Z. (2006, November 13). A new Mccarthy era dawns in America. *New Statesman.* Retrieved March 21, 2007, from: http://www.newstatesman.com/200611130028.

Sardar, Z., & Davies, M. W. (2004). *American dream, global nightmare: Celebrity, politics and the American empire.* Thriplow: Icon.

Sontag, S. (2004, May 24). What have we done? *The Guardian, G2*, p. 3. Retrieved March 21, 2007, from: http://www.commondreams.org/views04/0524-09.htm.

Todd, E. (2003). *After the empire: The breakdown of the American order* (C. J. Delogu, Trans.). New York: Columbia University Press. (Original work published 2002).

UK House of Commons. (2004). *Civil Contingencies Bill: Session 2003-04.* London: Stationery Office.

UK House of Commons. (2006). *Terrorism Bill: Session 2005-06.* London: Stationery Office.

UK Statutes. (1997). *Protection from Harassment Act: Elizabeth II, 1997, Chapter 40.* London: Stationery Office.

UK Statutes. (2000). *Terrorism Act: Elizabeth II, 2000, Chapter 11.* London: Stationery Office.

UK Statutes. (2001). *Anti-Terrorism, Crime and Security Act: Elizabeth II, 2001, Chapter 24.* London: Stationery Office.

UK Statutes. (2005). *Prevention of Terrorism Act: Elizabeth II, 2005, Chapter 2.* London: Stationery Office.

UK Statutes. (2006). *Terrorism Act: Elizabeth II, 2006, Chapter 11.* Norwich: TSO.

US Department of Defense (1992). *Defense planning guidance:* [Draft]. Retrieved March 21, 2007, from: http://www.pbs.org/wgbh/pages/frontline/shows/iraq/etc/wolf.html.

US Statutes (2001). *Uniting and Strengthening America by Providing Appropriate Tools Required to Intercept and Obstruct Terrorism Act of 2001 [The Patriot Act], Public Law 107-56.* Washington, DC: Office of the Federal Register.

US Statutes (2002). *American Service-members Protection Act of 2002 [The Hague Invasion Act], Public Law 107-206.* Washington, DC: Office of the Federal Register.

Vidal, G. (2002, October 27). The enemy within. *The Observer.* Retrieved March 21, 2007, from: http://www.ratical.org/ratville/CAH/EnemyWithin.html.

Walker, J. (2002, March). Panic attacks: Drawing the thin line between caution and hysteria after September 11. *Reason Online.* Retrieved March 21, 2007, from: http://reason.com/news/show/28345.html.

GLOBALISATION: THE BATTLE FOR SOLIDARITY AND EFFECTIVE RESISTANCE

Yacob Mulugetta

Introduction

The dominant discourse on globalisation describes it as an uncontrollable, inevitable and unstoppable process that promises enormous rewards. It is a force that is closely tied to a liberal economic model (neo-liberalism[1]) of an integrated and coordinated division of labour that privileges market forces. The transition to open markets and policy discipline may have undesirable consequences in the short-term, but the long-term benefits associated with an open economic model are tremendous. Hence, countries need to pursue the "right" policies, which permit a free, market-mediated, flow of capital and goods in the interest of prosperity and higher living standards. The countries that place barriers to investment and free trade through obstructive regulatory measures, tariffs and capital controls not only deny their people access to goods and services at attractive prices, but also interfere with the entrepreneurial impulses of their citizens. In effect, countries need to pursue specific policies that reduce labour costs, reduce public expenditures, and make work

---

[1] Neo-liberalism is a set of economic policies that have become widespread during the last 25 years or so. It is a political-economic philosophy that has had major implications for government policies since the 1970s. It strongly emphasises deregulation, privatisation and reduction of the state in the economy to facilitate freer movement of goods, resources and enterprises, in a bid always to find cheaper resources, to maximise profits and efficiency. The terms "neo-liberalism" and "economic globalisation" will be used interchangeably in this paper.

more flexible. These are some of the basic arguments put forward by the advocates of neo-liberal globalisation; a group that includes business, economic theorists and, to some extent, the popular press. Behind this group are some of the world's most powerful governments and financial institutions, such as the World Bank and the International Monetary Fund [IMF], with the power to coerce and discipline countries to adhere to prescriptions that would set them on the "right" path.

In practice, the globalisation project is often criticised for developing a world order that is politically imposed by powerful forces whose interest it represents: financiers, stockholders, industrialists and conservative or social-democratic politicians. The visible effects of neo-liberal globalisation are palpable. We have witnessed increasing poverty in a large number of countries, even in the most economically advanced societies. We also see the extraordinary growth in income differences, the transfer of service delivery from public entities to private agencies, and the heavy burden of external debt, which forces many poor countries to reduce their expenditure on social services. Quite often, much of the sacrifice for these problems rests on the backs of poor communities, who have experienced an erosion of social welfare programmes and public services under the weight of neo-liberal structural adjustment. To complicate matters, alliances between local elites and the lender communities have resulted in blind acceptance of adjustment conditions. Today, the reach of neo-liberal forces is such that even national policies tend to be drafted at the IMF or the World Bank, before being forwarded for local endorsement.

Against this background, resistance to neo-liberal globalisation is growing. International and national social movements have proliferated as a direct response to the excesses of globalisation and corporate hegemony over

world economic instruments and resources. Often, such
groups consist of disparate constituents, such as
environmentalists, poor people's agencies, labour
movements, women's movements and Non-Governmental
Organizations [NGOs], each coming with its specific
demands and focus activities. Their convergence of
thought and action derives from the realm of values and a
sense of civic responsibility and reliance on their own
initiative to do the "right thing" (Oliveira & Tandon, 1994),
since their views and principles are not being addressed on
the conventional political platform by the official
leadership. Furthermore, there is a broad recognition that
local interventions alone, as encapsulated in the slogan,
"Think Globally, Act Locally", may not be sufficient to
effect change without engaging with the range of global
forums and processes.

The objective of this chapter is to examine in broad
terms the characteristics of globalisation, and to pose the
question of why this phenomenon is attracting extensive
public debate. In doing so, it explores the features of
economic globalisation and delineates who the "winners"
and the "losers" are in this increasingly Darwinian world
order. The chapter then outlines the complex political and
economic setting within which resistance to global
economic governance is currently articulated. This will
map out how and why traditional forms of resistance have
given way to new forms, exploring the degree to which
these new agents can realistically sustain a degree of
autonomy without making significant compromises of
principle. Finally, it will provide some insights into the
merits of analysis, alliance-building and concrete action.

Implications of Globalisation

Making sense of the dominant globalisation discourse

Globalisation is an extensively debated topic, around which little consensus has emerged as to its nature, meaning and implications. Given this situation, it is worth deliberating on some of the meanings ascribed to globalisation by various scholarly orientations that have attempted to unpack this rather elusive, yet omnipresent, concept.

There are those who view globalisation within a political and economic frame. They offer a materialist analysis, whereby globalisation is explained by the emergence of a transnational capitalist class who employ the discourses of national competitiveness and sustainable development to further the interests of global capital (Robinson & Harris, 2000; Sklair, 2001). This historical bloc, to use the Gramscian terminology (see Gramsci, 1971), consists of corporations and financial institutions, state managers, media conglomerates, technocratic elites and intellectuals, all contributing to the construction of a new, transnational, hegemonic order. In short, this understanding of globalisation places emphasis on the alliance of elite actors in both the North and South, who use their great material and cultural power to promote a particular vision of society and implement policies that facilitate global capital accumulation and production. In pursuit of this outcome, transnational economic integration takes precedence over a state-centred world, in which this form of "internationalisation of state" converts nation-states into "transmission belts and filtering devices for the imposition of transnational agenda" (Robinson, 2001, pp. 174-175; see also Cox, 1987).

Another group of scholars offer a structuralist view, giving primacy to the interplay between political factors, state actions, transnational regulatory bodies and the

growing power of NGOs to explain the basis and
consequences of globalisation (Smith, Chatfield &
Pagnucco, 1997; Tarrow, 2001; Held & McGrew, 2003).
According to this group, there is a high degree of fluidity
in the nature and shape of globalisation, as there are
multiple factors and social spheres that influence the
direction it takes. While acknowledging the primacy of the
market and the dominance of neo-liberal ideology, they
argue that the era of globalisation does not necessarily
reduce politicians' power, but simply complicates their
tasks. Held (2004) believes that the current era of
globalisation is characterised by "the appearance of a
territorial policy, leadership that combines the local with
the global, the deterritorilisation of decision making, the
development of international law, the appearance of new
labour relations and the transnationalisation of politics".
In other words, there are many more critical factors that
need to be considered than can be addressed within a
straightforward Marxian class analysis to make sense of
global processes.

Others argue that the concentration of mass media and
the "space-time compression" of the modern world have
unleashed new channels through which culture,
consciousness and identity are expressed (Harvey, 1989;
Giddens, 1991; Dodgshon, 1999; Scholte, 2000). Some of
these scholars would argue that the rapid rise in the
electronic and computerised form of communication has
transformed the global space. Notwithstanding the
unprecedented speed with which capital can travel from
one corner of the world to another, advances in
information technology have also made it possible for
people in various parts of the world to connect with one
another and construct new forms of collective identity.
Castells (1997) refers to this cyber-driven phenomenon as

the "network society", within which new ideas are negotiated, identities formed and global relations shaped. The proliferation of social movements operating at a global level is itself one visible outcome of globalisation, which creates the rationale for such engagements, as well as the technical means through which dynamic alliances can be constructed.

The sketch presented above is somewhat coarse, and it would be beyond the scope of this chapter to provide a detailed review of all the different perspectives on globalisation. However, at the risk of making some untidy assumptions, I take the view that there are some underlying factors that impact on the nature of globalisation, regardless of the perspective. Indeed, there is nothing inevitable about neo-liberal globalisation, and it simply cannot operate independently of human agency. But there is also a growing literature that depicts human callousness and its insatiable needs as the main reason to be concerned about the future. Apocalyptic writers such as Homer-Dixon (2000) take the view that we (as humans) have created such complex and fast-paced systems that we now lack the resources, institutional control and ingenuity to extricate ourselves from the mess we find ourselves in. In short, we have checkmated ourselves, with a critical gap emerging between our need for practical and innovative ideas to solve complex problems and our inability to supply those ideas. Though such views appear to acknowledge the centrality of human factors in these complex systems, they seem to suggest that somehow humanity has suddenly become so irrational and "locked into" bad habits that, even with the imminence of its own self-destruction, it refuses to change course. However plausible this view may be, it tends to overlook the reasons why such "locked-in" behaviours have become so durable in the first instance. By presenting human problems within

a Malthusian perspective, the likes of Homer-Dixon appear
to be restricting their analysis to a conformist ideological
cubicle that exposes their aversion to alternative
possibilities.

I would favour the view that embraces the aphorism,
"Another world is possible", and that humanity still
retains its rational faculties, its creativity and its resources
to confront its problems. In arguing that the real problem
lies in the way power is distributed, I would pose the
following questions: "Who has control over resources?";
"Who has monopoly over 'knowledge'?"; "What kind of
'knowledge' is being propagated?"; and "In whose interest
are political and economic decisions often made?" My own
reading of the situation is that it is precisely within the
realm of economic globalisation and neo-liberal policies
that the real battle for human survival rests. This struggle
has many faces and takes many different forms. It refers to
battles waged at the global level against global warming,
ozone depletion, unfair trade, etc. It also refers to
countless local struggles around the globe fought by
individuals and communities for basic rights, resources,
livelihoods and dignity against repressive regimes,
unsympathetic financial institutions and predatory
corporations, often operating in partnership. Mobilising
these disparate voices of resistance against the excesses of
globalisation will be a challenge, but it forms the basis for
constructing a new world based on dignity and justice.

*Characteristics of economic globalisation and its intellectual
starting point*

Following the collapse of the ideologically bipolar Cold
War situation in the late 1980s, there emerged the unipolar
and confident dogma of "liberalisation and deregulation",
by which societies submitted completely to the exclusive,

unilateral logic of the market. This has given rise to a widening and deepening of international flows of trade, capital and technology within a single integrated global market; hence the term, "economic globalisation". The debate on economic globalisation has both staunch defenders and passionate adversaries. Its proponents are quick to make the case that economic globalisation will raise levels of income, expand consumer choice and widen opportunity. They argue that there is compelling evidence that economic globalisation plays an important catalytic role in accelerating growth and reducing poverty in developing countries. A report by the World Bank, *Globalisation, Growth and Poverty: Building an Inclusive World Economy* (2002), indicates that globalisation has helped reduce poverty in those countries that have accelerated the pace of integration into the world economy; and given that globalisation is an unstoppable force, there is little reason to wait. Hence, the sooner countries remove their barriers and integrate, the earlier they will embark on the path to economic prosperity. In a similar vein, the World Trade Organisation [WTO] and the IMF also argue that the growth of trade between countries increases the wealth of everyone, provided that everyone agrees to abide by the rules of trade liberalisation.

The detractors of economic globalisation, on the other hand, view it as a sinister force, which increases inequality, promotes insecurity, degrades the environment, and creates a culture rooted in money and wanton consumption. Environmentalists view it as a potential source of ozone layer depletion and global warming and point at global corporations and international financial banks as the principal culprits. Labour movements fear that capital movements towards areas that promise profit maximisation will be deleterious to all workers, leading to competitive wage cutting and poor working conditions.

Globalisation: The Battle for Solidarity and Effective Resistance

Women's groups take the view that the very nature of neo-liberal policies tends to erode the quality of the public services that women rely on. Local community movements in the Third World and their supporters in the North view neo-liberal policies and structural adjustment programmes, promoted by the Bretton Woods[2] twins, as the main causes of global poverty and growing inequality. Consumer movements in the North have responded resolutely against unfair trade conditions that keep workers in the Third World in perpetual poverty and destitution, as well as against child labour, reminiscent of Victorian England.

Increasingly, policies are being formulated and decisions made by political units outside the nation-state, which invariably demand global responses. To illustrate this reality, the assets of Transnational Corporations [TNCs] have increased by six-fold since the early 1980s, largely assisted by the dramatic increase in the number of TNCs since the 1960s (Cohen & Rai, 2000). This increased consolidation of economic power by supranational institutions and corporations means that they can now bypass the state and its laws as they please. An interesting example of such phenomena is the tourism industry. Investment and competition policy in this industry has

---

[2] The World Bank and the International Monetary Fund are together known as the Bretton Woods twins. Created at Bretton Woods, New Hampshire, USA in 1944, the mandate of these institutions was to ensure that future conflicts were avoided by lending for reconstruction and development and by smoothing out temporary balance of payment problems. As Susan George (2001) argues, they were regarded as progressive institutions, that were there solely to assist countries, and had no control over individual governments' economic decisions and no sanction to intervene in national policy. Their complexion is rather different these days, as they have acquired full control over some Third World economies and the mandate to intervene on matters of national policy.

created an unstable situation, whereby calls for further deregulation in Foreign Direct Investment [FDI] may well contribute to further erosion of host countries' ability to control leakage of profits. Already, up to 90% of profits from the tourist industry leave the host country, with no additional loss of local control (Pera & McLaren, 1999).

One of the unique characteristics of contemporary capitalism is its resilience in the face of multiple and perennial crises. It is a system of continual self-transformation and adjustment to meet new demands presented by new social and political challenges. As such, the nature and shape of present-day capitalism, expressed in terms of global capitalism, is markedly different from previous variants, although the real motives of "capital accumulation" remain unchanged. Not only are the relationships between the spheres of production and consumption modified, but so are the ways in which present-day capitalism expresses itself through an assortment of control instruments, such as trade, aid, loans, debt management, international law, etc. What does not change is the fact that atomisation and fragmentation remain as fundamental aspects of capitalist production, regardless of its historical phase. In concrete terms, this implies that the principal purpose of production is moneymaking rather than human need, which becomes subordinate to the primacy of profit maximisation.

As such, the essential pillar of current neo-liberal strategies is the promotion, strengthening and consolidation of an awareness that regards market principles as omnipotent. Indeed, this in itself indicates that capitalism as we know it today appears to have emerged triumphant and strong, with a speed, inevitability and force unparalleled in history. New forces and agencies facilitate its consolidation and offset the growing view amongst the public that the unfettered global market is

creating a "winner-takes-all" society, with grave
consequences to the well-being of society at large and the
environment people live in. The horror statistics from the
United Nations Development Programme [UNDP] (1998)
are a poignant reminder that contemporary capitalism has
created a world severely polarised by income distribution
and assets; the 358 richest people in the world possess a
fortune equivalent in value to the combined income of the
poorest 45%. Despite these overtly negative effects, the
neo-liberal paradigm has demonstrated its ascendancy by
coercing individuals, communities and even national
governments to accept that competition is inevitable in this
new global economy. Even after it came under severe
attack for causing the Asian financial crisis and the
associated socio-political upheavals in the late 1990s, the
neo-liberal policy framework still remains the predominant
method of economic activity. The writer and campaigner
Susan George had the following to say about the resilience
of neo-liberalism:

> No matter how many disasters of all kinds the neo-liberal system has
> visibly created, no matter what financial crises it may engender, no
> matter how many losers and outcasts it may create, it is still made to
> seem inevitable, like an act of God, the only possible economic and
> social order available to us. (George, 2001, p. 9)

How did neo-liberalism come to be such an orthodox
viewpoint, as if it were the natural condition of
humankind? Part of the answer lies in the activities of a
small group of neo-liberal economists at the University of
Chicago in the 1960s, under the tutelage of Friedrich von
Hayek (and later Milton Friedman). This group was
generously funded by corporations whose business

interests corresponded with the ideas that they were generating. It created a huge international network of foundations, institutes, research centres, scholars and public relations firms to push their ideas and doctrine relentlessly (George, 2001). Then came the Thatcher-Reagan axis of "conservative consensus", which granted neo-liberal thinking its legitimacy and political endorsement at the highest level and which was automatically extended towards the International Financial Institutions [IFIs], including the World Bank and IMF. What then followed was the wholesale practice of deregulation, privatisation and public sector downsizing across the North and South, with the consequences of severely weakened labour movements and a concentration of wealth in the hands of a tiny minority of large investors.

The paradox is that, even with left-leaning governments such as New Labour in power in the 1990s, this market-driven doctrine continued to dominate economic and public policy. If anything, New Labour and others akin to it elsewhere have taken up neo-liberal policies with much gusto and enthusiasm, ironically bringing in policies that even Conservative governments in the past would not have had the audacity to propose, for fear of provoking a collision with the public. Of course, what this alludes to is the fact that the neo-liberal project has been an outstanding success and has been embraced, voluntarily or otherwise, by all mainstream political parties and institutions. This tendency is partly because of the perception that anything short of embracing neo-liberal economic ideology implies inhabiting the "political wilderness" and partly because virtually all the mainstream political figures of our time may well believe in the virtues of the neo-liberal system, as the only possible economic and social order available to society. Third World political institutions have also surrendered spiritually, as well as in practice, to the new

market-driven realism, in order to attain the necessary
level of competitive efficiency to survive in a global
market.

*The anatomy of changing resistance: The "old" and "new" voices
of discord*

One discernible consequence of globalisation is the "retreat
of the nation-state" to a much more peripheral position of
authority, which means that the state is no longer in a
position to fulfil its historical role in guaranteeing social
welfare. Rather candidly, Tilly (1995, p. 1) declares: "As
states decline, so do workers' rights". So where does this
leave the "old" labour movement, which has always
functioned within the established norms of the political
framework? Clearly, the terrain of struggle has
dramatically shifted over the past two decades, as "nation-
state-driven" capitalism gave way to the "global" variant.
Indeed, it has become increasingly difficult to build a mass
movement around traditional class lines, given the changes
experienced and the declining appeal of such media of
engagement for millions of workers (Adkin, 1998). Labour
movement struggles about the appropriation of surplus
value no longer have the same resonance they had a few
decades ago. If union organisations are to remain relevant
and not by-passed by other forms of collective action, then
labour movement struggles need to be broadened to
occupy multiple terrains of resistance. To some degree,
this may already have come to pass. The very fact that
more and more people join activist organisations such as
Friends of the Earth, Greenpeace and Amnesty
International these days and fewer and fewer are
interested in membership of trade unions or political

parties is testament to the fact that the old institutions have already lost much ground and are now playing catch-up.

Of course, broadening the arena of resistance does not imply doing away with "class" as an organising principle, but rather demands a reconceptualisation of collective action through establishing common ground with other social movements and connecting with specific identities and values, in order to frame a broad-based alternative movement. As Laclau and Mouffe (1985) argue, social actors must be understood in terms of multiple, interacting subject positions, in which "workers" cannot be separated from "women", "environmentalists", "immigrants", "anti-war activists", etc. Rather, these identities and others are embodied, in various combinations, within each individual. In fact, the appeal of "new" social movements is precisely because they are able to *empower* people with the capacity to intervene directly in problems they are concerned with and to *control* the choices they make to shape the type of future they would like to see. This is particularly the case with young people, who are not so steeped in the traditions of the labour movement or other conventional institutions as a means of addressing their demands.

In view of the fact that there has been significant "voluntary disengagement" of people from the mainstream political process, the space within which resistance is articulated has also shifted. With the few winners and masses of losers created by the globalisation process, voices of dissent are likely to increase, contrary to the view that humanity has arrived at the "end of history", with capitalism and liberal democracy providing an optimal mechanism to satisfy the deepest urges of humanity (Fukuyama, 1992). Certainly, a great number of

global civil society[3] movements consider economic
globalisation to be a force that adversely affects peoples'
livelihoods, communities and environments. Hence, they
see themselves as being at the forefront of a discursive and
practical challenge to economic globalisation, through a
wide range of informal and unconventional channels of
resistance. At a time when the state has somehow
relinquished much of its regulatory power, these civil
society actors appear to be fulfilling an important role in
representing citizen's demands.

At the same time, the implications of the present
economic order for civil society are considerable. These
actors, particularly those that have been active in
challenging neo-liberal policies from various angles, now
find themselves at a crossroad between continuing their
engagement without making compromises of principle or
working in partnership with corporations and financial
institutions that are prepared to enter into a dialogue. Both
routes present dangers. On the one hand, working
autonomously, free from the influence of dominant
institutions at national and global levels, presupposes that
there is such a thing as an independent public sphere. On
the other hand, co-operation with governments and global
institutions could compromise an NGO's image if it was
perceived that the money was more important than the
message. Furthermore, there is a perception that
corporations are in the "dialogue" simply to outmanoeuvre
their critics and improve their image, with the sole

---

[3] Civil society is a broad concept, encompassing all the organisations
and associations that exist outside the state and the market. It includes
an array of organisations: interest groups, NGOs, labour unions,
professional associations, chambers of commerce, ethnic associations
and social movements. In parts of this document, "civil society" and
"social movements" are used interchangeably, when deemed necessary
to underscore the latter's informal and spontaneous characteristics.

intention of increasing their competitive edge. The journalist and environmental activist George Monbiot argues:

> Environmental groups should not take money off companies and should not allow themselves to be used as an extension of the corporate, public-relations effort .... The dangers are that by co-operating with the corporations on their terms, environmentalists help to justify the company's more devious practices. (As cited in Rowell, 2001)

Clearly, the civil society field is by no means a homogeneous one. Some civil society organisations actively promote the neo-liberal project and receive support from institutions such as the World Bank and the WTO. Others seek to reform such institutions through "ameliorating" projects that would help correct the excesses of the free market. And finally, those within the rejectionist and radical camp consist of activists involved in anti-racist, anti-globalisation, anti-sexist and solidarity movements. What runs as a common thread through them all is the fact that they inhabit, and interact within, the orbit of modern-day capitalism. This rewards its friends handsomely and employs various tactics to handle its critics and opponents, who mostly originate from civil society. Capitalism has become extremely proficient at adapting well to changing circumstances and enlarging its boundary of containment; so much so, that new "opponents" and their concerns are swiftly absorbed and neutralised. In short, it has become a self-organising (sort of auto-poietic) system with the capacity to replicate or reproduce itself.

Globalisation: The Battle for Solidarity and Effective Resistance

An interesting example of capitalism's capacity for self-reinvention can be seen in the consequences of the 1989 European parliamentary elections. Following the commotion caused by news coverage about holes in the ozone layer, the UK Green Party took nearly 15% of the overall vote. Both main political parties in Britain, alarmed by the possibility of a new political force in their neighbourhood, set out on a concerted campaign to "mainstream" the environment debate by alerting the public to the idea that they too were on a race to save the planet. The then Prime Minister Mrs Thatcher, not especially renowned for her "green" credentials, made a series of high profile speeches in words that echoed those of the environmental movement, acknowledging that global environmental problems presented a new and serious challenge for humanity. That effort, which culminated in the signing of the Montreal Protocol agreement to curb ozone layer depleting substances, helped reverse the momentum gathered by the environmental movement, to prevent it from posing a serious challenge to the established political framework. Indeed, more than anything, this example shows how at ease the "forces" of capitalism have become over the years in entering any arena of engagement and overpowering those they regard as outsiders. They often employ both coercive and passive (consensual) tactics to achieve their aims, some of which are discussed in the next section.

Cooperation, dominance and resistance in today's world

While the state is in crisis in both the South and the North, its problems are far more severe in the South, and its capacity to re-establish control is becoming an ever more distant possibility. The collapse of the developmental state has left many countries of the South bereft of a shared sense of national purpose, with promises of freedom from poverty and despair broken (Sen, 1997). In concrete terms, this is reflected in the continual erosion of public services and institutions, growing internal conflict, expanding debt, and destruction of ecosystems, all of which contribute to heightened social and economic malaise. The structural adjustment programmes prescribed by the Bretton Woods Institutions [BWIs], intended to mitigate some of these systemic difficulties, have, if anything, exacerbated existing problems and given rise to new ones. These problems are highlighted by the former Senior Vice-President and Chief Economist of the World Bank, Joseph Stiglitz:

> I have seen firsthand the dark side of globalisation – how the liberalisation of capital markets, by allowing speculative money to pour in and out of a country at a moment's whim, devastated East Asia; how so-called structural-adjustment loans to some of the poorest countries in the world "restructured" those countries' economies so as to eliminate jobs but did not provide the means of creating new ones, leading to widespread unemployment and cuts in basic services. The media and the public have since become concerned about this dark side as well – globalisation without a human face, it is sometimes called. (Stiglitz, 2001)

Thus, the failure of the "Washington Consensus" has put the BWIs on the defensive. Recognising that their policies have not delivered the desired results of increasing prosperity across the board, they have began to address the concerns raised by representative and advocacy groups regarding social, labour and environmental issues. Their language has also changed; terms such as "participation", "poverty reduction" and "stakeholder society" are now

firmly embedded in their vocabulary. There are even some
limited debt relief initiatives targeted at helping the
poorest and most highly indebted countries, although
many argue that they do not go far enough. The same
sentiments are also expressed by a range of "forward-
looking" TNCs, which argue that they now appreciate the
value of consultation, dialogue and "building
partnerships" at all levels, to make their business practice
compatible with the healthy development of society. From
the rhetoric, this "new development paradigm" appears to
be different from its predecessor. However, it still shares
the underlying purpose, of building globally integrated
capitalism, and much of its essential methodology,
employing liberal economics to achieve its objectives. The
principal difference is the strategy adopted by the current
"paradigm" of inclusiveness and participation, which
looks to nation-states to take an active part in
strengthening institutions to support markets, expanding
internationally, and to involve the private sector, as a way
of installing the global system in local cultures and
societies.

The softening up of the international financial
institutions and TNCs has been accompanied by their co-
operation with Civil Society Organisations [CSOs], which
appear to have multiple functions. They are regarded as a
useful source of technical expertise, they provide capacity
building to other CSOs, they deliver services and, most
importantly, they provide representation and therefore
amplify the voices of the poor in decisions that affect their
lives (World Bank, 2000). It is assumed that CSOs often
have closer contacts with local communities and can offer
valuable insights and perspectives that differ from those of
donors and government departments. These important
functions have contributed to their rapid proliferation at

the global level. Over 40,000 international NGOs are currently operating, with numbers of domestic ones rising even more rapidly, together controlling a growing share of development spending, emergency relief and aid (Keane, 2001). It is estimated that well in excess of $10 billion of official aid is channelled through NGOs, and it is widely believed that they now disburse more money than institutions such as the World Bank ("Sins of the secular missionaries", 2000; Petras & Veltmeyer, 2001).

Critics who are sceptical of the established judgement that places CSOs as the conceptual "good guys" would argue that many CSOs and NGOs are increasingly becoming professionalised and operating much like normal businesses or firms, subject to the same set of administrative and structural constraints. This tendency forces them to rely heavily on the outside world for donations, grants, and contracts to sustain their work, which they regard as important, with much to contribute to the betterment of humankind. Those with a large public following, such as Greenpeace, still manage to raise substantial amounts of money from private individual donations, although this source of income is intermittent and may be contingent on the type of campaign that is taking place at a given time. But even Greenpeace is increasingly turning its attention towards forging partnerships with those who have big money to spend. The financial institutions and TNCs, at times beset with identity crises and ever so eager to improve their public image, make ideal partners – the NGOs with their "progressive credentials" and the banks (and firms) with their money. Hence, the demand for more money to continue their operations forces NGOs to enter into partnerships that, at times, may contradict their original mission and exhibit the hallmarks of "unholy alliances".

Once such "partnerships" are crystallised, these

seemingly independent and voluntary actors often end up
having to re-evaluate their outlook and original mission to
fall in line with the demands of co-operation. As Northern
governments and institutions step up their direct and
indirect engagements with NGOs and CSOs, then the NGO
linkages with communities may well become
compromised, given that donors often come with a specific
vision of development and expect civil society agencies to
sign up to this vision, albeit through "consultation"
(Mohan, 2002). Naturally, most donors providing support
to CSOs are prepared to promote liberal democracy and
economic liberalism, and to argue for the "removal" of the
state from its traditional mandate of delivering social
welfare. The implications of this are that the funds go to
support a small and select group of civil society agencies
established precisely to "cash in" on the available donor
money or to those CSOs that have moved away from their
traditional adversarial position and embraced the ideology
of promoting "self-help" and choice in society. According
to Hearn (2001), this apolitical consensus tends to conceal a
highly politicised and partial perspective of development
and denies the space for alternative perspectives to the
liberal doctrine to gain legitimacy. Petras and Veltmeyer
(2001) are especially scathing about the role of South-based
CBOs and NGOs in promoting the status quo of on-going
neo-liberal reform:

> The egregious effects of structural adjustment policies on waged and
> salaried workers, peasants and small national business people
> generate potential national popular discontent. And that is where
> the NGOs come into the picture, to mystify and deflect that
> discontent away from the direct attacks on corporate/banking power
> structures and profits towards local micro-projects, apolitical "grass

roots" self-exploitation and popular education that avoids class analysis and capitalist profit-taking. (Petras & Veltmeyer, 2001, pp. 128-129)

The case of the Shell Oil Company's plan to develop the Camisea gas project in the culturally and ecologically sensitive Peruvian rainforest, an area blessed with one of the world's largest natural gas deposits, is instructive of the way corporations are entering into a new arena of engagement to overcome potential objections to their operations. Shell knew that Camisea was going to be controversial and, having learnt from its experience with the Brent Spar and Nigeria debacles, the company opted for a dialogue with the "stakeholders". In an unprecedented move, Shell invited about 90 interested groups or "stakeholders" to a series of workshops in Washington DC, Lima and London between 1997 and 1998, to agree to a plan of action on how to proceed with the project. Many carefully selected NGOs attended, whilst the more radical groups were marginalised from the process. This meant that the broader question of whether or not the project should go ahead in the first place was not on the agenda (Rowell, 1999). Later, when Shell began to have misgivings about the cost of the project and disagreements over the infrastructure with the Peruvian Government, many of the supportive NGOs were recruited to lobby the government on behalf of Shell. Although Shell eventually abandoned the project, the company had understood the value of "getting engaged" with NGOs and CSOs as an important way of winning the simple public relations battle, which is an important feature of "sustainable" business practice these days.

The relentless campaign to co-opt potentially dissident voices or create new CSOs as part of the drive for transparency is not confined to the Third World setting. In the North, similar acts of co-option are taking shape. When a corporation wishes to oppose specific regulations, particularly environmental ones, or wishes to go ahead with environmentally "controversial" developments, it has two options at its disposal. It can either go ahead openly while justifying its activity itself, or it can bring in an effective assembly of citizens or experts as "front groups" to promote the agenda desired by the corporation, while "representing" the public interest. The latter option is now the preferred route for many corporations, given that the use of such "front groups" enables corporations to take part in public debates and government hearings as part of their drive for transparency.

A famous example of this NGO-industry "partnership" is one between the Environmental Defence Fund [EDF], one of the largest environmental organisations in the US, and McDonald's. In the late 1980s, McDonald's faced a stern campaign co-ordinated by the Citizens' Clearinghouse on Hazardous Wastes [CCHW] against its ozone-depleting polystyrene foam sandwich clamshells. Seeing a major business opportunity, the EDF approached McDonald's with a proposal to develop a joint waste reduction initiative that would replace the polystyrene foam sandwich clamshells with paper wraps and light-weight recycled boxes, along with a series of other packaging improvements; an initiative which effectively undercut the campaign of the CCHW. For the fast food chain, working with a respectable environmental organisation has been beneficial in terms of getting back to business and reversing the damaging publicity that was impacting on its corporate image. In fact, it is not an overstatement to maintain that the EDF/McDonald's alliance has given McDonald's a reputation as a "socially responsible" business. Since this period, additional initiatives, such as their most recent introduction of energy saving programmes at many of their restaurants, reducing consumption by 10% to 15%, have consolidated further this partnership (Reckess, 1999). Whilst it can be argued that the EDF/McDonald's alliance may have added a new dimension to the relationship between corporate and environmental organisations in providing "environmental results", it has only addressed issues concerning the "premises" of McDonald's. As yet, there is little sign that McDonald's has applied pressure on its suppliers to endorse an environmentally responsible position. Given that it remains a major player in US agricultural production and processing, this could have enormous environmental implications. Some may argue that, by getting too close to McDonald's, the EDF has effectively tied its hands in terms of being even more influential in the service of the environment and society. Meanwhile, the EDF will receive generous funding from McDonald's, because it will take a non-confrontational style of engagement and work within the system of "partnering corporations".

Another case example relating to McDonald's is worth deliberation, not least for providing another perspective on the fast food chain's conduct. In the early 1990s, McDonald's was embroiled in the high profile "McLibel" case, in which the company denied the allegations made by two environmental activists about a host of abuses, and sued them for libel. The activists, Helen Steel and Dave Morris, did the unthinkable. They took their place in legal history by facing up to this giant corporation, and used the opportunity provided by the trial to subject McDonald's to its most humiliating public scrutiny, relating to its contribution to low wages in the catering industry, rain forest damage, litter in the streets, etc. The case lasted for

seven years and the trial for three years (314 days in the
High Court), and cost McDonald's an estimated £10
million. Although the activists on trial were found guilty
on several counts, they were widely viewed to have won
the publicity war, as the judge upheld the allegations that
McDonald's was cruel to animals and guilty of poor
employment practices. Stressing that McDonald's had a
long history of intimidating its critics, Franny Armstrong
had the following to say in *The Guardian*:

> Over the past 15 years, McDonald's has threatened legal action
> against more than 90 organisations in the UK, including the BBC,
> Channel 4, *The Guardian*, *The Sun*, the Scottish TUC, the New Leaf
> Tea Shop, student newspapers and a children's theatre group. Even
> Prince Philip received a stiff letter. All of them backed down and
> many formally apologised in court. (Armstrong, 1998, p. 4)

Although McDonald's may argue that this rather
unedifying episode was the responsibility of its UK branch,
the McLibel case did entertain international attention. It
would therefore be difficult for the company to argue
convincingly that the Main Head Office in Chicago had no
part to play in the matter, particularly since the trial cost
considerable sums of money and posed a threat to its
corporate image. In many ways, what transpired in this
trial is illustrative of the company's irritation with its critics
and its coercive style of response, intended to silence and
neutralise groups that question its health and
environmental record, which in this case simply did not
materialise. Indeed, there are many similar long-drawn-
out cases between individuals (or communities) and brand
name giants taking place from time to time, with varying
outcomes. However, while these outcomes may well

remain different, the stance of the giant corporations is almost always predictably bellicose, employing every public relations campaigning means available to them. I would argue that the few critics who manage to "last the distance" of confrontation, often at great personal sacrifice and relying on their reservoir of courage and conviction, offer much hope and break new ground in the formulation of common targets around which struggles evolve into genuine networks of alliances of resistance.

Complementarities of global solidarity and local action

One essential principle that needs to be understood is that any reforms which have taken place in various historical periods did not just occur out of thin air, but rather through struggle. For example, workers did not win rights because owners happened to be men of great altruistic character. Rather, the logic of resistance is that no change comes without campaigners actively working towards its realisation, as in the cases of workers demanding fairer wages, women fighting for the vote and minorities struggling for recognition as equal citizens in the eyes of the law. As the freed slave and anti-slavery campaigner Frederick Douglass remarked in 1857, "Power concedes nothing without a demand. It never did and it never will" (1857/1985, p. 204). In the same vein, there are a great number of causes in contemporary society that demand and continue to demand active engagement for concrete outcomes to be pushed through.

What has changed today is not the nature of the problems per se, but the terrain of engagement. The landscape of political space has been reshaped by the globalisation of trade and production, supported by specific material factors, such as advances in IT communication and the mobility of capital. From this

perspective, globalisation is not solely a synonym of
disempowerment; it also creates certain conditions for
democratisation, decentralisation and empowerment, as
well as for centralisation and standardisation.
Globalisation opens as many doors as it shuts (Agnew &
Corbridge, 1995). Two recent cases, those of the Ilisu Dam
Campaign and the Chiapas-based Zapatista Movement,
may help to illustrate the contention that globalisation has
created the space for alliance building and the legitimacy
of co-ordinated global engagement.

The final design of the Ilisu Dam was approved in the
early 1980s, but remained on the drawing board until the
mid-1990s, when the Turkish government sought to raise
the necessary finance by offering to make Ilisu a Build-
Operate-Transfer project. A year later, when no bidder
came forward because of doubts about the project's
commercial viability, the Turkish government selected the
Swiss turbine manufacturer Sulzer Hydro as the main
contractor. Governments of eight OECD countries agreed
to extend official export credits or guarantees of about $850
million to private firms. From this period onwards, the
project was dogged by protests from a concerted national
and international coalition of civil society agencies, raising
concerns about the project's "appropriateness" from a
variety of political, social, environmental and
archaeological positions. The alliance between these
environmental organisations, human rights bodies,
Kurdish community groups, archaeologists, anti-capitalist
protestors and the trade unions held firm against a massive
public relations campaign by the proponents of the project,
supported by the various governments, to reverse the
rhetoric coming from the activist camp. As the Ilisu
Campaign continued to gather momentum, the
subcontracted engineering firms began to withdraw their

association from the consortium one by one, fearing shareholder backlash. At present, the Ilisu Dam Project appears to be "consigned" to some uncertain future, when the Turkish government can successfully raise the necessary funds to go ahead with it. For the time being, the Ilisu Dam Campaign has won a major victory in stopping the project from proceeding, and demonstrating that a well-organised and committed civic engagement movement can go a long way in challenging the outcomes of controversial projects far away from home.

The second example, the Zapatista Movement, is even more remarkable in terms of the way in which it successfully challenged the Mexican Government and the neo-liberal thinking that underpinned its economic policy. The early 1990s saw the wholesale privatisation of public sector enterprises in Mexico, a strong wage-containment policy, and the rapid expansion of export-oriented industries (*maquiladoras*) by the Salinas Government, as part of its preparation to join the North American Free Trade Association [NAFTA]. Mexico's remarkable reversal from its historic position of inward-oriented development to the wholehearted embrace of market-driven interventions was taking place with no real consultation and was never subjected to domestic debate (Barkin, 1999). This may be partly because the government felt it had a mandate from the people to chart out what it perceived as a "prosperous" future, and partly because there was no alternative to neo-liberal policies at the end of the Cold War, when progressive forces everywhere were on the retreat. However, on the 1st January 1994, the day NAFTA was coming into effect, the Zapatista National Liberation Army [ZNLA], composed of poor indigenous Mayan peasants, came out of the jungle to occupy several towns in the state of Chiapas. It came with a variety of demands: electoral reforms, the creation of new municipal areas, ethnic representation in Congress, schooling in native languages, health and education infrastructure development, and land reform. These demands reflected the injustices people in Chiapas have endured for too long – the majority suffer from malnutrition, lack potable water and sewage facilities, and are amongst the poorest people in Mexico. Given that the region has a huge petroleum reservoir, provides 10% of the country's electricity and exports large quantities of coffee, the level of abject poverty amongst the indigenous Indian population is nothing short of a scandal. Initially, the news of this conflict was greeted worldwide as another Latin American guerrilla adventure. But as time passed and the Zapatista Movement began to gain publicity through various media outlets, the world came to know that it had no grand aims other than to enable people to live in dignity and to participate in the simple task of building a new world. The overt military clashes between the Zapatistas and the Mexican Army lasted only a few days and were followed by several years of sporadic political negotiations, which in itself amounts to a political victory for the Zapatistas. Massive protests in Mexico and abroad forced a halt to overt offensive action on a number of occasions when hope of a negotiated settlement was fading. This conflict still continues, despite the Government's acceptance of some of the Zapatistas' demands. However, the Zapatista experience is of particular interest to the practice of networked resistance to globalisation. Not only has this movement generated widespread support, it has also set in motion the beginnings of a worldwide mobilisation to find new and effective ways of bringing together a wide variety of different struggles, based on a common "ideology" that respects difference, processes, and above all, the humanity of the struggle for liberation (Bond, 2001).

Implications of Globalisation

At present, the widespread mobilisations for various causes across the world remain disconnected and atomised and, in the absence of innovative ways of interlinking, their ability to fulfil their objectives will remain limited in scope. Both the Ilisu Dam Campaign and the Zapatista Movement provide interesting narratives, showing that globalisation can paradoxically open new political space for contestation as it weakens existing patterns of relations between the state and civil society (Stahler-Sholk, 2001). In both cases, political alliances have been far stronger between local activists and international supporters, revealing the growing importance of global networks and universal rights, as well as local identities. This indicates an important alternative strategy of "globalisation from below", based on the recomposition of civil society across the globe on priorities that are compatible with the aspirations of people who are left out of the dominant development discourse.

The task of building and nurturing globally connected solidarity movements is beset by a number of pitfalls, many of which rest on the ability of particular civil society bodies to remain outside the influence of consultative processes initiated by governmental and supranational institutions. Such processes are already underway, with "reformist" civil society organisations entering into "mutually beneficial" dialogues with such institutions. This may well limit their repertoire of civic action in exchange for, as they see it, bringing together diverse talents and perspectives to formulate a common vision, firmly based on realism and achievable outcomes. Moreover, the number of new CSOs has been growing at a considerable rate since international financial institutions and corporations began to link up with non-governmental actors to push forward their vision of development and democracy. This trend cannot be mere coincidence, given the involvement of financial institutions in providing the funds to support these competing CSOs. Nor can it be regarded as a positive development, since the survival of many newly established CSOs is now dependent on keeping their sponsors happy. Naturally, their primary objective is to keep in line with their backers' expectations, knowing that their continued operation is conditional on a willingness to promote a particular vision that they took no part in creating. This process of "incorporation" leads to problems of legitimacy for CSOs in the eyes of people who regard corporations and international institutions as the source of their problem. In the long run, it may contribute to an erosion of trust in these seemingly non-governmental entities.

With a long history of co-option and neutralisation as a guide, grass roots and CSO groups will need to re-examine carefully their position with regard to the type of dialogue and co-operation to which they commit themselves. Their historic role as proponents of social justice and radical-democratic values is what forced the international financial institutions and corporations to embrace a "dialogue" and "collaborative" stance in the first place. Despite the creation of new CSOs and the co-option of existing ones, the social, economic and environmental problems associated with neo-liberal programmes are still with us, and there is little sign that better days are on the horizon. Against this backdrop, progressive social movements and CSOs are faced with a neo-liberal adversary engaged in a two-pronged macro- and micro-strategy of exploitation and containment. This will therefore require a two-pronged counter-hegemonic response: working with multiple social actors and facing up to NGOs and CSOs loyal to the neo-liberal agenda on the home front, while widening the scope of alliances with like-minded organisations on the international front. These actions need to be well synchronised and integrated into a mutually supporting system, feeding off the gains and strengths at the different levels to allow for a coherent interpretation of the mosaic of experiences. A predominantly local focus would only yield results that are disjointed and insular; similarly, ignoring local dimensions in favour of the international sphere is incompatible with the goal of constructing viable global structures that are firmly rooted in local reality. Such is the struggle against the bad effects of globalisation that global and local actions need to approach as part of the same resistance continuum.

References

Adkin, L. E. (1998). Ecology and labour: Towards a new societal paradigm. In R. Munck & P. Waterman (Eds.), *Labour worldwide in the era of globalization: Alternative union models in the new world order* (pp. 199-217). Basingstoke: Macmillan.

Agnew, J., & Corbridge, S. (1995). *Mastering space: Hegemony, territory and international political economy.* London: Routledge.

Armstrong, F. (1998, June 19). Why won't British TV show a film about McLibel?: Is it really so dangerous? *The Guardian,* p. 4.

Barkin, D. (1999). Financial globalisation and sustainable development in Mexico. In W. Wehrmeyer & Y. Mulugetta (Eds.). *Growing pains: Environmental*

Globalisation: The Battle for Solidarity and Effective Resistance
management in developing countries (pp. 58-73). Sheffield: Greenleaf.

Bond, P. (2001, August). Strategy and self-activity in the global justice movements. *Foreign Policy in Focus, Discussion paper #5.* Retrieved July 4, 2006, from: http://www.fpif.org/papers/gjm.html

Castells, M. (1997). *The power of identity.* Malden, MA: Blackwell.

Cohen, R., & Rai, S. M. (Eds.). (2000). *Global social movements.* London: Athlone Press.

Cox, R. W. (1987). *Production, power and world order: Social forces in the making of history.* New York: Columbia University Press.

Dodgshon, R. A. (1999). Human geography at the end of time?: Thoughts on the notion of time-space compression. *Environment and Planning, D: Society and Space, 17* (5), 607-620.

Douglass, F. (1985). The significance of emancipation in the West Indies. In *The Frederick Douglass Papers, Series One: Speeches, Debates, and Interviews; Volume 3, 1855-63* (J. W. Blassingame, Ed.). New Haven: Yale University Press. (Original work published 1857).

Fukuyama, F. (1992). *The end of history and the last man.* New York: Free Press.

George, S. (2001). A short history of neo-liberalism: Twenty years of elite economics and emerging opportunities for structural change. In F. Houtart & F. Polet (Eds.), *The other Davos: The globalization of resistance to the world economic system* (pp. 7-16). London: Zed Books.

Giddens, A. (1991). *Modernity and self-identity: Self and society in the late modern age.* Stanford, CA: Stanford University Press.

Gramsci, A. (1971). *Selections from the prison notebooks* (Q. Hoare & G. Nowell Smith, Eds. & Trans.). London: Lawrence & Wishart. (Original work published 1948-1951).

Harvey, D. (1989). *The condition of postmodernity: An enquiry into the origins of cultural change.* Oxford: Basil Blackwell.

Hearn, J. (2001). The "uses and abuses" of civil society in Africa. *Review of African Political Economy, 28* (87), pp. 43-53.

Held, D. (2004, July 26). *Globalization: An empirical assessment and an analytical interpretation* [Speech at the Barcelona Forum 2004]. Retrieved January 17, 2005,

Globalisation: The Battle for Solidarity and Effective Resistance from:

http://www.barcelona2004.org/eng/banco_del_conoci miento/documentos/ficha.cfm?IdDoc=1628

Held, D., & McGrew, A. (Eds.). (2003). *The global transformations reader: An introduction to the globalization debate.* Cambridge: Polity Press.

Homer-Dixon, T. (2000). *The ingenuity gap.* London: Jonathan Cape.

Keane, J. (2001). Global civil society? In H. Anheier, M. Glasius, & M. Kaldor (Eds.), *Global civil society 2001* (pp. 23-47). Oxford: Oxford University Press.

Laclau, E., & Mouffe, C. (1985). *Hegemony and socialist strategy: Towards a radical democratic politics* (W. Moore & P. Cammack, Trans.). London: Verso.

Mohan, G. (2002). The disappointments of civil society: the politics of NGO intervention in Northern Ghana. *Political Geography, 21* (1), pp. 125-154.

Oliveira, M. D. de, & Tandon, R. (1994). *Citizens: Strengthening global civil society.* Washington, DC: CIVICUS.

Pera, L., & McLaren, D. (1999, November). Globalisation, tourism and indigenous people: What you should know about the world's largest industry. *Planeta: Global*

Journal of Practical Ecotourism. Retrieved July 4, 2006, from:

http://www.planeta.com/planeta/99/1199globalizatio nrt.html

Petras, J., & Veltmeyer, H. (2001). *Globalization unmasked: Imperialism in the 21st century.* London: Zed Books.

Reckess, G. Z. (1999, December 28). Unlikely allies set example for sustainable society. *Environmental News Network.* Retrieved July 4, 2006, from:

http://www.enn.com/arch.html?id=34878

Robinson, W. I. (2001). Social theory and globalization: The rise of a transnational State. *Theory and Society, 30,* pp. 157-200.

Robinson, W. I. & Harris, J. (2000). Towards a global ruling class?: Globalization and the transnational capitalist class. *Science and Society, 64* (1), pp. 11-54.

Rowell, A. (1999, March). *Internet activism vs. "Dialogue PR".* Paper presented at the N5M Conference, Amsterdam. Retrieved July 4, 2006, from:

http://www.xs4all.nl/~evel/n5m/andytxt.html

Rowell, A. (2001, August). Sleeping with the enemy [Electronic version]. *BBC Wildlife Magazine.* Retrieved July 4, 2006, from:

Globalisation: The Battle for Solidarity and Effective Resistance http://www.andyrowell.com/articles/sleeping_with_the_enemy.html

Scholte, J. A. (2000). *Globalization: A critical introduction.* Basingstoke: Macmillan.

Sen, G. (1997). *Globalization in the 21st century: Challenges for civil society: The UvA Development Lecture 1997.* Amsterdam: University of Amsterdam.

Sins of the secular missionaries. (2000, January 29). *The Economist,* pp. 25-28.

Sklair, L. (2001). *The transnational capitalist class.* Oxford: Blackwell.

Smith, J., Chatfield, C., & Pagnucco, R. (Eds.). (1997). *Transnational social movements and global politics: Solidarity beyond the state.* Syracuse, NY: Syracuse University Press.

Stahler-Sholk, R. (2001). Globalization and social movement resistance: The Zapatista rebellion in Chiapas, Mexico. *New Political Science, 23* (4), pp. 493-516.

Stiglitz, J. (2001, October). Thanks for nothing [Electronic version]. *The Atlantic Monthly, 288* (3). Retrieved July 4, 2006, from:

http://www.theatlantic.com/doc/prem/200110/stiglit
z

Tarrow, S. (2001). Transnational politics: Contention and institutions in international politics. *Annual Review of Political Science, 4*, pp. 1-20.

Tilly, C. (1995). Globalisation threatens labor's rights. *International Labor and Working Class History, 47*, 1-23.

United Nations Development Programme. (1998). *Human development report, 1998.* New York: Oxford University Press.

World Bank. (2000). *Working together: The World Bank's partnership with civil society.* Washington, DC: Author.

World Bank. (2002). *Globalization, growth and poverty: Building an inclusive world economy.* Washington, DC: Author.